Women and the Islamic Republic

Based on extensive interviews and oral histories as well as archival sources, *Women and the Islamic Republic* challenges the dominant masculine theorizations of state-making in postrevolutionary Iran. Shirin Saeidi demonstrates that despite the Islamic Republic's nondemocratic structures, multiple forms of citizenship have developed in postrevolutionary Iran. This finding destabilizes the binary formulation of democratization and authoritarianism that has not only dominated investigations of Iran but also regime categorizations in political science more broadly. As non-elite Iranian women negotiate or engage with the state's gendered citizenry regime, the Islamic Republic is forced to remake, oftentimes haphazardly, its citizenry agenda. The book demonstrates how women remake their rights, responsibilities, and statuses during everyday life to condition the state-making process in Iran, showing women's everyday resistance to the state-making process.

SHIRIN SAEIDI is Assistant Professor of Political Science at the University of Arkansas. She has published articles in journals including *International Journal of Middle East Studies*, *International Studies Review*, and *Millennium: Journal of International Studies*. She is a member of the Editorial Board of the journal *Citizenship Studies*.

Cambridge Middle East Studies

Editorial Board

Charles Tripp (general editor)
Julia Clancy-Smith
F. Gregory Gause
Yezid Sayigh
Avi Shlaim
Judith E. Tucker

Cambridge Middle East Studies has been established to publish books on the nineteenth- to twenty-first-century Middle East and North Africa. The series offers new and original interpretations of aspects of Middle Eastern societies and their histories. To achieve disciplinary diversity, books are solicited from authors writing in a wide range of fields including history, sociology, anthropology, political science, and political economy. The emphasis is on producing books affording an original approach along theoretical and empirical lines. The series is intended for students and academics, but the more accessible and wide-ranging studies will also appeal to the interested general reader.

A list of books in the series can be found after the index.

Women and the Islamic Republic

How Gendered Citizenship Conditions the Iranian State

Shirin Saeidi

University of Arkansas

CAMBRIDGE
UNIVERSITY PRESS

CAMBRIDGE
UNIVERSITY PRESS

University Printing House, Cambridge CB2 8BS, United Kingdom

One Liberty Plaza, 20th Floor, New York, NY 10006, USA

477 Williamstown Road, Port Melbourne, VIC 3207, Australia

314–321, 3rd Floor, Plot 3, Splendor Forum, Jasola District Centre, New Delhi – 110025, India

103 Penang Road, #05-06/07, Visioncrest Commercial, Singapore 238467

Cambridge University Press is part of the University of Cambridge.

It furthers the University's mission by disseminating knowledge in the pursuit of education, learning, and research at the highest international levels of excellence.

www.cambridge.org
Information on this title: www.cambridge.org/9781316515761
DOI: 10.1017/9781009026574

© Shirin Saeidi 2022

First published 2022

A catalogue record for this publication is available from the British Library.

Library of Congress Cataloging-in-Publication Data
Names: Saeidi, Shirin, 1980- author.
Title: Women and the Islamic republic : how gendered citizenship conditions the
    Iranian state / by Shirin Saeidi.
Description: Cambridge : Cambridge University Press, 2021. | Series: CMES
    Cambridge Middle East studies | Includes bibliographical references and
    index.
Identifiers: LCCN 2021034733 (print) | LCCN 2021034734 (ebook) |
    ISBN 9781316515761 (hardback) | ISBN 9781009013000 (paperback) |
    ISBN 9781009026574 (epub)
Subjects: LCSH: Women–Iran–History–21st century. | Citizenship–Iran–
    History–21st century. | Iran–Politics and government–21st century.
Classification: LCC HQ1735.2 .S225 2021 (print) | LCC HQ1735.2 (ebook) |
    DDC 305.40955/0905–dc23
LC record available at https://lccn.loc.gov/2021034733
LC ebook record available at https://lccn.loc.gov/2021034734

ISBN 978-1-316-51576-1 Hardback

With honor and gratitude for the people of Iran, especially

Katayoun Alaedin, Nur Sadat Mousavi, and Aslan Saeidi

by the witness and what is witnessed

wa shahidin wa mash-hud (Quran 85:3)

Contents

Acknowledgments

This project began as a doctoral dissertation at Cambridge University. My supervisor, Glen Rangwala, read many versions of the manuscript and offered insightful comments that empowered me to move freely toward my own intellectual ideals.

I have presented sections of this book in different venues, including the Centre for Global Cooperation Research in Duisburg, Germany, and the University of Oklahoma. I am grateful to all the participants who provided feedback during these presentations. Abbas Edalat, Vahid Jalili, Seyedeh Azam Hosseini, Najib Ghadbian, Pearl Dowe, Joel Gordon, Ted Swedenburg, Mohja Kahf, Rania Mahmoud, Fatemeh Delavari Parizi, Zahra Abbasi, Shohreh Pirani, Amirhossein Vafa, Omid Azadibougar, Salvador Santino Regilme, and K. Soraya Batmanghelichi were intellectual inspirations as I wrote this book with their erudite interventions, but they were also dear friends who nurtured and sustained me. Anne McNevin, Paola Rivetti, Manata Hashemi, Amirhossein Vafa, Mateo Mohammad Farzaneh, Nayereh Tohidi, and Gamze Cavdar all read portions of this manuscript and offered critical feedback. My colleagues in the Department of Political Science at the University of Arkansas have supported my research by creating a collegial environment, and I'm most grateful for their presence. I owe a special thank you to Paola Rivetti, who taught me so many things, but above all her loving friendship enabled me to write through a frightening time.

Many thanks to Engin Isin and Peter Nyers for their scholarship and support of junior scholars in the discipline. Shahla Talebi commented on this project in various stages and offered invaluable support during my ethnographic and archival research on the Iranian left. Interviewees in the United Kingdom, Germany, and Sweden opened their hearts to me by recounting leftist experiences in Iran before and after the 1979 revolution. I thank them for those unforgettable moments we shared; I continue to reflect upon them.

I refined my arguments and curbed my passion because of interactions with students and faculty members at the University of Tehran, and

I appreciate their patience and engagement with my research. It was at the University of Tehran where I developed my teaching skills shortly after completing my doctoral degree. My experiences as a visiting assistant professor in the political science department also transformed the connection I made between my research and teaching agenda. This book came into existence due to the support of many individuals in Iran and abroad that sacrificed their time to not only make me feel at home in Tehran but also facilitate my research. I am unsure how to express gratitude for such acts of generosity and selflessness. I can only hope that the analysis offered in this volume demonstrates my commitment to the pursuit of scholarship that can be read in multiple languages. It is my wish that as my interlocutors and those who supported the production of this book skim through the following pages, they can see how intensely I thought about our conversations long after we parted ways.

Aslan Saeidi and Katayoun Alaedin, my parents, dealt with a very unruly daughter. This book would have been impossible without your capacity to let go. You encouraged me to not only think about, but also search for, freedom. You are my first teachers and greatest inspirations. I am blessed to have Nur Sadat in my life. Your light has made me stronger, and I thank you.

1 State Formation and Citizenship
An Investigation beyond a Eurocentric Gaze

1.1 Introduction

Women and the Islamic Republic's central argument is simple: If we shift our gaze from institutions and elite political contestations to everyday encounters, we will see how the Islamic Republic's hybrid governance structure produces citizens who cross, abide, and (at times) manipulate the state's formal boundaries. This pushes the postrevolutionary state toward a balancing act to pacify its female population.

More specifically, by exploring the experiences of diverse groups of women during the Iran–Iraq war (1980–1988) and in the postwar years, this book demonstrates how women's contextually contingent remaking of their rights, responsibilities, and statuses in postrevolutionary Iran also intermingles with, shifts, and conditions the state formation process as a consequence of what was, at least initially, an imposed war (Hiltermann, 2010). Previous investigations of non-elite women's and other populations' everyday encounters have shown how the state employed "women" as an important trope for the postrevolutionary state, as well as how women, in turn, used the trope to make the state answer to their concerns (Bayat, 2010a; Deeb, 2006; Mir-Hosseini, 2000; Moallem, 2005; Osanloo, 2009). *Women and the Islamic Republic* contributes to these studies by addressing a significant gap in this literature: I explore the effects of the Iran–Iraq war *on the status and formation of women's rights, roles, and responsibilities* in conditioning the state's formation. Each chapter illustrates the different forms and scales of citizenship that my interlocutors performed in postrevolutionary Iran within the broader milieu of legal inequality and ambiguous governance. My interlocutors also negotiated citizenship within the context and legacies of the Iran–Iraq war, as well as the Shi'i foundation of the state, which venerates female religious figures who crossed public/private boundaries (Povey and Rostami-Povey, 2012).

By studying statecraft as entailing acts of citizenship, *Women and the Islamic Republic* contributes to feminist political theory and the feminist struggle to move beyond resistance in discussions of women and the state. The importance of my non-elite female interlocutors to the conditioning of the state formation process is not tied to the Iranian context. Rather, my exploration of gendered citizenship in contemporary Iran can more broadly help us understand the substance of citizenship, as well as the state formation process for hybrid regimes in the region (De Souza and Lipietz, 2011). This book, then, does not take citizenship as central to state formation because of the Eurocentrism that plagues political science despite being a "global discipline" (Acharya, 2014, p. 649). Instead, by sidelining a Eurocentric gaze, I join other scholars who question their own assumptions to demonstrate what the post-1979 Iranian experience teaches us conceptually about citizenship and the art of statecraft.

1.2   Postrevolutionary Conflicts: Numbers and Logistics

The Iran–Iraq war, as well as the emergence of a civil war between the state and its opposition, placed the Iranian state in a unique position to shape women's rights struggles in postrevolutionary Iran. As such, this section will briefly historicize the 1980–1988 period. The victory of the 1979 revolution and conflict between different oppositional forces after the fall of the Shah coincided with the start of the Iran–Iraq war. In September 1980, Iraq invaded Iran, beginning what would be an eight-year war. Farhi (2004) has argued that coherent statistics do not exist regarding the number of people who participated in the Iran–Iraq war during different periods. This renders all estimations problematic.

There is limited scholarly research and social analysis of the Iran–Iraq war, and the Islamic Republic continues to dominate this discourse (Saghafi, 2001). However, for the purpose of presenting a broad statistical perspective, I offer the following data, which I verified through several and mostly reliable sources. This conflict resulted in the death of an estimated 188,000–213,000 people at the front; approximately 16,000 were killed in city bombings and attacks (Ghasami, n.d.; Sepahe Pasdarane, Revolutionary Guards website). According to Farhi's research, between 1.5 and 3 million people participated in the war, with Iran's population growing from 35 million in 1979 to 50 million toward the end of the war in 1986 (Farhi, 2004).

Different sources seem to suggest the following regarding women's participation in the war: According to one source, 6,601 women are considered martyrs of the war by the Islamic Republic, but approximately 100 of these women were killed by the Pahlavi Monarchy prior to the revolution (Ghasami, n.d.; Saeidi, 2008). Estimates suggest that 27 percent of these women were martyred in Khuzestan, southern Iran, parts of which were occupied from 1980 to 1982 (Safavi, 1389/2010). During the war, about 22,808 women volunteered as first-aid medics on various warfronts. Scholars based in Iran argue that 2,276 female doctors also worked on the front lines (Anon., 1390/2011; Ghasami, n.d.). In 1984, the Revolutionary Guards trained 4,000 female volunteers to carry out intelligence-gathering operations (Moghadam, 1988). While these statistics are hardly definitive, we can surmise that Iranian women had a significant presence in the Iran–Iraq war.

The number of Marxist groups, organizations, and parties grew in the aftermath of the 1979 revolution. As Behrooz (1999, p. 105) argues:

While prior to the revolution there had been perhaps a dozen such groups, after it their numbers grew to perhaps over 80, and this number increased as Marxist groups began to fragment into smaller units. Indeed, after the revolution it became common for any gathering of a few Marxist activists to call itself an organisation or party and claim to be the rightful vanguard of the working class. Hence, it is neither possible, nor perhaps necessary, to produce an account of all Marxist organisations, parties, and groups in the post-revolutionary era. It is safe to suggest that whatever happened to the major organisations and parties also broadly happened to the smaller ones.

Women and the Islamic Republic focuses on different Marxist groups. One of the largest Marxist organizations post-1979 was the Fadaiyan. In June 1980, it split into two factions: aksariyyat (majority) and aqaliyyat (minority). While the aksariyyat were willing to negotiate with the newly established regime, the aqaliyyat believed in armed resistance against the regime. During this time, the organization had fewer than 100 members, but it was estimated to have had over half a million devoted supporters (Behrooz, 1999, p. 105).

Paykar was a small organization that had between thirty and fifty influential members (Behrooz, 1999). Paykar is believed to have had thousands of supporters that were former Muslim Mojahedin who had moved away from religion and toward Marxism (Behrooz, 1999). The organization was influential in the Kurdistan region, where it ideologic-ally supported militant Kurdish groups, such as the Komoleh. The Tudeh was another Marxist organization that lacked popular support in post-1979 Iran. This was partly because it could not garner significant popular support after the 1953 coup. In 1980, it sided with the aksariyyat faction and revamped its ideological framework (Behrooz, 1999). By 1981, the Tudeh Party had lost its connections with other leftist groups, including the aksariyyat. The Tudeh and aksariyyat both collaborated with the newly established regime to suppress other leftist groups

(Behrooz, 1999). Smaller organizations such as the Organization of the Worker's Path (Sazman-e Rah-e Kargar) were important not because of their large support base – which did not exist – but because of their approach to instigating discussion among Iranian leftist organizations (Behrooz, 1999).

Another Marxist group with an insignificant number of supporters was Communist Unity (Sazman-e Vahdat-e Komonisty), but between 1979 and 1981 it continued to generate debates within the left through publications by a small circle of intellectuals (Behrooz, 1999). The Communist League of Iran (Etehadieh Komonistha-ye Iran) was a Maoist organization that began an armed struggle against the Islamic Republic in 1982 (Behrooz, 1999). The Iranian left grew post-1979 but did not enjoy popular support the way Ayatollah Khomeini did. Nevertheless, their experiences within prisons clarify leftist women's engagement with the postrevolutionary regime's gender policies in a space that continues to be of great importance in current Iran.

People from various backgrounds fought and died in defense of Iran, including members of the Islamic Mojahedin and the leftist Feda'iyyin guerrilla group (Saghafi, 1378/1999; Tagavi, 1985). Efat Mahbaz (2008), a supporter of aksariyyat, remembers this: Her brother Ali, also connected to aksariyyat, was arrested and executed a month before he was to leave for the front to offer medical support. Ali Mahbaz was an expert in laboratory science and a supervisor of the laboratory at Sarkhah Hasaar Hospital prior to his execution in the fall of 1981. Moreover, leftist political prisoners were not indifferent to Iran's war with Iraq. Efat Mahbaz (2008, p. 271) remembers being freed after seven years in prison:

As we were freed from prison, many Iranian prisoners of war were also released by Iraq. Like many other Iranians, I too went to greet these prisoners near Azadi Square upon their return to Iran. They had sorrowful faces with cold smiles on their lips. They were given red roses to hold. The suits they had on appeared to be in pain. Most of the people [that had come to welcome them home] were crying. Everything came together in a way that I instinctively began to compare them to political prisoners.[1]

The Iran–Iraq war served as a backdrop to the experiences of leftist political prisoners from behind bars, but it also shaped the Islamic Republic's view of its opposition. In another illustration, memoirs of Iranian prisoners of war have claimed that in the last few years of the war Iraqis relied on members of the Islamic Mojahedin as translators

---

[1] Translations are my own and occasionally edited by my dear friend Zahra Abbasi.

during interrogation of Iranian fighters (Hosseinipour, 1391/2012). The war was understood from and lived in different perspectives, many of which still require further investigation.

After the 1979 revolution, different political factions initially thought that supporters of Khomeini, who had quickly gained popular support, would share power with them (Arjomand, 1988). This would not, however, be the case. In the 1980–1985 period, women (and men) associated with Marxist–Leninist organizations or the Islamic Mojahedin faced mass imprisonment and execution as the Islamic Republic Party gained control of institutions under Khomeini's leadership (Shahidian, 1997). Many believe that a second revolution took place from 1980 to 1983, as well as a civil war, following the establishment of the Islamic Republic in Iran.

In 1981, the Islamic Mojahedin retaliated against the consolidation of power by the Islamic Republic Party and its human rights violations in prisons by killing over 1,000 influential clerics and laymen in bombing attacks (Iran Human Rights Documentation Center, 2009). One local nongovernmental organization (NGO) in Iran estimates that the Mojahedin killed close to 17,000 armed and unarmed Iranians between 1980 and 2012, with most of the killings having taken place between 1980 and 1988.[2] Mahmoud Amjadian was a prisoner of war in Iraq when he was killed by the Mojahedin only twenty-five days before he was to be released following six years of imprisonment. The following is his friend's reaction to witnessing his death, as shared with Amjadian's family:

The free spirit Shahid[3] engaged in the combats accompanying his brothers and was also a prisoner of war. He was martyred by the filthy hands of the hypocrites.[4] You, family of the free Shahid Amjadian! The night of Mahmoud's martyrdom, you were not there to mourn his death. It was unbelievable how the whole campsite was in grief of his death! In the campsite where I was imprisoned, the doors were closed and prayers were already said. That night, after Salah[5] was observed, every single one of the men there was stricken with inconsolable grief.

His friend continued:

Even though they did not know yet if he had been martyred for sure, they faced to Qiblah[6] and mourned his death. The sound of crying and mourning made one

---

[2] Shaheed (2012, p. 13). For more on these killings, see the website for Habilian, a local NGO in Iran that has documented the names of victims and locations of their deaths: Habilian, Iran, accessed in 2012, www.habilian.ir/en/.

[3] The Iranian prisoners of war are called *Azadeh* (free), signifying their free spirit.

[4] In the Islamic Iranian jargon, the term *Monafeqin* (hypocrites) refers to the Islamic Mojahedin.

[5] An obligatory religious duty in Islam that must be observed five times a day.

[6] Mecca: In Islam, all Muslims face Mecca at the time of prayers as an indication of unity.

Iraqi soldier (guards of the prison) so curious that he had come behind the doors to see if we were making trouble. The mourning stopped, but sound of grief was heard occasionally. The guard called me and said: "Come out! Go wash your face. Your brother is not dead yet!" The guard tried hard to stop the mourning, but in vain. Believe me, they cried so uncontrollably and loudly that the Iraqi soldier told me: "Go tell others that your brother is not martyred. Do not worry!" The enemy knew that our brother was already martyred. (Amjadian, 1381/2002, pp. 18–19)

This narration illustrates the heartache that Iranians experienced because of the Mojahedin's acts of violence. Viewing prisoners mainly through their group identity, the Islamic Republic in turn carried out mass arrests and executions of all opposition forces. Some imprisoned members of the Islamic Mojahedin were connected to those who were actively fighting the Islamic Republic outside prison. For instance, Nasrin Parvaz (2002, p. 99), a member of the Union of Communist Militants (which merged with the Komoleh shortly after the revolution) who was initially given an execution sentence, stated that imprisoned members of the Islamic Mojahedin would steal money from leftist prisoners to send to their organization outside prison. She describes the complex system Islamic Mojahedin had created to support their organization (Parvaz, 2002, p. 122):

They were Mujaheds that had become penitents [*tavvabs*] in prison. After some time, their organisation establishes relations with the organisation outside of prison. At the same time, they continued to work closely with interrogators. This collaboration was so extensive that at one point they were able to sneak a film of someone's torture out of prison. They were even able to steal the files of some of their friends and save them from execution. The interrogators trusted them so much that they were allowed to go home and rest for a few days, and then return to prison.[7]

Within this context of attacks and counterattacks, the precise number of political prisoners from 1980 to 1988 is impossible to determine. Indeed, most researchers agree that only certain individuals within the Islamic Republic's ruling elite could verify this information.[8] However,

---

[7] I have both interviewed Parvaz and read her work. Parvaz's memoir is over 300 pages and in Farsi. Parts of the memoir have been translated into English; see Parvaz and Namazie (2003). Her writing and poetry can be downloaded here: www.nasrinparvaz.org/web/. Parvaz's claims here regarding the Mojahedin's complex interaction with prison officials are also supported by Talebi (2011, p. 80).

[8] This question was posed to Shadi Sadr, Ervand Abrahamian, and Reza Afshari via online communication. All three are experts on the plight of political prisoners in postrevolutionary Iran, and none were able or willing to offer an estimate. On March 11, 2012, in an email exchange, Abrahamian stated that it is "impossible to give even half-estimates" as prisons were "revolving doors" during the 1980–1988 years. In an email

we do know this for certain. From 1981 until 1988, mass arrests and summary executions were common. We also know that the terror and mass arrests that followed the 1979 revolution resulted in the relocation of 4 million Iranians to the West, particularly the United States (Afshari, 2001). And, during the 1988 massacre, up to 1,000 prisoners in Tehran's Evin prison were executed; many more in Karaj's Gohardasht prison met the same fate (Robertson, 2011, p. 75).

Abrahamian (2008, p. 181) estimates that at least 8,000 executions took place between 1981 and 1985, and most of the executed were members of the Islamic Mojahedin. Between 1980 and 1988, 10,588 political prisoners are believed to have been executed in total.[9] Prisoners believe that everyday prison conditions improved between 1984 and 1987. This was a period when Ayatollah Montazeri's followers occupied key administrative positions (Robertson, 2011, p. 35). Afshari (2001, p. 105) argues that Montazeri and his followers had a significant role in removing the fanatical networks that maintained power within the prison system.

Additionally, prisoners remember resisting the state more forcefully during this period. They recall being more confrontational with guards, even attacking them when they heard news that the state was nearing collapse from relatives, visitors, and other prisoners who would join at later stages (Robertson, 2011, p. 36). For instance, in 1988, when news reached prisoners that fewer Iranians were willing to go to the front lines of war, Marxist prisoners refused to observe the Muslim fast during Ramadan (Robertson, 2011, p. 37). However, at times when Iran was losing at the front, such as the 1988 period when it was forced to end the war, prisoners also experienced the worst treatment, including summary executions and increased lashings.

While the level of violence fluctuated, dominant trends in the conditions at Evin prison in Tehran and Gohardasht prison in Karaj, as well as in the treatment of political prisoners, allow us to draw some tentative conclusions about female prisoners' experiences. The former political prisoners included in this study were held either with the general population or in solitary confinement. During the most difficult torture, they were held in solitary confinement, itself a form of torture (Mesdaghi, 1383/2004). Men and women were oftentimes held on different levels of

---

exchange on March 13, 2012, Afshari added that it becomes particularly difficult to make an estimate given that we still have limited knowledge of prisons in the provinces that are distant from Tehran.

[9] These data come from www.iranrights.org/farsi/memorial-search.php?pagenum=0. Many thanks to Leila Mouri and Shadi Sadr for helping me find this information.

the Evin and Gohardasht prisons. They saw each other in the corridors and during visitations, and they were sometimes placed in the same room when brought in to see the dead bodies following an execution (Mesdaghi, 1383/2004). Forcing prisoners to see and touch the corpses of their former comrades was, for prison officials, a "teaching moment" they believed would encourage other prisoners to submit to the demands of interrogators (Mesdaghi, 1383/2004).

Discussions around the use of rape in prisons circa 1980–1988 are rampant and controversial. In a 2011 report, Sadr argues that rape was common during this period in Iran's prisons. In my interviews with fifty former political prisoners (2008–2009) now living in Germany and Sweden, however, interviewees were adamant that rape was not widespread at the time.

Significantly, Sadr and I had interviewed some of the same women. During a conference in 2012 at Oxford University, I saw Sadr and some of our interviewees. I asked the interviewees why they had given us different responses to the question of rape. Most ignored my effort at starting a debate, but one woman became outraged that I would suggest that prison rape was not widespread and mentioned it had long been settled in memoirs. She believed that because many former prisoners, including Nasrin Parvaz and Iraj Mesdaghi, had discussed the rape of women in prison, I should not be concerned about this inconsistency, and she viewed my curiosity itself as an indication of my carelessness.

I will always remember the faces of a few leftist men sitting next to her at the lunch table changing color as they physically leaned in toward me with looks of disgust. It was one of the few times during my research where I lost my confidence. I was scared. My fear was not of a physical confrontation but of the scholarly concern of hurting my interlocutors in the process of research. As more prison memoirs were published, this issue became hazier. For instance, Shahrnush Parsipur (2013, pp. 38–39) observes,

In truth, I never heard prisoners talk about sexual abuse. But it was rumored that on their final night, young girls sentenced to death were wed to the guards so that they wouldn't be buried as virgins. It was said that if a girl was buried while still a virgin, she would lure a man to follow her to the grave. My only proof that this might have been happening were Shahin's last words [this prisoner had stated that her interrogator had touched her breasts, and she felt this meant she would be executed. Indeed, she was executed shortly after the alleged incident]. I did know a couple of other prisoners who had gotten close to having sexual relations with the guards, but in one instance it was a prisoner's strategy to stop her torture, and in another, deeply affectionate feelings had developed between an interrogator and a prisoner.

These inconsistencies capture the complexity of working with memories, as well as of the formation of analysis in qualitative research, and raise many questions: What is at stake in such claims for a feminist lawyer living in exile (Sadr) versus former political prisoners who are also living in exile? Given the conservative elements in Iran's left as well as the political work that the terms *rape* and *prostitute* carry out in Iranian society, could it be that shame, self-care, and self-preservation prevented some women from discussing rape with me, an outsider?

These questions will continue to unsettle me and complicate the possible uses and boundaries of ethnography in general and interviews in particular. Reflecting on such moments of the research process reminds me of Hartman's (2008) emphasis on recognizing what may never be retrieved in the lives of the marginalized. At the same time, Hartman insists on thinking imaginatively about that which we cannot know for certain by using, with restraint, innovative reading practices such as an investigation of narratives.

1.3 Intersections between Ambiguous Citizenry Structures and War in a Hybrid Regime

Feminist scholars generally agree that women's citizenship is often compromised in postrevolutionary periods as they are pushed back into the home (Hatem, 2000; Joseph, 2000; Tetreault, 1994; Vickers, 2008). Iran's formal citizenry framework and unique experience with war in the postrevolutionary period animated the possibility for innovative gendered approaches to citizenship. My investigation of citizenship in the postrevolutionary Iranian state illustrates that, in addition to explicit legal inequality, the ambiguity surrounding the legislation of Islamic law engenders what Nyers (2011) has identified as "irregular citizenship": namely, that "citizenship has not been revoked per se, but ... rendered inoperable, or 'irregularised.'"

Minoo Moallem (2005) asserts that the Islamic Republic implements a citizenry agenda through the transnational notion of an *Islamic Ummat* to downplay the diversity among Muslims in Iran as well as abroad. Moallem (2005, p. 24) states: "The patriarchal control of women's bodies and sexuality as a major subject of religious and cultural discourses converges with hegemonic notions of sexuality that privilege heteronormativity in the context of modernity and postmodernity. Thus, both gendered and sexual citizenship are created (and of course contested) as sites of exclusion and inclusion."

The Iranian constitution explicitly addresses civic rights as well as social rights. The problem is that these rights are inconsistently upheld and overshadowed by a vague notion of Islamic authenticity. For instance, as Paidar (1995) has argued, the Iranian constitution identifies the state as being responsible for adhering to Islamic law with respect to women, but the constitution refers to Islamic law "as an extra-constitutional criteria in many of its articles" (p. 261). Paidar has illustrated, for instance, that Article 21 – which addresses the protection of mothers and the family – identifies the state as being responsible for also protecting women's rights within an Islamic legal framework. However, there isn't any clarification on what women's rights are or what qualifies as Islamic law. I agree with Paidar's assessment that "this resulted in the subjection of the constitution to a divine law outside and above it" (p. 261). *Women and the Islamic Republic* demonstrates that in addition to conflict over explicit legal inequalities, citizenship's irregular nature in Iran has intensified elite and non-elite contestation over the term in practice as well as theory.

In another example, Paidar (1995, p. 261) notes that Article 151 identifies the state to be responsible for providing military service for all citizens within the boundaries of Islamic law. Whether women should be permitted to defend the country in the context of war remains vague, though. In some instances, the law is unambiguous regarding women's rights but equally irregular. While Iranian law does not ban women from biking, for example, in 2016 Iran's Supreme Leader, Ayatollah Khamenei, identified women's cycling in public as impermissible.[10]

While Khamenei's fatwas in relation to social issues are national law according to Article 110 of Iran's constitution, they are not legislated the same way throughout the country because of the controversy that surrounds the exceptional amount of power the position of Supreme Leader has been granted in Iran's post-1988 constitution. Khamenei's rulings, then, are not equally and consistently abided by in practice by other state agents, including his representatives, or by the population at large.[11] Iranian women in Kurdistan's province of Marivan, for instance, have been prohibited from cycling in public. As a result of such

[10] See BBC Persian's reporting on this topic: www.bbc.com/persian/iran/2016/09/160918_126_khamenei_cycling_women_forbidden. See also the Supreme Leader's official website: http://leader.ir/fa/content/16227/دوچرخه-سواری-بانون.

[11] In another instance, while Iran's law and the Supreme Leader view music concerts as permissible, Ayatollah Alamolhoda, who is the Supreme Leader's representative and the leader of Friday prayers in Mashhad, does not allow music concerts to take place in the holy Shi'i city: www.entekhab.ir/fa/news/285820/چرا-توریست-به-مشهد-نباید-بیاید-دیگر-نباید-سر- کنسرت-با-مردم-با-برخی-لان-مسئول-کوته%80%E2%فکر-چانه%80%8C%E2نی-کرد-اگر-کنسرت-میخواهی. انداخته-راه-درکشی-رضا-ر-امام-مقابل-در-کن-زندگی-دیگری-جای On Alamolhoda's position and how it conflicts with the Supreme Leader's views on this issue see: www.ghatreh.com/news/nn33212192/حجتی-کرمانی-اظهارات-علم-الهدی-صدر-صدد-خلاف-نظر-رهبری-است.

inconsistencies, women in different parts of the country experience conflict over this issue in everyday life.

Another important contextual factor in the formation of gendered citizenship during the 1980–1988 period in Iran was that the postrevolutionary leadership was unprepared for the Iraqi invasion. As an indication of Iran's unpreparedness, Khomeini suddenly ordered the release of ninety American-trained pilots who were imprisoned for months due to allegations of treason (Stempel, 1981). The unexpectedness of the war also affected how women living in southern Iran remember how their lives were interrupted. Narges Aghajari, a medical assistant from Abadan, states the following about the day the war began:

I was 20 when the war started. The Youth Organization at the time, or Hilal Ahmar today [Iran's equivalent of the Red Cross], offered training courses, such as typewriting, and sewing ... I had signed up for typewriting. On the morning of the 31st of Shahrivar [September 22], I was getting ready to attend my class. My brother came home, and when he found out I wanted to go to class he said, "so you don't hear these sounds?"

He then went on to inform her about the Iraqi attack on Iran. She continues:

Then when I saw the war planes and heard the sound of bombs and missiles, I realized that yes! There is a real attack on our soil. Like many families in the city, my family insisted that I leave Abadan. In fact, they said the city must be evacuated. But we pleaded with my father until he allowed us to stay. He would not accept our request easily but he was a committed man, we continued to insist, and finally he allowed us to stay. ("Revayat-e Zan-e Emdadgar-e Abadani az Ruzhaay-e Jang," 1396)

Saham Taghati is an Iranian-Arab from Khorramshahr and one of fifteen women who stayed and defended their hometown as medical assistants at the onset of the war. She recalls the beginning of the war in the following way:

Exactly on the 30th of Shahrivar [September 21] I was at the bazaar with Fakhri [her sister] and two of our friends: Nabati and Alieh Hajipour. They were both seamstresses and wanted to buy some fabric and sew themselves *manteau* [Islamic garment]. It was about 7 pm, but the sun had not set yet, and suddenly we heard the sound of a few loud explosions. We were close to the Jamae Masjid [a popular Mosque in Khorramshahr]. We turned toward the Seif Bazaar. We were trapped between the waves of people that were moving. Everyone was saying something different. Most people stated that "they have attacked the *bandar* [port]." Alieh hit herself on the head and screamed "my father is dead!" That day it was her father's turn to work at the port's customs. We went to their house very quickly. Their father knew his family would be worried and he arrived just as we did. Alieh was delighted that her father was alive. We said goodbye to them and returned to our own home. There was no security anywhere, and if we were killed, we did not even have identification documents on us. We walked toward our home. Our neighborhood was 200 meters from customs, and they were attacking that area aggressively. I told Fakhri, from tomorrow we have to wear sneakers and have identification on us in case something happens. Unlike the environment outside, our home was calm. (Soleimani, 1381/2002, pp. 15–16)

The context of invasion meant the war was "imposed" in the view of the Iranian state and parts of society, at least initially. This view on the invasion of Iran by Iraq was also instrumental in engendering long-term volunteer participation in the war with little state compensation in return. This understanding challenges the historical top-down approach utilized to study the connection between war and citizenship formation (Kage, 2010; Mann, 1987; Markoff, 1996; Marwick, 1988). The Iran–Iraq war was a people's war for the Islamic Republic, and the leaders of the new regime would have been unable to carry out the war without popular support (Gongora, 1997). In fact, one of the reasons the war came to an end was precisely that popular participation in the war waned by the mid-1980s (Gongora, 1997). This is also an important reason why the Iranian people felt it necessary that the postrevolutionary state respond to *their* needs – because they participated in the effort to fight against the invasion and support the Islamic Republic. Now the postrevolutionary state needed to heed their aspirations, demands, and desires.[12]

According to the Islamic Republic's own records, the invasion of Iran by Iraqi forces was unexpected. For instance, The Center for War Studies and Research states the following:

The Islamic Republic had no preparation or readiness for getting involved in classic warfare between 1357 and 1359 [1978–1980]. Iran's national security and defense strategy were completely disrupted. Among the state's armed forces (the army, police, Revolutionary Guards, and Basij) there was extensive discoordination, so much so that foreign observers, including Iraqi military elites, believed the following: "Iran is lacking reliable defense forces." Similarly, Iran was also short on military supplies because all of the country's military relations were cut-off, and all military contracts were suspended. The armed forces of the country were not ready to respond to the invasion of Iraq. (Markaze motalat va tahgheghate jang, 1378/1999, p. 100)

This lack of preparation and coordination meant that much of the defense was popular and spontaneous (Basij Jamaah Zanan-e Keshvar, 1391). In fact, Iran's main advantage in the war was its manpower – a population that stood at 45 million in 1985, more than three times the

---

[12] Thank you to the reader who made this connection during the clearance review of the book.

size of Iraq's population (Farhang, 1985, p. 662). Additionally, during the 1980–1988 period, Iranian society was emerging from a revolution guided by the utopian vision of creating a new society (Bayat, 2010a).

A young and enthusiastic population was already mobilized and ready to make sacrifices prior to the Iraqi invasion of Iran because of the 1979 revolution (Skocpol, 1988). For instance, young female students associated with the Academic Center for Education, Culture, and Research (*jihad daneshgahi*) – established after the 1979 revolution in different parts of the country – volunteered at fronts in the south, washing soldiers' clothing and preparing their meals (Basij Jamaah Zanan-e Keshvar, 1391; Judaki, 1395/2016, p. 91).

In other instances, there was little institutional support for organizing women's volunteer work (Akbari, 1390/2011). For example, women living in southern Iran individually volunteered at local hospitals and washed soldiers' bloodied clothing (Judaki, 1395/2016, p. 91). The estimated fifteen women who stayed at Khorramshahr when the city was attacked in September 1980 remember burying the dead to prevent the corpses from being eaten by dogs (Soleimani, 1381/2002; interview, Tehran, June 2008). During the early days following the revolution, many hospitals were not equipped to handle the amount of laundry. Iranian women, particularly those geographically close to the front lines, carried the emotional and financial burdens of the war by caring for refugees and the families of martyrs with visitations and distribution of clothing, food, and other material goods (Akbari, 1390/2011).

Women from across Iran volunteered to become medical assistants and received short-term training before joining various warfronts (Jafarian, 1381/2002). Iranian women wrote letters to soldiers, as well as their own fathers, brothers, and husbands. See, for instance, a letter titled "A Small Contribution" from a woman who identifies as a martyr's wife to men on the warfront in 1366/1987:

I am the wife of one of the martyrs who gave their blood for the revolution. After being injured four times, my husband finally paid the ultimate sacrifice for Islam in Esfand [March] 1365 [1986] during the successful operation of Karbala 5. In addition to a corporeal jihad, he went on a financial jihad as well. For that purpose, he saved some of the foreign currency that he used to take care of his basic needs during travels abroad. This amounted to more than 300 British pounds. He donated all of this money to the National Development Fund. Likewise, I have gathered all of the jewelry that I was gifted by this martyr during my marriage, and I am bestowing it to the Revolutionary Guard Corps. I hope with this small step, I am able to contribute to the freeing of Hossein's Karbala. (Shirazi, 1387/2008, pp. 22–23)

Shamsy Sobhani, a medical assistant who volunteered in southern Iran, remembers how the local women of Andimeshk, in the Khuzestan province, would offer washing powder to the Shahid Kalantari Hospital's laundry room:

The local women would come to help. Although there was plenty of washing powder in the hospital, they would bring powder and bleach. There was an older lady who had sold her chickens so she could buy washing powder for us. No matter how much we stressed that the hospital has enough, please don't do this, it did not matter. (Jafarian, 1381/2002, p. 115)

Saham Taghati, who worked closely with ten other women in Khorramshahr to support soldiers, remembers going to Abadan once a week with five or six of these women to take a shower:

In Khorramshahr, they had shut off the water. To be more exact, there was water only during certain hours, and we rushed to store as much as we could for necessary tasks. Once a week, five or six of us would take a shower in Abadan! We did not know anyone there [in Abadan]. We knocked on people's doors and asked "can we use your bathroom?" The women of the home would usually agree. Sometimes as we were taking a bath, the homeowner would put our clothing in the washing machine. When we came out of the bath, we would put on clean clothes and say goodbye to the homeowner. (Soleimani, 1381/2002, p. 25)

Similar to women in other contexts, Iranian women participated in the war in a variety of ways that included emotional, physical, and financial support of the warfront. They also supported each other.

Iranian war studies expert Jalili (1396/2017, p. 48) states the following with regard to the role of the people in the war and the significance of the revolution to mobilizing popular support for the war in the postrevolutionary period:

Our war differed greatly from other wars in the world. One of these differences was the popular nature of the defense. Our war was not taken forward by organizations such as the Revolutionary Guards or the army. The revolutionary guards and the army were influential. The bulk of the work, however, was carried out by everyday people. This is what makes our war unique. Certainly, it is bad that we had two armies, and still the war fell on the shoulders of Basij volunteers. At any rate, this was the case. The reality of the war was that our soldiers departed for warfronts from mosques.[13] Even a lot of military training took place in mosques. The place from which all sorts of preparations were made was the Basij headquarters. From the commanders to jams and food stuff, it all came spontaneously from the people. Therefore, while the state's formal military

---

[13] Mosques were crucial centers of mobilization for Islamists before the 1979 revolution as well. For more on this see Ghodsizad (1383/2004).

organizations should have taken the lead in the war, their role was less significant than that of the people.

Iran's dire situation, but the people's optimistic outlook, can also be noted in the writings of Iranian feminist scholar and women's rights activist Mehrangiz Kar. Visiting the Khuzestan province in southern Iran only four years after the end of the war, Kar offers some of the initial sociological observations on the destruction that the region had endured. In *Nakhl haye Sukhteh* (Scorched Palm Trees), Kar (1379/2000) discusses her first moments in Abadan in 1371/1992, although the book was published several years later:

I gave my directions to the driver. Homelessness, instability and pain have taught him the lesson of patience. He is peaceful and kind. During the drive, my attention goes toward homes that are ruined. I tell myself that these are the same homes prepared for employees of the oil company. Those beautiful homes had many amenities, but there is no trace of the colors, the green grass, the gardens, and facilities that are still in our dreams. Homes that have been rebuilt resemble second-hand patchwork clothing, and bring great sorrow to my heart. (pp. 12-13)

Kar notes the destructive impact of the war as she travels in Khuzestan and poses questions about the slow reconstruction process that many in the region still complain about (Kar, 1379/2000, pp. 12–13).

The context of the war demanded popular support and cooperation, and wartime urgencies undermined the political boundaries that the Islamic Republic sought to formalize through legal and structural mechanisms (Saghafi, 1378/1999). There were also specific temporal, regional, and historical contingencies that at times supported women's participation in the war and established situated forms of citizenship. As Koolaee (2014) has argued, unlike the Iraqi experience, Iranian women were not invited into the public sphere during the war due to a lack of human resources. Instead, the 1979 revolution and the Iranian constitution politicized women and encouraged them to pursue their interests, desires, and justice-oriented goals in the postrevolutionary state. There were also regional norms that enhanced the possibility for women's involvement with the war. For example, Kar (1379/2000) states the following about the women of Khuzestan:

Unlike the city, where women had the right to appear as they wished and be demanding as they worked in most offices and training centers, the women living on the margins of the city or in villages worked in the most difficult conditions. They did not even ask for any salary or rights in return. These barefoot women were involved in both production and distribution of homemade products.

Kar goes on to explain how the working conditions of women living in southern Iran prepared them to engage with extended war conditions:

At dawn, they would put black cloth on their heads and place their black pots on top of it, and they would take their products to the city for distribution. Their system for distribution did not include any machinery and was exacting, extensive, and non-stop. These women managed a complicated process with great agility and ease. As such, by sunrise, on every street corner there was a bin of rice milk, a bin of fresh cream, a scale with a few rocks, and a plastic bag for collecting cash. Additionally, there was an alert woman present greeting customers. (pp. 24–25)

As Kar explains, gender relations in Khuzestan were traditionally more relaxed than in regions such as Mashhad and Qom. This meant that women could more readily engage with the public fronts of the war, including those in southern Iran. Additionally, the women who lived in the small villages that bordered Iraq also had a history of involvement in the informal economy and hard physical labor. Prior to the onset of the war, Revolutionary Guards had trained women who supported Khomeini to confront various armed resistance groups targeting the Islamic Republic (Jafarian, 1381/2002; Judaki, 1395/2016, p. 71). With the start of the war, many of these women, such as Maryam Amjadi and Sakeeneh Hoorsi, trained other women and men in armed resistance (Judaki, 1395/2016, p. 71). As another illustration, Maryam Seyaaval trained male soldiers in Iran's Kurdistan during the war (Judaki, 1395/2016, p. 72). Mothers who had sons at the warfront also managed rest stops and centers where they washed and prepared clean uniforms (Judaki, 1395/2016, p. 72). Within at least some segments of Iranian society, there was an embedded readiness to carry the weight of the war where the state was lacking. As I will shortly discuss, many women – particularly those living in southern Iran and in the border regions – participated.

The power structure in postrevolutionary Iran relied upon parallel institutions that depended extensively on popular participation (Bayat, 2010a; Ehsani, 2009; Kamrava, 2000). Unlike classic cases of state formation and warfare in the West (Tilly, 1985, 1990a), the postrevolutionary Iranian state was unable to consolidate its power or establish a unified citizenry body within the context of the Iran–Iraq war. Ehsani (2017) has argued that in Iran political and institutional fragmentation became a hallmark of the postwar period. The already ambiguous citizenry guidelines in a hybrid regime with republican elements intersected with the unexpected invasion of Iran by Iraq. But the postwar fragmentation of the power structure fashioned the situated nature of women's gendered citizenship, which continues to condition the state formation process. Additionally, the centrality of sacred female figures in the Shi'i faith, such as Hazrat-e Fatemeh, daughter of Prophet Mohammad, and Hazrat-e Zeinab, his granddaughter, gives the Islamic Republic a particular readiness to recognize issues pertaining to women's concerns (Shariati, 1356/1977). The following chapters illustrate how historical contingencies made the state an important instigator of gendered citizenship. This chapter sets *Women and the Islamic Republic*'s tone by arguing that in post-1979 Iran the flux in state regulatory measures has been central to the expression of micropolitics and formation of unrehearsed acts of citizenship from within society.

1.4 Citizenship and State Formation: Toward a New Approach

Coupled with the ambiguities that define the interplay between Islamic law, women's rights, and their application within society, the Iraqi invasion meant that different expressions of acts of citizenship develop. These expressions are contingent on the context, opportunities, and limits that specific historical moments forge.

Women and the Islamic Republic draws upon the more recent generation of state formation literature to construct an original theoretical framework for studying the art of statecraft through acts of citizenship. Popular claim-making efforts and the state's cultural dimensions have been examined, particularly within ethnographic studies of the state, but without a lens on acts of citizenship (Chatterjee, 2004; Coronil, 1997; Das and Poole, 2004; Gupta, 1995; Hansen, 1999; Hansen and Stepputat, 2001; Joseph and Nugent, 1994). Additionally, studies of state formation have depicted the state as the "effect" of particular practices (Migdal, 2001; Mitchell, 1991, 2002, p. 77) and stressed the importance of studying political practice "as it is" (Abrams, 1988, p. 82; Biersteker and Weber, 1995; Doty, 2003; MacKinnon, 1989).

I argue that this unstable nexus between statecraft and particular enactments (Dunn, 2010; Strauss and Cruise O'Brien, 2007) makes acts of citizenship integral to the state's conditioning. Importantly, "the state then is not the focus of the story: the process of crafting the state, which is constantly being performed in a variety of ways, is the focus of understanding political authority and power. Statecraft is highly contextual and is a crafting, a process with a multiplicity of particular instantiations" (Auchter, 2014, p. 5). While we know that citizenship is about governance and an important attribute of the modern state (Faulks, 2000), we also know that the subject-making process is contested during everyday life to complicate how citizenship is studied (Ong, 1996).

Women and the Islamic Republic retheorizes Engin Isin's notion of acts of citizenship as a lens to understand how the non-elite women I interviewed conditioned the state formation process in post-1979 Iran. For Isin, agency on the local terrain results in intervening acts or the making of "scenes" that demonstrate self-actualization by disrupting the status quo or the regime's governing tactics, as feminist scholars have rightly argued within Middle East studies and citizenship studies (see, e.g., Kandiyoti, 1991; Sayigh, 1998a,b). Drawing on the work of Arendt and Butler among other philosophers, Isin argues that once an act is performed it produces unpredictable effects within society between "others" and the "Other." This particular component of Isin's theorization allows me to illustrate how agency constructs anything beyond one's own subjectivity or disposition to external forms of oppression like patriarchy, which is an important feminist task in political science and beyond (Kantola, 2006; Zerilli, 2005).

I understand Isin's work to argue that citizenship can take different forms that might be considered more or less top down or bottom up but can become scripted and acts of citizenship interrupt those established scripts – but not necessarily from one direction or the other.[14] I read acts of citizenship not necessarily as merely acts of agency or self-actualization because this suggests an intentionality and predictability that Isin argues may not be present.[15] Isin contends that acts of citizenship are breaks or interruptions of established scenes or scripts, which may or may not have longevity or transformative effects in the longer term. We therefore must not overemphasize individual acts of citizenship and attribute an unrealistic level of influence to individual interventions (Abu-Lughod, 1990; Bayat 2010a). As such, I contextualize acts of citizenship within the broader historical contingencies that women encountered during different time periods in postrevolutionary Iran. As the Islamic Republic addressed women's rights, roles, and responsibilities grounded in prevailing citizenry frameworks interwoven with republicanism, Shi'i reverence for female Muslim figures, and the Iran–Iraq war (and manipulation of its legacies), women and men also entered into this negotiation with the state.

I use acts of citizenship as a working concept (Slaby, Mühlhoff and Wüschner, 2019) that discloses how citizenship forms in momentary bursts through contentious politics aimed at the state and/or society

---

[14] I thank Anne McNevin for explaining this argument to me.
[15] I thank Anne McNevin for discussing this point with me further.

(Abdelrahman, 2013). While Isin conflates acts of citizenship with "the right to demand rights," I refrain from this approach. At least in the Iranian context, acts of citizenship are at times forged through commands that fall outside the "right to demand rights" framework. By looking at citizenship as appeals made to the state and its institutions, we place limits on women's engagement with rights.[16] For instance, in Chapter 3 I highlight spiritual acts of citizenship – interventions evolving out of the historical contingencies of the 1979 revolution and geared toward preserving the revolutionary citizen that one had created with care through familial and community support, as well as erudite poetry. In another illustration, as I show in Chapter 4, people sometimes exert their agency from within society with acts of citizenship centered on belonging and togetherness – not in the name of rights alone but instead grounded in moral assessments. Nevertheless, Isin's notion of acts of citizenship and the attention he draws to claims of specific rights in contextualized moments permit me to consider the interventions of people living with irregular citizenry frameworks in relation to conditioning of the state formation process.

Each chapter illustrates the diverse, complementary, and conflicting notions of rights, roles, and responsibilities that the women included in this study express through their rights demands, pursuit of spiritual growth, moral calculations, and formation of belonging during different moments of postrevolutionary Iranian history. Moreover, each chapter demonstrates how in particular moments research participants' acts of citizenship uphold, and in other instances destabilize, larger power structures in the Islamic Republic. Acts of citizenship, as I employ them in this book, do not collapse this insight with claims of a homogeneous identity for those performing citizenry acts in an effort to offer a view of an "essential self."

The term "citizen" is used in official state newspapers and media productions daily (Pourreza, 1397/2018) by scholars based in Iran who write in Persian for an Iranian audience (Shaditalab, 1397/2018). It is also used to demand specific rights during assemblies. "Citizen" is employed by women's rights activists today to defend their rights from behind bars (Baniyaghoob, 2011/1390). Young Hezbollah cultural activists[17] also use "citizen" to discuss the subjectivities of male soldiers who volunteered in the Iran–Iraq war (Kashfi, 1385/2006). There is even

---

[16] I am grateful to reviewer one for bringing this point to my attention.

[17] Hezbollah is usually associated with the Lebanese movement. However, there is a diverse and evolving Hezbollah faction in Iran that carries out pro-Islamic Republic cultural activism.

a chain department store in Tehran called *Shahrvand* (citizen). Yet, perhaps due to the nondemocratic elements that exist in the Islamic Republic, the non-Islamic roots of the term, or the academic tendency to connect citizenship to the state (instead of the city, for instance), the word "citizenship" remains controversial in contemporary Iran.

During my years of living in Iran and traveling in the country, I continually encountered people who expressed confusion over (or complete rejection of) their citizenry status. This happened *despite* documentations of contestations over citizenship rights and responsibilities in the postrevolutionary constitution, as well as such striking illustrations of citizenship theories and practices in Iranian society. The feeling among Iranians that they are not citizens has been addressed in novels such as Mahmoud Dowlatabadi's *The Colonel* (2011). The novel addresses post-1979 Iran's social complexities through the ordeals of a retired colonel who has children involved in Islamist and leftist activism. Two of his children are executed in prison for their leftist activism, one is martyred in the warfront, and one is confined to the house as a disappointed revolutionary. In this context, we encounter his daughter, Farzaneh, who is married to an abusive husband. She correlates her abuse to the experience of the nation after the 1979 revolution, finding a sense of commonality: "I'm a stranger in my own home! The tragedy of our whole country is the same: we are all alienated, strangers in our own land. It's tragic. The odd thing is that we have never got used to it. Yet, woe betide us if we do" (p. 91). The sentiment of not being a citizen but acting like one anyway came through in my fieldwork as well. My book captures this response to life in postrevolutionary Iran by imagining Isin's notion of acts of citizenship through ethnographic research in a context "beyond the West."

Acts of citizenship, as I conceptualize them, do not signify an identity or a reliable "map" for thinking through postrevolutionary Iranian politics (Slaby, Mühlhoff and Wüschner, 2019, p. 3). Citizenship and state formation are inextricably interconnected. Acts of citizenship, then, are not a "definitive concept" in *Women and the Islamic Republic*. Instead, I "merely suggest directions along which to look" when we explore nonelite women's roles in conditioning the state formation process (Blumer, 1954, p. 7). *Women and the Islamic Republic* traces the endurance of the past in the present to consider the import of religion and warfare on the making of postrevolutionary Iran.

I locate my analysis at the intersection of the situated social circumstance in which people live, the real-time contingencies that they experience, and their individual capacity for creativity (Boltanski, 2011). Recognizing that people do not generally "invent an entire ontology of actions from scratch," what follows reveals the situated historical contingencies that engendered my research participants' variegated approaches to what are, at times, surprisingly unruly expressions of citizenship (Velleman, 2013, p. 27). Acts of citizenship, as I came to understand them during this project, are not "unilaterally imposed" by society. Instead, they "are transmitted and translated through negotiations with situated religious and citizenship norms" (Ong, 2011, p. 27). The Islamic Republic's political structures, Shi'i foundations, and political experiences cannot be sidestepped for a glorification of women's desires, thoughts, and acts.

1.5   Methodological Rationale: Pushing the Boundaries of Political Science

My research was "driven by an interest in investigating concepts and theories through deep contextuality" (Iqtidar, 2011a, p. 23). My approach is similar to Iqtidar's (2011a). As an Iranian American raised in the Washington, DC, area, I saw firsthand how noncontextualized concepts such as "Islamism," "secularism," "state," and "hardliners" stripped Iranian politics (but also the broader global Muslim community) of particularities that not only could have enriched the field of political theory but also might have forged more productive US engagement with Muslim Americans, Iran, and the broader Middle East.

In this section, I will briefly show how up-close engagement with interlocutors and analysis of textual documents helped me theorize how non-elite women's acts of citizenship condition the state formation process. My decision to rely on qualitative methodologies stemmed from studying hybrid regimes. Given that I sought to capture a view of "social processes as they unfold" (Tilly, 2006, p. 410), I chose methods that allowed me to "zoom in" and "zoom out" (Nicolini, 2013) of case studies and individual interviews. For instance, extensive political ethnography permitted me to build long-term relationships that were fostered through in-person interactions and also via social media. I used participant observation to understand what citizenship meant to my interlocutors and interviewees (Lichterman, 1998).

Through a preliminary analysis of interviews carried out in 2007 and 2008, I began seeing citizenship and conditioning of the state formation process as interlinked in real time. I gained insight into the daily lives of interlocutors and how they navigated macrolevel structures by remaking microlevel politics (Benzecry and Baiocchi, 2017). At the same time, "shadowing" participants during a variety of events – including commemorations of loved ones lost to the war or state executions – revealed the contexts, social networks, and limitations that interlocutors struggle with. Also, by shadowing Hezbollah affiliates as they participated in Islamization projects, I not only studied the artefacts they were creating (Miettinen, 1999) but also saw the different layers and scales of governance taking place within cultural institutes. I noted in real time how Hezbollah affiliates engaged with the ambiguity of governance in these spaces.

I also had to educate myself on the production of war and prison memoirs in postrevolutionary Iran. With respect to memoirs written by former political prisoners living in Europe, I have interviewed nearly all of the women whose memoirs I use in this book. These up-close interactions with different women and men during fieldwork in Europe guided my selection of books. I also relied heavily on discussions with Shahla Talebi, a professor and former political prisoner, to discuss the ideas and quality of the memoirs.

In exploring war memoirs produced in Iran, I relied on a similar strategy of consulting with the younger and more critical generation of war studies experts based in Tehran. This generation is intimately connected to men and women who were impacted by the war; it actively produces research on the war, including managing publication of the renowned student magazine on the history and culture of the holy defense, *Habil*. The newer generation of Iranian war experts, such as Mazaheri (1392/2012) and Zibakalam (1385/2006), argue that memoirs addressing the participants in the Iran–Iraq war are oral histories. These oral histories, produced in recent years, contrast the memoirs written during the war, which focus mostly on issues pertaining to warfare that the state is invested in pushing toward a particular militaristic narrative. Oral histories, on the other hand, are not regulated by the state because they address one person's broader life experiences in the context of war. In many ways, oral histories of the war oppose the Islamic Republic's formal narratives of the war, or what Mazaheri (1385/2006, p. 4) labels as "governmental" narratives of the "holy defense."

Women and the Islamic Republic is grounded in interviews that gave me insight into how women framed their experiences during the 1980–1988 period. I also rely on oral histories to further contextualize the ideas introduced during interviews. My own experiences in speaking with women who have written memoirs reconfirm Mazaheri's (1392/2012) and Zibakalam's (1385/2006) analysis regarding the validity of these texts.

I found that there generally existed little state regulation of these books. Often, the conflicts that did emerge were between authors and narrators. There are also many cases where the woman whose experience is being recorded does not write her own memoir. Instead, she narrates it and another person, usually a younger woman, produces the actual memoir. For instance, during one disagreement that I witnessed, a martyr's wife had shared a story about life with her late husband that she did not want disclosed. Her amanuensis argued that it was in fact her right to determine what should go into the volume. Publication was halted indefinitely. By interviewing the women and addressing the production of their memoirs with them during face-to-face encounters, I accounted for the quality of these books, which do undergo some level of censorship, either state- or self-imposed.

As a member of a younger generation of Iranian studies scholars, I felt that there existed far too much essentialization of Iran as a case study. Povey (2012) has illustrated that Iran's experience with colonialism, women's rights struggles, war, religious reform, and postcolonial aspirations are important similarities that it shares with regional neighbors. She insists that Iran's women's movement and intellectual contributions to "religious reformism" have influenced Muslims in the region and the Muslim minority in the West (Povey, 2012, p. 169). *Women and the Islamic Republic* centers on what non-elite women's struggles during everyday life meant to them. I argue that the concepts of "hybrid regimes," "citizenship," and "state formation" can "travel" to other countries in the region and beyond, although not seamlessly (Collier, 1993; Landman, 2000; Sartori, 1970). My methodological approach highlights the potential for thinking comparatively without making universal claims geared toward broader applications.

I refrain from universal claims on these terms or even generalizations of Iranian women's experiences through my case studies. I concur with Singh (2018) that scholarly claims on "mastery," even in postcolonial texts, are undergirded with a writer's illusions of individual transparency and desires toward control of something. I reject this colonial practice while recognizing that, despite my intentions, my vantage point may also generate new forms of exclusion. Nevertheless, my findings demonstrate how acts of citizenship helped me understand the ways that non-elite women can condition the state formation process in postrevolutionary Iran by remaking their statuses, rights, and responsibilities.

Inspired by the work of Cooper (2015, 2016), I understand there to be many ways that the state is imagined and enlivened. Focusing on how my interlocutors condition the state-making process through acts of citizenship, *Women and the Islamic Republic* invites others to examine this process with different lenses and a focus on a variety of national and transnational social groups. As I demonstrate how acts of citizenship developed to condition state making during different moments, I also reveal the conceptual problems associated with a binary formulation of democratization and authoritarianism, Western and non-Western. Comparing women's acts of citizenship in Iran during the war and in the postwar years not only uses concepts that are relevant elsewhere but also allows us to further develop those concepts through case studies and draw inferences without making general or universal claims (Landman, 2000, chapter 2).

Women and the Islamic Republic creates "a breach of self-evidence" and takes readers into the specific moments where women conditioned the state formation process by drawing attention to the conditions, structural spaces, and opportunities that intersect with their acts of citizenship (Burchell, Gordon, and Miller, 1991, p. 76). This methodological approach also lends itself to a triangulation of my findings and allows me to demonstrate the variations that exist in the ways acts of citizenship have emerged among diverse social groups in the postrevolutionary state. Instead of offering an absolute response to non-elite women's role in conditioning the state formation process, *Women and the Islamic Republic* illustrates the different forms and scales of citizenship that the women in my study enacted to condition the state formation process. In what follows, I bring out as many possible directions of meaning to see the complex ways in which notions of citizenship are addressed, without insisting upon a singular logical substructure.

1.6   Disrupting Categorical Boundaries: Positionality, Affect, and Understanding

The narrative or practice turn in international studies has been closely linked with a renewed investment in interpretative methodologies. An initial observation during long-term ethnographic research on practices is that there is a need to develop stronger qualitative methodology skills. The significance of research skills to the study of politics from below has also been noted by feminist scholars. Debates regarding feminist uses of gender and sexuality as categories of analysis have once again been rekindled within feminist studies. In her 2006 essay "Beyond the Americas: Are Gender and Sexuality Useful Categories of Historical Analysis?", Najmabadi, a historian of modern Iran, chronicled her struggles with surpassing gender and sexual binaries while using them as categories of analysis in her path-breaking *Women with Moustaches, Men without Beards* (2005). Najmabadi (2006, p. 18) asks, "How can we bring out as many possible directions of meaning to see the complex node at which notions of gender and sexuality are worked out, without seeking a singular logical underpinning?" A methodological concern with assumptions of singularity that conceal the historical specificities and multiplicities of genders and sexualities as analytical categories was also at the forefront of US historian Boydston's thought-provoking 2008 paper "Gender as a Question of Historical Analysis." Boydston similarly questions the usefulness of gender as a category of analysis when the historical processes of gender are often explored uniformly and with binary associations that efface understandings of nonlinear interrelationships between multiple forms of the social.

Feminist scholars of conflict studies have also initiated this debate, and this variant of the debate is my focus here. Vickers, for instance, argues that because Western feminists have systematically relied on specific approaches to studying gender and the nation, their scholarship is currently unable to capture the complexities of this association in different contexts as it lacks contextually appropriate theories and methods (Vickers, 2006; Daulatzai, 2008). Elshtain (2009) has also joined this conversation, voicing her dissatisfaction with the routine application of gender as a category of analysis in feminist studies of war. She too laments that we have lost sight of the analytical variations that can be noted if closer attention is paid to historical contexts, suggesting that citizenship and identity formation may generate more nuanced feminist analyses of conflict.

Despite these cautionary notes, mainstream feminist studies of conflict exemplify the continued uncritical deployment of gender and sexuality as categories of analysis. I heed the above concerns regarding a lack of focus on the particularities of case studies in some feminist investigations of conflict. These scholars persuasively argue that the use of sexuality and gender as imported categories of investigation can impede the production of knowledge in studies of the global South and North when one particular categorical routine becomes "common sense for our work" (Boydston, 2008, p. 561).

Boydston (2008) suggests that by letting go of categories we may begin to respond to less scripted questions of gender and sexuality that emerge from the specificities of our studies. However, gender and sexuality can simultaneously be categories, questions, and tools. This complexity makes it methodologically impractical to (de)prioritize gender as a category. More importantly, I am unsure as to how we can make gender less central to our perceptions in contexts where feminist consciousness (Stanley and Wise, 1993) – multiple visions of social reality that account for various forms of inequalities, discriminations, and imaginations – supports investigation. Using gender and sexuality as categories of analysis is not intrinsically (and need not be functionally) restrictive. If we are paying attention, then, in unpredictable moments during the research process, these categories can transform into conceptual tools for analyzing and revising interconnected epistemologies that ultimately develop whole projects.

More specifically, this section demonstrates this: By analytically engaging with the affective questions that the research process generates, gender and sexuality as analytical categories can gradually account for greater theoretical and empirical variance by interrogating positionalities and demanding adjustments in the researcher's feminist consciousness for the duration of a specific project. While feminist scholars of conflict readily address their positionalities and emotional relationships to their projects, rarely is affect connected to methodological frameworks.[18] The transformations that emotional labor engenders in the researcher's own subjectivity could reveal associations and evidence that remain invisible without an awareness of one's own positionalities.

Scholars of both conflict and Middle East studies have voiced methodological concerns over the limits assumptions pose for researching politics. Barkawi and Brighton (2011) contend that within the social sciences war is primarily believed to be a destructive force, and this "anti-militarist" stance has historically limited domains of enquiry. From a different angle that also speaks of the importance of recognizing the emotional labors of research for methodological purposes, Schayegh (2010) asserts that the complexities of state–societal relations during the Pahlavi Monarchy, which ruled over Iran prior to the 1979 revolution, have yet to be adequately addressed in Iranian studies. Schayegh (2010, p. 47) argues that this is because "in the West, many historians of Iran are Iranians, for whom monarchy and revolution were deeply personal experiences."

Similarly, Chehabi (1998, p. 495) postulates the following concerning studies of Iran's Pahlavi Monarchy: "the upheavals of the post-revolutionary years have preoccupied scholars so much that the detailed and dispassionate analysis of Iran under its last dynasty is still in its infancy." Methodologically accounting for our priorities, questions, and patterns by repositioning ourselves and allowing, when necessary, for shifts in our consciousness permits submerged perspectives to infiltrate investigations and develop more robust empirical analyses and theoretical prisms.

---

[18] Weiss (2011) argues that even when we address our positionality and the situated nature of knowledge creation, we may still be evading aspects of our knowledge production journey.

1.7 Subtle Interventions and Remaking Categories: Fieldwork on Iran's 1980–1988 History

Women and the Islamic Republic illustrates how evidence gathered through personal narratives in case studies can develop into theoretical propositions when researchers analyze encounters with emotions as evidence and remain open to shifting their positionality and consciousness. I demonstrate this by showing how gender and sexuality can also be tools for deciphering narratives, as well as that there also exists an "epistemology arising from ontology," when researchers are prepared to rethink their categories and even let go of their embedded explanations (Wickramasinghe, 2010).

I conducted more than twenty-four consecutive months of fieldwork in Iran, Sweden, Germany, and the United Kingdom (2007–2009; 2012–2014). My research practices included participant observation, narrative analysis, and in-depth interviews using the snowball sampling method. When possible, the interviews were recorded. I participated in the daily life of participants, non-elite women and men whose lives crossed paths with national politics during the 1980–1988 period. I did so through conversations and interactions, by observing, and sometimes by participating in activities (e.g., religious ceremonies, regime-run activities for families associated with the war, and human rights gatherings among former political prisoners in Europe).

Broadly, I was interested in understanding women's and men's citizenship in everyday life during different periods in postrevolutionary Iran. These years included the 1980–1988 Iran–Iraq war and other moments of national and international conflict. The 1980–1988 period is understood as a particularly violent and isolated time in contemporary Iranian history because of intersections between local and international violence due to the revolution's unexpected outcomes. My study focused on a range of different spaces. I interviewed the following social groups: former Islamist volunteers of the Iran–Iraq war, women who entered Iran's religious seminaries after the revolution, nurses employed during the war, and leftist political prisoners whom I interviewed in Europe. Part of my work examined the legacies of the Iran–Iraq war on different and at times conflicting social groups, including families of war martyrs and post-2009 Iranian Hezbollah cultural activists.

I analyzed interview data thematically and linked emergent themes with individual narrations of experience. I also relied considerably on my field notes, including recordings, scribbles, commentaries, questions, and analyses. These reflected, regrouped, and prepared me for further interviews and archival research (Barz, 1997, pp. 45–62). These interpretations were vital for gaining insight into my own positionality during the interviews and archival work, as well as for shifting my consciousness when it circumscribed the horizons respondents' narratives assembled. I relied on my field notes analytically in and out of the field. By engaging with the affective questions the research process generates, gender and sexuality as analytical categories can gradually account for greater theoretical and empirical variance by interrogating positionalities and demanding adjustments in the researcher's feminist consciousness.

When this project began, I had already been an anti-racist feminist of color for close to a decade, and intellectually I was familiar with the relevance of power relations in the production of knowledge. I had not, however, thought extensively about the visceral dimensions of this understanding. While feminist scholars of conflict readily address their positionalities and emotional relationships to their projects, rarely is affect connected to methodological frameworks. The transformations that emotional labor engenders in the researcher's own subjectivity could reveal associations and evidence that remain invisible without an awareness of one's own positionalities.

During my 2007–2008 fieldwork, interviews revealed my unconscious perspectives, as respondents demanded recognition of their emotional positionality toward me. The questions this process generated subsequently became material knowledge and informed my use of categories of analysis. For example, while meeting with Parvin H., a former political prisoner, and her teenage son, the subject of going without sexual intimacy while in prison came up during our discussion. Without intending to, I said, "But that must not have been a problem for you," to which my interviewee quickly and sharply responded, "Yes, it was actually."[19] As an Iranian American woman from the diaspora, my nostalgic perspective lay behind this categorical assumption and was at play in my method of interviewing and analysis. Subconsciously, I imagined "real Iranians," the ones raised in Iran, had more self-control than those living in non-Muslim societies. Apparently, I was uncomfortable talking about sex in front of her son and assumed that she felt the same way. As a younger woman, I struggled to envision that a woman from her generation wished to follow through with her sexual desires.

In another instance, the daughter of a war martyr, Sahar A., was discussing her dedication to modest clothing, and again I unconsciously interrupted by saying, "But that's easy for you," to which

[19] Personal interview, Cologne, Germany, April 2008.

she retorted, "It is the hardest of all sacrifices Islam requires."[20] My assumption about an uncomplicated set of negotiations for Muslim women who practice their faith was shaded by a simplified understanding of Islam as simply someone's way of life – not possibly a constant struggle within the self for maintaining one's piety. By being reminded of my bodily unconsciousness through these affectively charged retorts from respondents, I strengthened a feminist consciousness that was suspicious of claims regarding the omnipresence of silences, as well as my own impulse to respond in place of other people, to "find" their voice.[21] The responsibility and necessity to listen with curiosity, without taking refuge in the boundaries that gendered points of reference constructed, was integrated into my categorical universe and interviewing methods.

Together, the unexpected responses above called for attention to the specificities of my case studies. Interlocutors wanted me to begin moving toward them through an intimacy that I had not previously shared with strangers. However, I quickly learned that this repositioning, created by breaking down the emotive boundaries between participants and myself, was structured. Field notes indicate that interviewees contested my emotional engagements during the interview process, which included not only a series of suppressed assumptions that prevented sympathetic listening but also a lot of crying on my behalf over the losses women endured due to political violence – that is, their presumed victimhood. In short, respondents thought my life and living "at the intersection of individual and social dynamics" while carrying out the field research prevented me from sufficiently appreciating the complexities surrounding their histories (Maynes, Pierce, and Laslett, 2008). The following comments are a sample of what I was told.

Maryam Nouri, a former political prisoner affiliated with aqaliyyat, mother, and author, stated, "I will never forgive you if you misrepresent my criticisms of other prisoners," as I left her home after a week-long stay that included interviews with other former political prisoners to whom she had introduced me.[22] Laleh Z., a war veteran, housewife, and mother, made the following statement at the end of our interview: "I hope that you will share your work with all of us that have participated in these interviews. I hope that you write what we have told you."[23] Halimeh E., a Bakhtiari (an Iranian tribe) mother of three war martyrs, stated as I was leaving her home in Ahvaz (a city in southern Iran), "[T]hey [her sons] were like pieces of my body and soul. I gave them

---

[20] Personal interview, Tehran, Iran, May 2008.   [21] Gallagher (1995, pp. 225–244).
[22] Personal interview, Cologne, Germany, April 2008.
[23] Personal interview, Shiraz, Iran, July 2008.

[to the war]; that's okay. View them as your brothers, there is no difference."[24]

The symbols, metaphors, and timing used to address intersections between my position as a researcher and interviewees' accounts of individual experiences suggest that they wanted me to express solidarity in an empathetic manner as a "feeling-with" (Bartky, 2002, p. 81). This strikes a balance between losing oneself in other people's stories and leaving sufficient distance to acknowledge the individuated nature of their pasts. While they welcomed me into their homes, showed me the physical marks of torture that remained on their bodies, shared photos and stories of dead loved ones, and embraced my identities and affection, interviewees finalized our encounter by reclaiming their love, survival, and loss as uniquely their own. For example, as her concluding words, Halimeh E. chose to identify her sons as pieces of her "body and soul" but projected a more distant relationship, that of sister, onto me. In Iranian culture, some mothers have a closer relationship to their sons than other women in the family, including even a man's wife. Recognition of narrators' frustration with my emoting over their experiences of political violence posited gender and sexuality as context-specific categories that form through the intersubjective relationship between individual participants and myself, and not my systemized lens for analysis (Maynes, Pierce, and Laslett, 2008).

Interview dynamics revealed the methodological significance of the conscious and unconscious assumptions I held, forcing my feminist consciousness to work its way through verbal and visual narratives without "preconceived conceptual schema" (Maynes, Pierce, and Laslett, 2008, p. 116). Simultaneous repositionings, in light of interviewees' responses, felt like blindness. I relied on my standpoint politics for motivation while navigating rapid movements as my perception readjusted to analysis without the security of familiarity in sight and sense. I had to stop analyzing discourses through my own preferences. During this light but intense journey, the underpinnings of my "categorical vision" (Boydston, 2008, p. 561) were also fragmented. This is because I could no longer recognize as significant the rhetoric that captured my attention the fastest, reached my core the quickest, or the binary frameworks I felt most at home with as an Iranian American student of gender, race, and sexuality studies.

I became accustomed to continually moving between people, feelings, claims, and ideas during interviews and archival work until the specific

---

[24] Personal interview, Ahvaz, Iran, July 2008.

complexities at issue became apparent – not depictions of gender and sexual categories as I understood them through my own history, solidarities, and education. Repeated and strategic totalizing statements in the written text or during interviews, such as frustration toward the West for supporting Iraq in the war, also informed my analysis. For instance, the relevance of Iran's international isolation during the war and its connection to local political interventions initially emerged through these discourses. However, I did not allow the most well-established discourses or the most articulate individuals to distract me from noticing anomalies, additional logics within narratives, or overlaps between social processes, where they emerged. After all, isolation was not only caused by US and regional policies toward Iran; it also developed out of a radical remaking of cultural and social norms within a state that was in transition to becoming an Islamic Republic. However, interviewees were less forthcoming about this information due to their concerns regarding privacy and security. In contrast, when asked specifically about everyday processes – education, marriage, mourning, and child-rearing – narrators elaborated on the manifestation of emotions that traversed through them in a postrevolutionary state at war.

I began noting respondents' interventions that at first glance may have been overshadowed by a storyline's larger claim to "coherence and common understanding" (Scott, 1988, p. 38). Put somewhat differently, I learned to navigate the architecture of narratives that cemented past experiences with desires for current action through the standard plot of beginning, middle, and end. How stories of sexual violence and harassment during the war were told reveals how personal narratives were developed first into arguments and then supported a reconsideration of mainstream theorizations of citizenship and nationalism theories.

In the summer of 2008, I had two interviews with Somayeh R., a war veteran from southern Iran who was an active member of the women's Basij, a paramilitary force. She told me that the popular claim made by the Revolutionary Guards and Basij that a group of Iranian Arab women and girls were raped and murdered by Iraqis in Susangerd (a city in southern Iran) was publicized and memorialized before an official investigation could take place.[25] I also had another revealing interview with Ali Q., a former male member of Basij. Ali informed me that some Iranian female members of the Mujahedin, who had participated in the

---

[25] Personal interview, Tehran, Iran, June 2008.

1988 operation Eternal Light, were raped by Iranian soldiers.[26] Another interlocutor, Habibeh R., recalled how some Iranian men sexually harassed women on the streets of Khorramshahr (a city in southern Iran) at the onset of the Iraqi invasion, though she was adamant that this was not common.[27]

We remember in the present. These narratives were likely performances used to express interviewees' disapproval of, or allegiance to, reformist or conservative political movements in Iran. Yet, and perhaps outside of their intentions, they also displayed how state-sponsored associations between gender, sexuality, and the nation during war might be acted upon on the ground. I found the multiple interventions within recurring discussions of sexual harassment and rape – such as disruptions of the male hero image or depictions of silent females standing by male soldiers – to hold deeper narrative insight than the claim of wartime sex crimes alone.

When reading memoirs and other archival literature, repositioning myself and questioning my "categorical vision" was slightly more complicated, simply because no one was present to question my thinking and perspective. I was aware of how important this process was due to my previous experiences with interviewing. During archival research, scholars often feel that their subjectivity destabilizes through engagement with writing. This experience may not, however, occur so readily for everyone. Some might lose sight of the urgency in monitoring their relation to sources. Similar to conducting interviews, when reading memoirs and other literature, we can create methods out of our affective engagements with books to move toward the specificities at issue and away from unjustified simplifications engendered by our egos.

I slowly learned that close readings offered the best protection against making unfair general claims. However, I needed methods for performing this task in isolation. I therefore began to write immediate summaries of the literature I was reading (particularly for the war and prison memoirs), which I shared with my then-supervisor by email. The trust that had developed between us and the speed with which he saw my analyses meant that the very act of this exchange made me feel *responsible* for the writing. I would otherwise not have felt this responsibility that strongly while undertaking archival work; often, there is no one else present while we look through libraries across the globe in search of data

---

[26] Operation Eternal Light took place in 1988 after Iran accepted the ceasefire. Male and female members of the organization invaded Iranian territory from neighboring Iraq. Personal interview, London, UK, September 2010.

[27] Personal interview, Tehran, Iran, June 2008.

for our projects, and it is easy to simply select data that fit our categorical and other assumptions. I would reread my emails to him that same day or the next and question my analysis, repositioning myself accordingly. My interpretations were also not readjusted in accordance with his judgment or preferences; neither of us would have allowed or wanted such a methodology. Rather, this self-reflection in front of another person forced me to acknowledge my own unfair readings. Often I would go back and reread memoirs or at least sections. My own rereadings of the emails, in front of an audience that I had now created through my supervisor, made me feel *accountable* to my readers. A method for holding ourselves both responsible and accountable, and for shifting our positionality, is needed if we are to read and analyze sensibly with the intent to possibly create new approaches or theoretical propositions. We are not writing alone as scholars, and our write-up experience is indeed a relational one connected to different people and communities.

With careful attention to narrative themes and structures, I also detected popular gender interventions into the state's war propaganda through the analysis of memoirs published in Iran.[28] Although memoirs of the Iran–Iraq war may undergo some censorship, the Iranian people have skillfully mastered the art of disclosing suppressed histories. For example, in *Khabarnegar-e Jangi* (Wartime Journalist) (Raissi, 1383/2003), Maryam Kazemzadeh writes in the prelude that the men she encountered during her time at different warfronts can be "role models" for "all generations" in search of exemplary figures to emulate. The Islamic Republic continues to manipulate the identities of war martyrs to impose its narrative of heroic youth, and Kazemzadeh's introductory sentence converges with such an agenda.

However, throughout the memoir, she also narrates how male soldiers and journalists dismissed her, refused to collaborate with her, and deliberately scared her. It was only through the radical support of a few key individuals, such as Mostafa Chamran, Chief Commander of the Revolutionary Guards during the early days of the Iran–Iraq war, that she carried out her professional duty and personal desire to work as a female journalist reporting from the warfront.[29] Despite state interference in publishing, readers were given a sophisticated description of her struggles and her eventual success in creating a space for herself in an

---

[28] There are currently over 200 memoirs written or narrated by Iranian women regarding their experiences as nurses, fighters, or relatives of war martyrs during the Iran–Iraq war. Memoirs written by political prisoners during this same period are also flourishing in the Iranian diaspora.

[29] See, for example, Raissi, 1383/2003, pp. 27–28, 59, 70–71.

unwelcoming atmosphere. As such, readers can formulate a specific understanding of her historical experiences as a female journalist in postrevolutionary Iran, one that runs counter to the state's broader war agenda and gender politics enacted both at the time and today.

Based on the evidence I gathered during interviews and from memoirs, I began to suspect what in the later stages of my work would become more detailed: Through their spatial and rhetorical disruption of, and at times compliance with, the state's wartime propaganda system, it was also possible for people, including state elites, to destabilize the conventional gender and sexual associations that upheld state-promoted nationalisms and citizenship in the first place.

However, this finding also meant that *how* I understood intersections between the state, nation, and citizen had to be rethought, a process that I delve into further throughout *Women and the Islamic Republic*. I was hearing provocative histories; meetings and interviews continually posed new questions for me. This meant that I conducted more interviews than I'd originally planned, resulting in approximately 200 in-depth interviews by the conclusion of the project. Not all were necessarily useful. Where I had further questions regarding my field notes, I contacted respondents once again. I had continued my conversations with several interviewees after the end of my fieldwork. When still uncertain, I shared my analyses with former interviewees to obtain their comments. Chiefly constructing arguments through a terrain of ambiguities, I also sought feedback from a colleague who had directly experienced Iran's prisons in the 1980–1988 period. Today she is a social scientist and university professor in the United States; she has also had extensive conversations with political prisoners and families involved in the Iran–Iraq war, and she commented on significant portions of my analysis.

Another colleague, who lost her father in the Iran–Iraq war, also read and commented on my work. Additionally, analyses of in-depth interviews and informal exchanges were conducted with a metaphorical eye on other documents to capture the range of meanings and implications that interpretations offered. Because of the emotional labor of many individuals, I became comfortable with changing my positionality and consciousness, collecting and connecting pieces of an uncultivated story through multiple feelings, languages, spaces, and discourses.

1.8   Structure of the Book

This book consists of two parts that illustrate the different forms of gendered citizenship that have developed in post-1979 Iran as well as how within different historical contingencies women's acts of citizenship remade their statuses, rights, and responsibilities to condition the state formation process. I begin by questioning the validity of a linear conceptualization of women's rights struggles in modern Iran. Chapter 2 explores how much Iranian women rely on memories of women's activism in modern Iran as they challenge and reconsider their own statuses, rights, and responsibilities today. The chapter demonstrates that both during the 1980–1988 period and today, the women I encountered relied significantly on their own immediate memories to engender their acts of citizenship.

The next two chapters introduce readers to the different forms that acts of citizenship took from 1980 to 1988. In Chapter 3, I present the notion of spiritual acts of citizenship as geared toward preserving one's status as a revolutionary citizen. Building on the work of Ghamari-Tabrizi (2016a) and his investigation of Foucault's notion of political spirituality, this chapter demonstrates that if we account for women's subjectivity, political spirituality did more than engender a move toward martyrdom or a fascination with death. Islamist and leftist women's spiritual acts of citizenship were also interspersed with familial love, erudite poetry, and literature that enhanced their capacity for self-preservation. This chapter contributes to our understanding of subjectivities during the 1980–1988 period, which remains an understudied dimension of politics in postrevolutionary Iran.

Chapter 4 operates more as a hinge chapter, exploring more fully a proposition that seeps through in Chapter 3: During conflict, opportunities for conditioning the state formation process become feasible for non-elite women. The chapter illustrates that the process of self-preservation addressed in Chapter 3 was entangled with acts of citizenship geared toward the formation of collectivities. Women's conceptions of collectivity involve a sense of personal responsibility toward unifying a community that is on the verge of disintegration due to the isolation and fear that violent conflict entails. This chapter recognizes the productive potential of the isolation and loneliness that constitute political struggles during everyday life within conflict zones. It argues that this sort of isolation propelled different Iranian women to use their bodies for the making of polities, as well as to destabilize the heteronormative underpinnings of the regime's state-building endeavor through moral assessments grounded in the postrevolutionary pious worldview. In this chapter, affect is understood as an emotive backdrop, or that "feeling in the air" that we sense, but it also interfaces with emotive connections between people.

Women's spatial movement into new spaces during conflict is widely recognized as one of the outcomes of war (Berry, 2018). This process in

Iran was met with opposition from state and societal forces, but it also provided women with the means to build new political communities to support their own and others' survival. As Martin and Miller (2003, p.145) have argued, "space is produced through social relations and structures." To interrogate issues pertaining to morality in a postrevolutionary context, Iranian women used their bodies to galvanize polities that upheld women's individual and collective visions of a more egalitarian and just society. While the body has been central to Western feminist thought, the body's flesh and material capacities have commonly been sidestepped for its metaphorical usages; this trend exists in feminist studies of conflict and citizenship as well (Beasley and Bacchi, 2000; Davis, 1997). The second point the chapter illustrates is that there was a tension between how state and societal forces wanted these women to function in public spaces and how they wanted to live. This conflict pushed women to self-determine their public and private subjectivities and destabilize the heteronormative structure of state-building in wartime where men are the protectors of the nation-state and where the ideal female citizen is a wife or mother who quietly sends her loved ones to war.

Studies grounded in multiple sites of conflict have argued that within the context of violence women often make significant gains, but these transformations can also be undermined in the aftermath of war (Baumel, 1999; Berry, 2018; Bop, 2001; Enloe, 2000; Thomas and Bond, 2015; Sharoni, 1988). As Berry (2018) has argued, very few studies have relied on a gendered lens to explore war's long-term effects. Chapters 5 and 6 investigate how two social groups – families of war martyrs and Hezbollah cultural activists – perform acts of citizenship, as well as what their enactments tell us about the legacies of war for women's remaking of their statuses, rights, and responsibilities. As social groups understood to be close to the state because of their commitment to the notion of an Islamic state and close association with the Islamic Republic's religious interpretations, families of war martyrs and Hezbollahi citizens are entrusted by the state to continue the ideals of the 1979 revolution. One conclusion that emerges from both chapters is that, despite the state's effort at placing these social groups above others in society as first-class citizens, their practice of Islam is heavily embedded in the experiences they share with the rest of the Iranian nation. Women affiliated with these two social groups continue to enact varied performances of acts of citizenship that at times push back on the state's enforcement of women's statuses, rights, and responsibilities in the postwar period – often in unexpected ways.

The state depicts war martyrs' wives and daughters as embodying a higher level of morality and religiosity than others. This gives them significantly more political power than other segments of Iran's society. Chapter 5 examines the legacies of the first decade of violence in the postrevolutionary state. Studying Islamist politics after the reform movement (1997–2005), the chapter illustrates how political orientation is often dependent on larger national political trends, as it also draws attention to generational differences. With a focus on how Islamist women use their memories and moral power, I argue that these women have significantly transformed since the 1980–1988 period, although they claimed to be dedicated to the notion of an Islamic government as Islamists (at least until 2008). Today, the activism of these women explicitly engages with the rights of others as they construct a more pluralistic society and challenge the state's exclusivist approach to citizenship through acts that invite more Iranians into the national body. In fact, the underlying aspiration for citizenry equality among wives and daughters of martyrs is one reason that the state began to draw attention to the mothers of war martyrs and families of nuclear energy martyrs in post-2009 Iran.

Yet, while families of war martyrs directly rely on their political power to advance others' interests, female Hezbollah cultural activists – who are positioned as another group following the path of war martyrs – perform acts of citizenship that in certain moments remain uninterested in others' communities and rights. Through case studies of different Islamization projects, Chapter 6 argues that a new form of collectivity has emerged among Iranian women after the 2009 conflict. Discussing Hezbollah cultural activists' engagement with the Islamization of the social sciences and women's rights in post-2009, this chapter also illustrates that, for the first time in postrevolutionary Iranian history, some non-elite Iranian women who identify with the transnational Hezbollah movement in Iran have begun to defend other women's rights by activating morals and sensibilities similar to those held by the rest of Iranian society. This trend was not predominant among Islamists during the 1980–1988 period but has slowly transformed through the interventions of families of martyrs and other privileged Islamist social groups in the postrevolutionary state. Nonconnectivity was a significant feature of women's rights struggles during the 1980–1988 period, and it was visibly surpassed in 2009. Chapter 6 shows that at the same time as bringing about such developments, acts of citizenship can also be used to uphold the state's authoritarian tactics and do not necessarily move the state toward democratization. The concluding chapter addresses some of the major themes that the previous chapters shed light on.

One final note: I have used interviewees names only when they gave me permission, and in other instances I have used pseudonyms. Some leftist women did not want to highlight or acknowledge the political organization the state accused them of collaborating with, and I have omitted that information to protect their privacy.

2 Reflecting on an Idealized Past
Memory and Women's Rights Struggles
in Postrevolutionary Iran

This chapter asks the following questions: Do women's postrevolutionary rights and roles progress linearly, connecting post-1979 rights struggles to the prerevolutionary era? How do the women I encountered, either during interviews or through memoirs, appraise and relate to this sometimes idealized past? During my time as a visiting professor at the University of Tehran (2012–2014), I met two female PhD students with shared research interests. Quite excited to be with scholars from my own generation, I immediately began to discuss how influential the history of Iranian women's activism had been in my life. As I reviewed this history from the Qajar period to the Pahlavi years and postrevolutionary Iran, the two women gave me blank stares and an almost prerehearsed look of disapproval. They then began to question me on the histories of colonialism. The connection and friendship that I had hoped to establish suddenly seemed unsettled.

Through several months of close interaction, I noted that the two women were critical of the status of women in Iran, but the point of reference to conceptualize or rectify their concerns was rarely guided by a recounting of past women's rights struggles or national gender policies. Even the recent history of the 1980–1988 period was rarely reflected upon, despite the reality that one student's father had served in the Iran–Iraq war. They complained about their struggles to find suitable partners and their frustration toward men who dismissed them due to their age and high academic credentials. One of the students, for instance, told me sadly that she had to reject a proposal from a young man living abroad because he was a follower of the Supreme Leader and she felt that this meant they were culturally incompatible. She also discussed how her strict wearing of a hijab among the faculty was due to her sense of respect for one faculty member in particular and that she (like the rest of us) did not dress that way outside the university.

These two PhD students were also vocal about the vagueness of citizenship rights in Iran. During one late-afternoon group discussion, a debate emerged about satellite television. I stated that everyone having access to it suggested that the state was not serious about preventing people from watching Western television programs. One of the PhD students intervened: "Yes, but it's illegal. We don't want to be categorized as criminals. Do you know that such offenses can prevent us from getting good government jobs?"

I was also surprised when one of the PhD students, who identified with the Hezbollah movement, laughed at my interest in the Islamization of women's rights. She replied, "Are you serious? You came all the way from the other side of the world to study this? There is no such thing as Islamic rights or Islamic social sciences! These are just a bunch of people getting large sums of funding, and it will all end soon when Ahmadinejad leaves."

Over the course of a few months, I realized that the two women did not conceive of, remember, or connect with women's activism in modern Iran the same way that I did. Instead, they relied on their own immediate memories and goals to move into action. These memorable exchanges guided my attention toward a larger trend that emerged in my research: Often during my interactions, women did not try to locate their acts of citizenship within an established historical narrative on women's rights struggles.

Influential feminist studies of Iran suggest that Iranian women continue a liberal rights struggle that materialized during the democratic activism of the Qajar period, resistance movements of the Shah era, and political contentions in contemporary Iran (Afary, 1996; Afkhami and Friedl, 1994; Moghadam, 1992). Historical time is imagined in terms of a progressive move toward a liberal democratic state. For instance, Mojab (2007, p. 13) states:

The number of women participants in the first revolution [The Constitutional Revolution, 1906–1911] was indeed small. However, step by step they gained more prominence and launched their organizations and publications during numerous struggles that continued until the second revolution of 1979.

Carrying the same linear connection between the past and present with respect to women's rights, Sedghi (2007, p. 21) states that "the most striking continuity across the past hundred years of Iranian history and politics has been the growth of women's agency, its strength and potency."

My purpose in this chapter is to concentrate on the individual's own remembrance of the past and how she renews memories to move history forward in accordance with her own imagination, as well as to focus on the broader constraints and opportunities that shape her present life. The interaction that takes place between individual and collective remembrance requires further attention in the social sciences and within memory studies (Hirst and Manier, 2008). This trend permits the formation of a distorted conceptualization of how change occurs and at times results in overinvesting in a linear progression of history.

I marshal various sources of evidence – including a special issue published by a Hezbollah cultural institute, some of the analyzed articles from which are not publicly accessible – to argue this: At least one reading of Iranian women's conceptualization of their status and formation of rights, roles, and responsibilities in the postrevolutionary era is its nonlinearity and connection to individual goals and memories. I contextualize women's own words from memoirs and other texts within long-term histories of activism in modern Iran and consider the conditions, structural spaces, and opportunities that made their acts of citizenship visible and, at times, invisible. This is a vital context to the more microlevel analysis that follows in the remainder of *Women and the Islamic Republic*. By including this detail on how my interlocutors engage with the history of women's rights, I better illuminate their political consciousness.

I illustrate that there were two dominant tropes that emerged in how women who were politically active during the 1980–1988 period reflected on the idealized history of women's rights in Iran. First, for these politically active women, their individual and diverse memories within the family and community defined their activism. What is missing is a linear reading of the historical past, as in both interviews and memoirs women did not connect their activism to the history of women's rights struggles. I was surprised to find that, among my interviewees, there was no appreciative glance back at activist history in Iran during the Pahlavi Monarchy or the Qajar period.

Second, there was also a strong intergenerational learning process for some women. Both during interviews and in memoirs, women of the left and supporters of Ayatollah Khomeini remember being motivated by their distinct identities as women, by their familial histories (with forced marriages, physical abuse, and unexpected solidarity from male elites), and by witnessing the lives of female relatives who never reached long-held personal desires. Leftist women's emphasis on women's rights and concern with issues pertaining to gender discrimination are also recounted by Tabari and Yeganeh (1982, see especially pp. 143–170). Shahidian (1996, p. 51) notes that leftist women's political interests were significantly shaped by their reflections on Iranian society's patriarchal norms. Afary (2001) has shown that, for some Islamist women, a desire for independence was central to their participation in the revolution and Iran–Iraq war.

In the final section of this chapter, I highlight how the activism of women affiliated with the post-2009 revamping of the Hezbollah movement has been impacted by remembering their own gendered experiences, those of others in Iranian society where they carry out community outreach work, and the knowledge they gained through friendships forged in Hezbollah cultural institutes with other pious women from different post-1979 generations. I show how this historically contingent experience within Hezbollah cultural institutes encouraged Hezbollahi women, who had initially volunteered for participation in an anti-feminist movement, to challenge this state gender policy. I also demonstrate that a backward gaze at women's rights struggles does not shape Hezbollahi women's activism.

2.1   Politicization and Leftist and Islamist Women's Motivations for Activism from 1980 to 1988

Juxtaposing the similar motivations that brought leftist and Islamist women into revolutionary activism – albeit in different camps – highlights the similarities that leftist and Islamist women shared in their backgrounds. Both leftist and Islamist women were motivated by similar familial and sociopolitical experiences to embrace political activism, and their development into activist citizens was rarely articulated as a devotion to the history of women's rights movements in modern Iran. More specifically, women's immediate gendered experiences and intergenerational exchanges underpinned their politicization. Gendered acts of citizenship were borne out of their specific contextualized realities as non-elite women.

For women affiliated with the left, personal experience with gender boundaries influenced their decision to become politically active. Soudabeh Ardavan was loosely affiliated with the leftist organization aqaliyyat; she spent close to eight years in the Evin and Ghezel Hesar prisons. She was also a sculptor, designer, and sketch artist. Of her reason for becoming a political activist, she notes:

My family was always worried that people would talk bad about me because I frequented rug shops [to sell her rug designs]. They did not want to be embarrassed before friends and acquaintances, so they tried to convince me to stay away from the bazaar. I was determined to show them that I was cleverer than the men that ran the rug shops in the bazaar. I wanted to show them that I was stronger and "more manly" than those men! Our home was a cold and closed place. My father's rigid attitude had made life difficult for my three brothers and me. My mother was under more pressure than anyone else. She lost her mother when she was six years old, and a few years after that, she lost her father. She ran away from her strict brother at the age of 16 and moved to Tabriz from Maragheh.

She goes on to discuss how her difficult upbringing impacted her understanding of women's rights:

An atmosphere of constant crisis in our home pushed my brothers and me to think further about the violation of our rights. We were in search of a way to tolerate our difficult circumstances. I should add that I was under more pressure than my brothers. They could go into the streets or play outside. However, because I was a girl, I was denied these rights, and I was forced to sit in the house. Therefore, I took refuge in my drawings. All alone and in the dark, I made a world for my life through color and design. I became familiar with the poetry of Forugh Farrokhzad. As such, I could give meaning to my loneliness and understand it. However, I still did not know what I was to do with the injustice that I saw taking place around me or where I was to receive support from. (Ardavan, 1382/2003, p. 7)

Before the 1979 revolution, the idea that women had to protect their bodies from the male gaze, and that men were responsible for monitoring female relatives' bodies and movements in the name of honor, was more prevalent in the country than it is today (Mir-Hosseini, 2017). Ardavan had to struggle against this historical backdrop as she entered a male-dominated public space.

Other leftist women I interviewed also remembered the injustices that they witnessed within the home shaping their decision to join the resistance against the Shah and, later, the Islamic Republic. Ardavan's gendered experiences pushed her toward political work during the revolutionary period. Familial conflict over women's physical movement into public space has been noted by other scholars of gender and the Middle East (Sadiqi and Ennaji, 2006).

It was not only women of the left that came into revolutionary work in spite of familial experiences with gender discrimination. Mina Kamaii was a teenager during the revolution and lived in Abadan. Her older brother was a father figure. Like most women from southern Iran, her movement and agency were limited due to the region's conservatism. She reflected on her brother's presence in her life:

Mehran did not allow us to participate in demonstrations. But we used to go anyway without telling him ... Mehran had activities that he would participate in during this time, and he would attend demonstrations. He was in touch with others in the mosque that were active. But he did not allow us to go anywhere. Once my three sisters and I insisted on going, and finally he allowed us to accompany him. I told my mom that I wanted a chador to wear, and she fitted one of her chadors for me. We took Shahram [younger brother] with us too. Many people were there. All the kids from school, the youth that were active in the mosque, and ... [her digression here]. The ghods mosque was near our home, and the kids from the neighborhood guided us. (Mohammadi, 1381/2002a, pp. 16–17)

Kamaii also remembers how she and her sisters were not allowed to walk home from school, although the school was adjacent to their home. The sisters had to wait under a tree for Mehran to chaperone them. When the war began and Kamaii wanted to stay in Abadan and help behind the front lines, her family objected. In the fall of 1979, Mehran forced her to leave the mosque where she was preparing food. Once they arrived at home and Kamaii refused to evacuate their home, he kicked her in the face and left her with a black eye that lasted twenty days (Mohammadi, 1381/2002a, p. 30).

The revolution did not enable Kamaii to leave the home and participate in sociopolitical activities. Instead, it was a moment of contention within the family over a woman's place, as well as a battle that she was able to legitimize for herself and the women surrounding her.

Kamaii and her sisters could return to Abadan once their mom decided that living with extended family was not conducive to their well-being. Their mother was also impacted by their resistance, which included going on a hunger strike to stress their opposition to leaving Abadan. Kamaii was one of twenty women from Abadan that supported the war efforts by working as volunteer medical assistants. For some women, male guardianship and the limits it posed encouraged them to seek refuge in their role as caregivers in the context of war and also reach out to other women for help. Kamaii's memoir also suggests that domestic violence was at the very least a marginal part of the experience during the revolutionary and war period for pro-Khomeini women who wanted to enter the public sphere. Yet domestic violence rarely appears in the narratives written by or for pro-Khomeini women.

As Milani (1992) states, both women and men are expected to participate in preventing themselves from seeing one another. Adhering to modesty through a series of practices, such as lowering their gaze, is understood as an act of piety. Segregation of genders is more stringent for Islamist women and men, although separation of *mahram* and *non-mahram* (those related and not related) is expected of everyone in public space (Khosravi, 2008). For women such as Kamaii, participating in the war was hardly an easy task due to such gendered norms, which governed Iranian society and public space at the time (as they continue to do today).

For some women, familial relations refined and enhanced their activism. Monireh B. (2009) affiliated with the Marxist group Revolutionary

Workers Organization [Rah-e Kargar], spent time in prison before and after the 1979 revolution. She states the following about her motivations; family factors into her reflection on the past but from a slightly different perspective than Ardavan's and Kamaii's familial memories:

I was acquainted with political issues because both my brother and sister were arrested during the time of the Shah. All my cousins were in prison. One of my cousins committed suicide under the Shah after being tortured in prison. My house was filled with political discussions. Naturally, when I entered university at the age of 19, I was drawn to political activities. I was not really affiliated with any particular group. The reason I was arrested under the Shah was because I was trying to smuggle in a communiqué to my brother, who was being held in prison. I was held for six months at that time.

Monireh then goes on to discuss how her family history intersected with her own views on women's rights:

I was very active during the Revolution. After the Revolution, I was active because I did not believe that the new situation reflected the principles upon which the Revolution was based. In particular, I disagreed with the compulsory veil, the increased role of the clerics in the courts and Parliament, as well as the censorship of the press, which had led to the banning of most of Iran's newspapers. I became active with a Marxist group, Revolutionary Workers Organization [Rah-e Kargar], and was in this group for about a year and a half before being arrested. The activities were above-ground. We had a student cell, which distributed leaflets in the street about our group's ideals, and we started debates and discussion of important issues in the street and we recruited new members. Our group never believed in armed struggle. (Monireh B., 2009, p. 63)

Monireh frames the origins of her political activism within her familial history of resistance. In another volume (Hadjebi-Tabrizi, 1383/2004), Monireh remembers watching her brother pray with great concentration; she assumed that he was a member of the Mojahedin. Although she considered herself a leftist, she was mesmerized by his dedication. He shared with her books addressing resistance and revolution in other countries, such as Algeria. He also took Monireh mountain climbing, which was another opportunity for her to connect with his politically active friends. Memories of familial activism – cousins, brothers, and sisters that had resisted during the time of the Shah – shaped women's decisions to resist the establishment of an Islamic Republic in Iran. Issues pertaining to women's rights were only one reason for politicization, and families also impacted their political decisions.

Positive family relations were also remembered by followers of Khomeini as instrumental to their decision to participate in the war. Some 6,428 women were martyred in the war, and 500 of them were warriors at the front lines ("Amaar-e Shohada va Esargare-haye Zanan dar Doran-e Defa Moghaddas," 1395). The family of Maryam Farhanian, who became a martyr in the early days of the war while supporting other fighters as a medical assistant in Khorramshahr, remembers the important role her father played in her politicization. According to a close family friend:

Haj Latif [Maryam's father] was mindful of his kids' morality, behavior, and religiosity. He also allowed them to freely decide on their social activism. During that time, you could not find many fathers that permitted all of their sons and daughters to participate in activities having to do with the revolution. (Saalmee nejad, 1391, p. 21)

Farhanian's father is remembered as the person who encouraged and legitimized her activism. Her brother, however, introduced the family to the "message of the Islamic Revolution" (Saalmee nejad, 1391, p. 48):

Mahdi Farhanian was the son of Haj Latif and the first person to bring the message of the Islamic Revolution into the home and introduce the family to Ayatollah Khomeini. The family was religious and this made them receptive to Imam's messages, and Haj Latif and Naneh Hadi had no objections with regard to Mahdi's activism. In fact, it was quite the opposite.

Mahdi brought texts and stories about his activism into the home to further politicize Farhanian:

The entire family, especially Maryam and Fatemeh, gathered around Mahdi and asked to be included in revolutionary activism. Mahdi believed that one has to first strengthen his or her mind and then enter political participation. This is because if a revolutionary person cannot survive under the torture of SAVAK, they can inflict a heavy loss to the revolution itself. Moving in this path came with many difficulties and risks. It required a strong motivation and dedication to the power of God. Mahdi preferred that members of the family, such as Maryam, Fatemeh, and Aghelah, become familiar with religious and revolutionary texts. Every time he brought a prohibited book home, he made it possible for his brothers and sisters to become acquainted with the revolution. (Saalmee nejad, 1391, p. 48)

Farhanian appears to have been influenced by her immediate context and the loving support of male figures. According to one of her sisters, as well as the letters Farhanian wrote to Mahdi after his martyrdom, she had a special affective bond with him (Saalmee nejad, 1391). The circulation of books between her brothers and sisters nurtured her desire to participate in the revolution and war. An appreciative glance at the history of women's rights activism in Iran is missing from Farhanian's story of activism in revolution and war.

During my interviews, I encountered women who did not highlight a politically significant familial background or specific gendered experiences with discrimination as the inspiration behind their politicization. Their gravitation toward leftist and Islamist activism was a "rite of passage" forged through teenage friendships and the broader revolutionary atmosphere (Mottahedeh, 2000, p. 66). As Sohrabi (2019) has recently argued, while the role of *tashkelat* (political organizations) has been studied by scholars as significant in shaping the actions of activists, the centrality of friendships to decisions made by political actors is overlooked. An interviewee affiliated with the Islamic Mojahedin, Haleh B., spent close to three years in prison during the early 1980s and described her motivation for political activism:

Having a political cause was an answer to people who asked you what service are you doing for your country or what do you believe in. It was fashionable at that time for the youth to be associated with a specific political group and have a political philosophy, even if they didn't really know it well. People would question you and call you pro-regime, elitist or *Taghuti*, if you wore fancy foreign clothes or would be uninformed. Everyone also had a common purpose, being against the Shah. The atmosphere early on was positive and everyone was engaged in dialogue and conversation about what is best and what is right.

In addition to being influenced by the atmosphere at the time, Haleh explains how her everyday life shaped her political path:

I first got interested [in politics] when I was probably around 13 years old. I was young and living with my mother and brother. My social life revolved around going to school and being with friends. I wasn't raised in a leftist and religious family. So that didn't have an influence on me. My parents were not supporters of the Shah. But they were also apolitical. Through a friend who knew Ali Shariati's family, I was also introduced to his work, which influenced me. Most of my friends at some point became involved with groups like Mojahedin. Some stayed a member. Others left to join other groups. When things got more dangerous, some also got afraid and tried to disassociate themselves from others. (Personal interview, Germany, 2008)

While discussing the production of literature and poetry during the 1980–1988 period, Ahmad Karimi-Hakkak (1985) has argued that where one stood in relation to the Pahlavi Monarchy and the establishment of an Islamic Republic in postrevolutionary Iran determined how a writer was perceived by his or her peers. Through his analysis of the era's literary production, Karimi-Hakkak captures Iran's sociopolitical, postrevolutionary atmosphere and eloquently frames Haleh's approach to relating to an idealized past with respect to women's rights. For Haleh, a particular friendship, and the resultant introduction to one thinker, Ali Shariati, was the origin of her low-level collaboration with the Islamic Mojahedin. The contextual significance of standing for something and having a political philosophy (even a uniformed one) was, for some, more important than one's grasp or even commitment to those ideas, as Haleh's reference to fading friendships after the state's crackdown suggests.

Similar to Haleh, Shamsy Sobhani (Jafarian, 1381/2002) remembers becoming politicized through friendships. Two years before the 1979 revolution at the age of twenty-three, Sobhani signed up for adult education night classes. During these classes in Tehran, where she had recently moved from northern Iran, she became familiar with the work of Morteza Motahhari and his discussion on the importance of hijab for women. She states:

> Reading these books, and friendships with women that were mothers and had a few kids, left a long-term impression on me. These women participated in printing and distributing leaflets on Imam's thought [Khomeini]. I felt like I had gotten some distance from everyday life. My mother would say "Shamsy! A girl must become a homemaker and settle down. You are twenty something years old, and what you are doing will not lead to a blissful ending." Those days I felt very lonely. I wished to speak with someone. Several times I decided to give Motahhari's book *Hijab* to Ruhangiz [her sister], but she was a happy nineteen-year-old that had no patience for reading such a book. (Jafarian, 1381/2002, p. 14)

Sobhani's parents were not aware of the extent of her activism, and the family was not politically active. In 1979 she joined the Revolutionary Guards and was stationed in Kurdistan prior to the start of the Iran–Iraq war due to the region's unrest. She served the Revolutionary Guards as a medical assistant in Kurdistan and later in the war. Exciting friendships, access to ideas that verified their transforming identities as pious women, and a break from the everyday labors younger women in large families endured made political activism appealing. There was no backward glance at the women's rights movement in modern Iran or even reflection on middle-class women's advancements during the reign of Mohammad Reza Pahlavi.

Relationships with women from other generations helped women negotiate their prison experience. Shahrnush Parsipur (2013, p. 155), the acclaimed Iranian writer who spent "four years, seven months, and seven days in prison," recalls that most of the women in prison were young and sought relationships with older and more experienced female prisoners who oftentimes were arrested for nonpolitical reasons. Many of these high schoolers, even after witnessing the execution of friends and family members, were unable to process the severity of their predicament. As an illustration, intergenerational relations within prison also influenced how Nasrin Parvaz decided to engage with the regime:

During our recreational time outside, we walked with mother Masturah and talked about our lives with her. It has been some time since she was transferred from the joint committee [*committee moshtarak*] to Evin. Raz and I took care of her. We washed her clothes, and we helped her in the shower. We treated her like our own mother because she was old and kind. She also refused to do as the *tavvabs* demanded. She never talked with the *tavvabs*, and she only had relations with us. She was arrested because the regime was looking for her sons.

Parvaz goes into further detail as to why she found Masturah endearing:

What I found interesting about mother Masturah was the following: although she knew the *tavvabs* were writing reports on her, she still preferred to side with us [Raz and Parvaz]. The code word she used to describe the *tavvabs* was "germs." One day the *tavvabs* told her that we were unclean [*najis*] and anti-revolutionary; therefore, she should not speak with us. She told them that there were only two humans in the room, and that was Raz and Parvaz. (Parvaz, 2002, p. 79)

Parvaz appears to be empowered by witnessing Masturah's resistance. Importantly, she was touched by the fact that Masturah was not motivated by an association with a resistance movement. Instead, the insistence of women from previous generations, often nonpolitical, on maintaining a level of personal independence, preference, and freedom emboldened both young prisoners.

Class issues were important catalysts for women's activism during the 1980–1988 period. This has rarely been acknowledged, especially within the formal narrative of the Islamic Republic with respect to non-elite participation in the war (Ahmadi, 2018). The Islamic Republic's formal narrative emphasizes the religious upbringing of most women who participated in the war. For instance, in a volume published by the Center for Documentation on the Islamic Revolution, it is stated,

We can state that most of the women that were active in the Sacred Defense were raised in middle-class and religious families. They grew up with Islamic teaching, and this contributed to their political and social awareness … from a religious perspective, they were highly committed, and during their participation [in the war], adherence to religious edicts was an important goal to them. (Judaki, 1395/ 2016, p. 67)

To document the centrality of Islamic norms to the lives of women who participated in the war, the volume offers several examples by referencing the major memoirs published in recent years. For instance, readers are reminded that some martyrs' mothers asked women with improper hijabs to leave their sons' funerals due to their commitment to Islamic attire, and some nurses refused to touch male patients without surgical gloves to make certain they did not touch a man who they are not religiously permitted to be in contact with because of their participation in the war efforts (Judaki, 1395/2016, pp. 68–69).

Similar to women affiliated with the left, however, followers of Khomeini remember their experiences with poverty and shed light on another view on intergenerational connections. While there are no certain figures, it is estimated that during the eight-year conflict there were 171 female Iranian prisoners of war ("Amaar-e Shohada va Esargare-haye Zanan dar Doran-e Defa Moghaddas," 1395). One was Masumeh Abad, a prisoner of war in Iraq for four years. She recounts how she felt when one of her teachers called her father a thief:

When he used the term "thief," my father's pious face appeared before my eyes. I wanted to scream. I wanted to yell louder than him. I wanted to say that it is true my father is a worker, but he is a great human being. If his body smells like oil, his spirit smells of decency. My heart ached for my father's hands, hands which worked and were worthy of kisses. (Abad, 1395, p. 74)

Like leftist women, Abad recalls her father's economic status and its ramifications on the quality of her life as she frames her politicization at a young age.

At times, then, intergenerational relationships and women's immediate memories intersected to shape their decision to take political action. For Islamist women, political action was not only defined in terms of participation in the war. Marriage to war veterans and men committed to Khomeini was also an important act of solidarity with the state (Akbari, 1390/2011).

Similar to Masumeh Abad, Mrs. Mehri remembers the poverty that her father was raised in when recounting his martyrdom and its impact on her decision to marry an injured war veteran: "My father was born into a poor family and at a young age became an orphan. Left with little choice, he began to work for my mother's father at a young age in our village. When he became a teenager, he started to work at a factory and married my mom" ("Vaghte hameh chez be khoda khatm meshavad," 1391, p. 24).

Coming from a small village in Mazandaran in northern Iran, Mrs. Mehri decided to marry her first husband, who was later martyred, because his commitment to religious practice was similar to her late father's. She was also aware of her immediate context as she recalls how her martyred husband allowed regular visits to her mother's home, which, during this period, was a right readily denied to married women (Abdolah, 2011). Mrs. Mehri's decision to marry her second husband, a paralyzed war veteran, was based on her dedication to her martyred father and husband. She states that her father wished for her to study nursing; she believed she made her father proud by taking care of a disabled war veteran. For some Islamist women, political action was engendered by an intersection between immediate memories, experiences with class, and intergenerational connections.

Following the 1979 revolution, a Kurdish uprising began in Iran's Kurdistan between the Sunni and Shi'i Kurds, with the Shi'i supporting the newly established Islamic Republic (McDowall, 1996; Prunhuber, 2010). Kurdish militant groups continued their warfare during the Iran–Iraq war, although the conflict in Kurdistan had subsided by late 1981. For many Islamist men and women who would become involved in the Iran–Iraq war in 1981, this initial conflict was a kind of practice at warfare in an Islamic Republic.

Maryam Kazemzadeh (Raissi, 1383/2003) argues that the conversations she had with Khomeini during a visit in Paris, where she had gone to take photos of him, encouraged her to think about continuing her career as a wartime journalist in Marivan, Kurdistan, during the Kurdish uprising in 1979. Kazemzadeh remembers her desire to be a journalist even as a child but briefly states that her familial and broader societal context did not support her career choice. Only toward the end of the Iran–Iraq war did journalism become a popular career choice for Iranian women; Kazemzadeh's presence on the warfront makes her a trailblazer (Farhadpour, 2012). When she asked Khomeini about the religious permissibility of women becoming journalists, he stated: "If the regulations of hijab are abided by, there is no problem" (Raissi, 1383/2003, p. 28). The mandatory enforcement of hijab had some positive effects: Women began to enter previously male-dominated fields of work, such as photography and journalism (Farhadpour, 2012). Nevertheless, Kazemzadeh recalls that a military commander told her the following when she arrived in Marivan, Kurdistan: "The truth is that we don't believe that a Muslim woman would have the audacity to travel to this region, unless she was an anti-revolutionary who had infiltrated a news outlet" (Raissi, 1383/2003, p. 28). Kazemzadeh states the following in response:

I waited for the commander to finish what he was saying. Once he stopped talking, I asked for permission to go to my room. I presented them with the written statement Imam Khomeini had given to me in Paris. I received this letter from Imam when I travelled to Paris from the UK. Given that I had a deep interest in photography and journalism, I wanted to know Imam Khomeini's views on female journalists; as a source of emulation (*marja-i taqlid*) and a religious leader his views were important to me ... When the commander saw Imam's handwriting, he was completely convinced and apologized for his behavior. (Raissi, 1383/2003, pp. 28–29)

For some female supporters of Khomeini, his support for women's participation in national affairs, as well as the solidarity of other male elites, enabled them to become political activists. Kazemzadeh also describes how the support of Mostafa Chamran, a revolutionary commander in Marivan and also a US-trained scientist who was later killed in the Iran–Iraq war, influenced her sense of self:

Dr. Chamran asked about my love and interest for photography and journalism. Although the reason for this conversation was something else, we talked past our evening prayers and dinner. Dr. Chamran had a warm and calm voice. I listened to his words with my heart and soul. That night we talked about everything. He discussed the life and resistance of Dr. Ali Shariati, his death in London, and I was eagerly all ears. I had developed my religious, political, and cultural awareness through the writing of Dr. Shariati, and I had a special interest in him.

She further expands on how Chamran showed an interest in not only her intellectual development but also gender identity:

After dinner, Dr. Chamran picked up my camera and spoke about art with me. I heard that he painted. He told me about a candle he had drawn, as well as a horse. He then discussed his daughter who was about my age. He said that seeing me became a reason for him to remember his daughter, who had been living with her mother in the United States for years. The warm voice of Dr. Chamran and his spiritual awareness made me feel more secure. That night I saw him as a psychologist. A person that knew and understood me better than myself. (Raissi, 1383/2003, pp. 31–32)

Kazemzadeh's immediate interactions with men such as Khomeini and Chamran emboldened her to become the only female reporter in Iran's Kurdistan during the Kurdish uprising following the 1979 revolution. From 1980 to 1981, she reported and also worked as a medical assistant throughout the Iran–Iraq war. She traveled to the warfronts of Kermanshah with her husband, Asghar Vasaali, who was a political prisoner before the revolution and sentenced to life. (He later fought in Kurdistan and the Iran–Iraq war, becoming a martyr in 1980.) She found the solidarity that her family and community of origin refused to give her, and which she remains silent about throughout the memoir, in elite Islamist men. Where this solidarity did not exist in men – for instance, when she wanted to join her husband in the Iran–Iraq war and he initially rejected her request – she was confident enough to demand the right to participate in the war. Kazemzadeh informed her husband that if he did not allow her to go with him to Kermanshah, she would seek a divorce. Her narrative of her political development does not include an appreciative glance at women's rights struggles in the past. Instead, it reaches into up-close experiences and intergenerational exchanges with male political elites to enliven her political activism. While most Iranian male soldiers and commanders in Kurdistan disapproved and reacted negatively to Kazemzadeh's presence at the warfront, she defended her right to stay and work because of the confidence she developed through interactions with Khomeini and Chamran.

2.2 Iran's Hezbollah and Remembrance of Marzieh Hadidchi Dabbaq: From Superwomen to Equal Women

Similar to the previous discussion on women's activism during the 1980–1988 period, for the younger generation of activists affiliated with Hezbollah, individual memories, experiences, and goals are prioritized over historical narratives on women's rights. Iran's Hezbollah has political roots that predate the 1979 revolution. However, in the post-1979 period this faction functioned as the coercive arm of the state by enforcing various Islamization projects onto society, including mandatory hijab (Sedghi, 2007).

This social group is significant for its close ties to the state, hence my focus on its activism. Many of the women associated with the Hezbollah faction, should they wish to stay involved in politics, will take up sensitive positions in the state's security, media, and diplomatic institutions. The newer generation of Hezbollah cultural affiliates do not remember the 1979 revolution or Iran–Iraq war. Similar to other Iranian youth, they negotiate the state's religious authority over their lives (Khosravi, 2008). As pious citizens, they are prone to collaborate with the Islamic state and oftentimes come from low-income families where reliance on the state for support is crucial to their livelihood (Khosravi, 2008). The age range for female cultural activists is anywhere from early twenties to early forties; as such, female Hezbollah activists understand the problems and issues women from different generations are facing. By participating in community outreach and grassroots activism as leaders in local mosques, the university, and state institutions such as the Islamic Republic of Iran Broadcasting, female Hezbollahi cultural activists also gain insight into the problems of noncitizens.

Following the 2009 presidential conflict, most independent women's NGOs were shut down by the state, and activism became more challenging for everyone but for women in particular (Mouri and Batmanghelichi, 2015). Moreover, feminism and women's rights activism were formally classified as threats to national security by the Revolutionary Guards (Sadeghi, 2009). The Islamic Republic invested heavily in pro-regime cultural institutes where pious youth were employed to reproduce the state through cultural and artistic work that animated the ideals of the 1979 revolution (Saeidi, 2017). As such, the two themes that existed in women's activism during the 1980–1988 period – personal histories and an intergenerational learning process – exist here as well.

This section illustrates the significant influence that pro-regime Hezbollahi women's individual memories and immediate surroundings have on how they approach the predicament of women in Iranian society today. I do this through an analysis of published and rejected essays submitted for a special issue on the life of Marzieh Dabbaq edited by a Hezbollah cultural institute where I carried out extensive fieldwork from 2012 to 2014.

Marzieh Hadidchi Dabbaq was an Islamist revolutionary close to Khomeini who later served the state in various formal capacities, including as a member of parliament. In November 2016, shortly after her death, one of the Hezbollah cultural institutes that facilitated my research prepared a special issue on her life. Dabbaq is a female role model for the Hezbollah front in Iran due to her anti-Shah activism prior to the revolution, as well as her unwavering support of Khomeini after the 1979 revolution. She represents the ideal woman for the conservative right in Iran – and the Hezbollah faction. For instance, she was trained as a fighter in Lebanon prior to the revolution and served conservative interests in parliament, but she was also the mother of eight and a wife. During the last few years of her life, she informed the Supreme Leader that she would like to go to Syria (*Banuye Enghelab*, p. 35), and he responded to her request by arguing that she was more needed in Iran. Her death was an opportunity for the Hezbollah front to explore how its female supporters assessed the state's current gender policies.

The augmentation of revolutionary female figures during the 1980–1988 period, such as the late Dabbaq, is central to the anti-feminist movement that the state supported after the 2009 presidential election conflict. The regime's ideal revolutionary woman, who supports men politically but also takes care of the home, was first promoted in Iranian society during the early 1980s to make distinctions between Iranian women (Farhi, 1994). The younger generation is expected to reproduce this image through their cultural activism.

Female Hezbollahi cultural activists' remembrance of religious role models such as Hazrat-e Fatemeh (daughter of Prophet Mohammad) and Hazrat-e Zeinab (his granddaughter), as well as their support of Dabbaq as a practical role model, is both grounded in the present condition of women in Iran and rooted in their own "autobiographical memory" (Isurin, 2017, p. 10). Since the Ahmadinejad presidency (2005–2013), there has been a significant production of cultural material on Iran and the region that focuses on the lives of female martyrs and women related to male martyrs (Basij Jamaah Zanan-e Keshvar, 1391). The public display of these national and international narratives solidifies the importance of women to Iran's 1979 revolution, the Iran–Iraq war, and regional transformations.

As I show below, in the process of consuming and promoting such cultural material, Hezbollahi women also reexamine their own lives in relation to this national and regional context. Additionally, working together in Hezbollah cultural institutes literally gives women *space* to connect with one another's gendered struggles. There is, then, an important contextual element to Hezbollahi women's assessment of an idealized past: The interpersonal knowledge that Hezbollahi women gain during interactions in cultural institutes shapes their assessment and relationship to an idealized past, even as activists have begun to critique the notion of the ideal revolutionary while working toward exemplifying her in Iranian society and in the broader international system.

In the first segments of the special issue, women and men who knew Dabbaq describe her different roles and responsibilities thus: She did her own cooking and did not waste even a grain of rice (*Banuye Enghelab*, p. 39); she watered her plants on a strict schedule (*Banuye Enghelab*, p. 32); she played for hours with the children of martyrs (*Banuye Enghelab*, p. 33); she did not own a piece of gold (*Banuye Enghelab*, p. 32); she worked for one pound a week as a maid in the United Kingdom when she left Iran prior to the revolution due to her anti-Shah activism (*Banuye Enghelab*, p. 6); when she had some loans to repay from her tenure as a parliamentary representative, she became a taxi driver to make ends meet (*Banuye Enghelab*, p. 8).

Dabbaq was also the first female commander of the Revolutionary Guards and is one of the theoreticians behind the special unit of the Revolutionary Guards that became known as the Quds Force (*Banuye Enghelab*, p. 24). She is remembered as a woman who made hard decisions but also stood by the consequences those decisions had for her life.

The special issue appears to take its lead from the papers submitted and indicates little forethought given to a formal message on Dabbaq's life. For instance, several people who knew Dabbaq personally argued that her husband was supportive, and as such an equality is depicted within Dabbaq's marriage. However, the special issue also includes a short interview with her husband, and his silences tell a slightly different story. He focuses on the challenges of a life with Dabbaq: "what a difficult life I had with Miss Dabbaq. Unlike the norms that ruled the Pahlavi era, we saw each other for the first time on our wedding night. I had never seen her before. At 29 years old, they wed me to a

14-year-old. When we moved to Tehran, I found her some teachers" (*Banuye Enghelab*, p. 20). In the remainder of the interview, he discusses his own prerevolutionary activism and the financial challenges he faced with eight children. He does not mention her again.

It appears that, either intentionally or unintentionally, the special issue initiated a debate on women's independence. For the younger generation of female Hezbollah affiliates, the narratives of Dabbaq's life also appear to tell a less visible story: She had much control over her decisions. This level of decision-making, at times, escapes the limits that the Islamic Republic's citizenry framework poses for women (Afary, 2001). Afary (2001) has discussed how Dabbaq left her children and husband to support Khomeini abroad and that she was involved in anti-Shah activism that placed her family in danger.

A former revolutionary activist, Agha-Mohammadi, states the following which supports Afary's (2001) claim: "when Miss Dabbaq left Iran for Syria, Lebanon and other places, Haj Hassan [her husband] had no contact with her and did not know where she was. It was not until Imam Musa Sadr stepped in and revealed where she was living that he was able to see her again" (*Banuye Enghelab*, p. 9). Her independence holds the different narratives of her life together. This did not go unnoticed by the younger generation of female Hezbollah affiliates, who, prior to 2012, were not given space in Hezbollah cultural institutes to work side by side with each other or their male counterparts (Az en Nasl Motefaker berun Nmi aayad, 1387/2008). Perhaps motivated by this marginalized narrative on Dabbaq's life that sets her above other Iranian women, the authors in the special issue call for equality between all women in post-1979 Iran.

The theme of gender equality is dominant in the published essays. One piece argues against the tendency within Hezbollah to place college-educated women and women involved in national affairs above the housewife, mother, and even women who do not identify with pro-regime activism. The hierarchy that this categorization produces denies women their right to decide who they want to be. The author, Sajdeh I., states:

The ideal woman embodies education, marriage, motherhood, and social activism in excellence. In turn, this is what is expected of other women. Women are forced to annihilate themselves and take on a strange form to fit into this model. We wanted this ideal, even if it meant destroying her inner identity, character and capacities. Creating one model for everyone meant that we overlooked an important reality: women's abilities, capacities, and the conditions of their lives vary. Therefore, there is a problem with this description. The woman that cannot become a mother feels empty. The girl that is unmarried is discouraged. The mother that did not continue her education sees herself as incomplete and useless. Very few women can actually fit into this model. We were critical of feminism because of its universal description of women. Yet unintentionally, we are taking steps in the same path. The perspective that can move us closer to our vision is one void of a stable and homogenous model of a revolutionary woman. We have to accept that the presence of all of these qualities in one woman is unlikely. Where it is possible, the presence of this woman will also entail some challenging conditions. We need a vision where Hazrat Zahra and Hazrat Zeinab are understood as ideal and complete women. We have to try to emulate them. We have to accept that the ideal woman is not human. She does not exist. The revolutionary woman is not a character. It is a spectrum. An excellent example of someone at one end of this spectrum is Miss Dabbaq. At the other end of this continuum, there are hundreds of women that fall within this range despite all the specific conditions of their lives. Being present on this scale, without any hierarchy or ranking, is praiseworthy. (1395/2016, p. 42)

Toward the end of the essay, she states the following when discussing women who do volunteer and perform community work in the post-revolutionary period:

It is possible that their hijab is not proper. But this does not lessen the value of what they are doing. With all of their limitations and merits, they are still an illustration of a revolutionary woman. Even if they cannot decipher their own identity, and do not define their activism as a form of service connected to the government, they are still revolutionary women. (p. 43)

For Sajdeh, the interplay between religion and gendered subjectivities is limited to the postrevolutionary period; little attention is given to gender and subjectivities in the prerevolutionary years. According to Sajdeh's understanding of the 1979 revolution, the revolution created myriad options for women, and all paths should be equally respected and available to her. She references the revered Shi'i female figures, Hazrat-e Zahra and Hazrat-e Zeinab, to undermine the state's hierarchy of worthy women by stating that Iranian society should see these female figures as ideals and that equality should exist between all Iranian women because ideals are not reality. This is a radical move that contrasts with how the Islamic Republic used female Shi'i figures during the 1980–1988 period to "displace, supersede, and even render impertinent Western anxieties about gender equality" (Osanloo, 2014, p. 250).

Closely related to the Islamic Republic's use of these sacred female figures for evaluating women's supposed purity, and subsequently creat-ing a citizenry hierarchy between women, Sajdeh questions the connec-tion between the chador and an enforcement of inequality between women (Farhi, 1994, p. 264). This stems from a contextualized historical factor: Beginning in 2005, the Ahmadinejad government pursued a campaign for a "culture of modesty," and Iranian women's style of dress became a point of national conflict again as morality police arrested poorly veiled women (Sadeghi, 2009, p. 51). Additionally, Sajdeh's critical perspective is also related to the timing of the special issue. Following the 2009 presidential election conflict, the Hezbollah faction attempted to disassociate itself from the Ahmadinejad government and its policies due to his conflict with the office of the Supreme Leader and Ali Khamenei himself (Sohrabi, 2011). In the aftermath of the 2009 conflict and the various forms of opposition it engendered, space was created for critiquing the Ahmadinejad administration's gender policies, which were a conservative interpretation of the Islamic Republic's foundational approach toward the gender question (Osanloo, 2014).

Ultimately, Sajdeh suggests that even women who identify closely with the regime cannot become Dabbaq for various reasons. Instead, she finds that the ideals of the sacred figures of Hazrat-e Fatemeh and Hazrat-e Zeinab are more practical role models because they lack an embodied presence that can then be commodified. Sajdeh thus believes that female religious icons are more accessible for the majority of the population because they are difficult to pin down and package. She calls upon these sacred female figures to enliven imagination for Shi'i women and enable them to articulate their visions and make their lives visible before a reluctant Hezbollahi audience and a broader patriarchal society. For Sajdeh, the 1979 revolution is memorialized as a watershed moment that made a variety of subjectivities possible to Iranian women. From this standpoint she reimagines the relevance of Dabbaq, Hazrat-e Fatemeh Zahra, and Hazrat-e Zeinab.

The insistence that the state expand its notion of revolutionary woman to include all women in Iranian society, and on equal terms, can also be noted in another piece that was included in the special issue. This concern is significant because since the establishment of an Islamic Republic in Iran after the 1979 revolution, Islamization has not been only about individual morality but also been a matter of constructing an identity, an appearance, that stands in opposition to all things perceived as "Western" (Martin, 2007). Given the close relationship that exists between revolutionary identity, body, and being Islamic, I argue that expanding the limits on who qualifies as revolutionary can be seen as an affront to the state's narrow Islamization project, which these women are supposed to be leading (Sanadjian, 1996). Zahra D., a PhD student in philosophy, states the following:

It seems to me that in contemporary Iran, the image we have of an ideal woman is that of a hero who can do all things. She has higher education. She married young and has at least three successful and happy children. At the same time, she is busy in her professional career, and in this domain too, she is highly regarded. The Iranian superwoman is in hijab and very devout. She does not speak to men who are strangers (*namahram*) unless it is absolutely necessary. At the same time, she may have many male colleagues. She does her own cooking, and her home shines of cleanliness. Her kids have a great peace of mind, which is the result of her extraordinary mothering. Her husband reveres her in all ways. What does this woman look like in reality? Many educated women are getting married later, having fewer children, or delaying their entry into the workforce. In all cases, women have prioritized some of their ideals above others. But the Islamic Republic's superwoman is perfect in all domains of her life, at once … What conclusions can we draw from the distance that exists between the reality and this ideal? (1395/2016, p. 44)

Khosravi (2017) has illustrated that, in contemporary Iran, a woman who is wealthy, employed, educated, mobile, and also domestic is depicted as a first-class citizen in the national media. This is indeed an image that most Iranian women will never be able to embody; it's also a remaking of the 1980s ideal of the revolutionary woman, which Zahra seems to also have in mind as she references the media's role in promoting an unrealistic depiction of women.

Similar to Sajdeh, Zahra also calls for an equality between all women in Iran and an appreciation for the different contributions that each woman makes to society:

The state's cultural narrative should illustrate to its children that it respects various forms of the ideal woman and that they are all equally valuable. Additionally, until it is able to demonstrate the different models of the ideal woman, it should help its superwomen realize their potentials. It is ultimately women's own responsibility to materialize their dreams. In a society where women have such a complicated situation, however, any support will have significant impact. (p. 47)

This heightened and public form of reflection on the predicament of women in Iranian society can be noted in analysis developed through other methods. Based on my experience living and working with female Hezbollah affiliates over several years, Zahra's essay could easily be based on the broken hearts and spirits that she encountered in her social group and her individual goal to rectify this situation. One evening in the winter of 2013, I was invited to edit a film I had coproduced with a female Hezbollah affiliate, Sara Z. The film addressed how war martyrs' mothers think about culture and cinema. After a few full days of filming, we were excited to do our own editing. We had also developed a friendship during those long days of filming and interviewing and began to enjoy one another's company. We were the only women in the building that night at the cultural institute, but the institute's supervisor was there. We both felt comfortable. Sara was a young, ambitious, and gifted undergraduate student in Tehran who was married to a fellow activist. She was also one of the leaders of the anti-feminist movement that gained momentum during the Ahmadinejad presidency. Despite her young age and lack of experience and expertise, Sara was readily invited into research institutes connected to various state organizations working on issues that relate to women's rights.

As we edited, I noted that she was stressed and anxious but preferred not to tell me what was going on. She was panicking, kept looking at the door, and had trouble focusing. I noticed that her husband was standing by the editing room and appeared agitated as he looked at us and erratically walked back and forth. Finally, around 8 p.m. with tears in her eyes, but still standing tall, she informed me that she had to leave but that she would be back tomorrow to review my editing and make any final contributions. Four years later, Sara was a women's rights activist, divorced, and a PhD candidate living alone in Tehran. Her political views had changed. She later informed me that one of the reasons for the divorce was that her husband had demanded she completely stop her education and social activism.

The authors who contributed to this special issue on Dabbaq's life write with a fluidity and insight that seems to come from experience and their individual goals and struggles. There is little analysis or comparison with women's rights struggles in even postrevolutionary Iran, much less prior to the revolution. Yet they are aware that the image of women like Dabbaq is no longer popular and that the state has moved on to promoting another image: a superwoman that also has a market in the West. This is perhaps why they spend an extended amount of time addressing the freedom they are in search of and then connect this desire to their personalized conception of Dabbaq and women like her.

Their novel interpretation of the lives of Dabbaq, Hazrat-e Zeinab, and Hazrat-e Fatemeh Zahra centering on independent women (which enhances equality between women because of their openness to scales and difference) is theoretically powerful. A consistent thread in Dabbaq's life is independence in decision-making, assessments, and activism – almost like a goddess that invoked endless ways to demonstrate the importance of the perspective she held and the power of her touch. The two authors view the lives of Dabbaq, Hazrat-e Zeinab, and Hazrat-e Fatemeh Zahra with a lens that steers away from the 1980s focus on purity toward one illustrating how women can be different but equal (Farhi, 1994, p. 264).

This reinterpretation of ideal womanhood from the 1980s creates much-needed room for women to maneuver. Importantly, both writers appear to be frustrated with the state's complete dismissal of feminism; this inability of the state to gain pro-regime women's full support when it comes to gender policies has been noted elsewhere as well (Sadeghi, 2009). They mention the social benefits that a feminist movement has garnered for Western societies, as well as how feminist and Islamic ideals can become unintentionally entangled. In the most immediate sense, then, their writing reveals that they can no longer remain quiet about the experiences of women in their families, networks, and society, and perhaps even themselves. Their reading of the Islamic Republic's original ideals is directly connected to their insight regarding the lack of independence that determines many women's lives in Iran, as well as to the problems associated with the regime's solution to its long-standing gender question: promotion of the superwoman persona.

2.3 Rejected Essays and New Possibilities for Equality between Men and Women

Perhaps surprisingly, the editors rejected analyses that were disconnected from the day-to-day reality of women's lives in Iran and that refused to acknowledge the gendered tensions within Hezbollah cultural institutions. These essays "failed interestingly" (Ellis, 2015, p. 7). As rejected documents, they highlight that engaging with Iranian women's gender struggles as equality between *men and women* has become significant for at least some Hezbollah cultural activists. The unpublished essays signify a turn in the gender politics of Iran's Hezbollah faction and a refusal to romanticize approaches employed during the 1980–1988 period. Together, the rejected essays suggest that gender equality – understood as equality between men and women – *can* be pursued among the pro-regime faction today and that at least some of the key officials in the Hezbollah movement are invested in changing the everyday lives and struggles that inequality engenders for Iranian women.

The first two essays I discuss depend heavily on a conception of women's rights styled as traditional, which fully denies the importance of legal equality or even a woman's right to the public sphere. This thinking on women's rights exists within cultural institutes and also among pro-regime families dedicated to conservative readings of the Quran (Tawasil, 2015). As such, the refusal to recognize the necessity of women's rights is tangible in the lives of pro-regime women, and yet these essays were surprisingly rejected for the special issue on Dabbaq's life organized by a Hezbollah cultural institute.

The third essay I discuss, however, is grounded in the author's inter-actions and experiences with women from other countries. The author identifies conversations and friendships with women from abroad to have been instrumental in piquing her interest in women's issues, and not her life or observations in Iranian society. She offers a unique experience connected to her background as a female leader in the movement. Hezbollah cultural institutes tend to send their most valuable and dedi-cated activists abroad to represent the regime in the international arena, but this is a privilege that few women in the movement are granted. This essay was also rejected perhaps because it transcends the inner workings of everyday life for women in Iran today. The author outlines how she came to value equality between women and in relation to men through interactions with the "Other."

One essay that did not make it into the special issue addressed mother-hood as the most important characteristic of a revolutionary woman. Yet the author, Mahnaz R., refers to women's activism in modern Iran to build her argument about the revolutionary woman:

Our discussions of a revolutionary woman should not be limited to the Islamic Republic. In the period before the revolution, we witnessed the actions of revolutionary women. An example would be Anis al-Doleh, the favorite wife of Nasir al-Din Shah who broke the Shah's hookah during the tobacco protest led by Mirza Shirazi. In reality, a revolutionary woman supports Islamic governance, stays in touch with the political causes of her time, follows the news, and analyzes with insight. When she feels her presence is necessary, she will be on the scene. She takes on any challenges for Islam and Muslims. A revolutionary woman feels a sense of responsibility to those around her. In fact, she feels responsible for the situations that arise before her. In her mind, individualism has no meaning, and she only sees herself as part of a collective. (1395/2016, pp. 1–2)

Mahnaz remembers women's activism during the Qajar period but with the intent to expand conceptualizations of revolutionary women without acknowledging the importance of a woman's right to independ-ence, movement, and public space. Later she not only stresses that motherhood is *the* characteristic of a revolutionary woman but also positions women's presence in the public sphere in conflict with their role as mothers:

Motherhood and married life are a priority for a revolutionary woman because these two roles are hers exclusively. This means that for these two roles there is no one else that can replace her. In other words, a woman that is a mother and wife, and has a career, will not be missed if she is away from society. This is because someone else can be found to replace her at work. However, if she does not spend time with her family, they will feel her absence. (1395/2016, p. 6)

Mahnaz's insistence on enforcing a correct formulation of life and society for women is probably one reason the piece was rejected. The published essays highlight a woman's right to determine how to balance the different domains of her life; this seems to be a notable legacy of Dabbaq's activism for both male and female Hezbollah activists. Her essay, then, simply does not fit into the collection. Additionally, she does not view the 1979 revolution as an opportunity for women to escape patriarchy or their roles as mothers. More than anyone in the special issue, Mahnaz referenced Iran's current Supreme Leader as well as Khomeini to support her argument that the revolutionary woman should stay at home for an undetermined period of time. The Hezbollah faction is understood to be closest to the Supreme Leader (Thaler et al., 2010). Yet in this instance, for the editors at least, their devotion to him did not include a dichotomy between the public and private sphere or predetermined formulations on a woman's place.

Another rejected essay also pursued a critical stance on the issue of women's independence and rights. Sahar M. explored how Persian literature in modern Iran has deciphered the revolutionary woman. After a vague and brief discussion of a few works that she finds to be feminist and therefore not organic (such as Zoya Pirzad's *I Will Turn Off the Lights*), she states the following, which relates to how Mahnaz understood women's rights demands in contemporary Iran:

Womanhood is the basis for sacrifice. Womanhood is not about asking for your share or demanding rights that you have lost. In my view, women's resistance is centered on elevating humanity. Through the upbringing of their children, women lead a struggle against oppression and human conflict. Such women are above all conceptions of gender. In my opinion, one of the reasons that our own national feminists are not interested in the revolutionary women that came to be during the Islamic Revolution, such as Dabbaq, is that the character of women like Dabbaq surpasses the stereotypical images that feminists have of the ideal woman. (1395/2016, p. 4)

Sahar also takes a critical stance with regard to women's rights struggles in contemporary Iran. Similar to Mahnaz, she elevates the conversation beyond Iran by drawing connections between all of humanity. This perspective seems to be forged through her reading of influential Persian literature and as such can be seen as a form of individual memory. While a dismissal of gender equality can be witnessed in Iranian society, state elites consider it an unreasonable policy path to take.

During my fieldwork, I was surprised to find that even among the conservative women's rights activists, research centers, and state institutions such as the Supreme Council for Cultural Revolution, there was no uncertainty about it: At least some legal-rights structures must change within the country to establish gender equality. The reality that critical views that dismiss women's struggles for legal equality are pushed out of the political front closest to the regime's decision-makers is notable. Not only does it illustrate that the Islamic Republic imposed constraints on some anti-feminist women's agency, but a focus on revising the legal structure to the benefit of women also shows that the regime has been unable (or perhaps unwilling) to overlook the decades of activism since the 1979 revolution.

The final rejected essay departs significantly from the pieces discussed above. Marzieh P. places the woman of the Islamic revolution, and not the revolutionary woman, in relation to the global woman and man. Her individual memories that forge this conception center on trips abroad, in particular a 2007 conference on the environment that took place in Bolivia on climate change. She focuses on her own experiences at the expense of discussing men, another distinctive characteristic of her writing.

Studies have indicated that after 1979 Iranian women have contested the public/private divide through the support of Khomeini (Keddie, 2000) and his emphasis on women's political presence in the public sphere. Women have also relied upon their own innovativeness in undermining spatial constraints by moving into new fields of work after being barred from some professions shortly after the 1979 revolution (Esfandiari, 1997). I argue that for the newer generation of Hezbollahi women, entering the international arena as politicians, scholars, and activists is a high-ranking priority that builds on the legacy of women's spatial politics in post-1979 Iran. For many Hezbollahi women, this desire to move toward the international arena is also an outcome of the long-held Iranian perception that Western media misrepresents Islam, Iran, and the Shi'i in particular (Martin, 2007; Sreberny-Mohammadi, 1995).

Marzieh begins her essay by introducing readers to how she became interested in women's rights and her own particular take on the woman's question using a discussion of her trip to Bolivia:

This was not the first or last time that I interacted with women from abroad. I have travelled to three neighboring countries for religious pilgrimages. I have been to Germany and the United Arab Emirates. I have also interacted with Americans, Europeans, and Asians that were travelling in Iran. I have spoken with women from different cultures and histories. I connected with these women and entered their lives for a short moment without the interference of the media or academic discourses. This context allowed us to develop a level of intersubjectivity and to pay attention to one another's situations, statuses, and horizons. (1395/2016, p. 2)

She goes on to connect her interactions with diverse women from abroad to questions pertaining to women's rights in Iran:

The woman of the Islamic revolution is a woman that was created through the Islamic revolution. She understands herself as someone that resists superficial views that deny her humanity. She also stands against perspectives that place a woman in opposition to a man, the family, and ultimately her own womanhood. … The woman of the Islamic revolution may be the wife or mother of a martyr, and/or a socially active woman, or perhaps she identifies with none of these roles. She is a woman, however, in search of the truth and God, and in this path she will deal with whatever may come her way. The woman of the Islamic revolution can be in the most masculine context, but she will fill it with love and sincerity. Her presence decreases violence and encourages global peace. (1395/2016, pp. 4–7)

Significantly, she locates the incitement of her interest in women's rights in interactions with those abroad. This illustrates the importance of individual memories to women's rights struggles in contemporary Iran. Her essay departs from a nationalistic stance and draws out questions and theories within an international framework concerned with the human condition. Iran's self-perception has historically been intertwined with a sense of grandiosity coupled with victimhood. Marzieh is possibly influenced by this line of thought, given her close proximity to political elites during this trip (Thaler et al., 2010). She might be using these international encounters as a tactic to bypass the state's concerns with a discussion on women's rights. As such, she can build her argument without pushing against the red lines.

It appears, however, that the larger issue is that the essay centers on her agency, and perhaps this made editors within the Hezbollah cultural institute uncomfortable. Large portions address her personal experiences, which are, linguistically, given a priority while other forms of knowledge are only brought in to support her own experiences. Importantly, men as active figures are missing from her story entirely.

Marzieh's attention to her own voice excludes men's agency. For this Hezbollah cultural institute, a recognition of male and female interactions on an equal terrain seems to have been an important objective for the special issue on Dabbaq.

Additionally, she is not discussing the "revolutionary woman" but has explicitly decided to address the women of the Islamic revolution, which includes all Iranian women. Toward the end of the essay, she radically redefines the postrevolutionary woman as a woman who makes mistakes, has regrets, and perhaps has endured pain. The suggestion that the ideal woman may have "political depression" (Cvetkovich, 2012) departs from the state's optimistic description of the postrevolutionary woman.

2.4   Conclusion

Women's political involvement in the postrevolutionary period has been dependent on their immediate memories and the contextualized histories they are dealing with at the time of their participation. This chapter explored how women affiliated with political movements during the 1980–1988 period, and those active in political movements today, reflect on and assess an idealized past.

The first section of this chapter illustrated that both leftist and Islamist women were impacted by the forms of gender discrimination they experienced as young girls and that their political participation was also impacted by intergenerational relationships where they were both empowered and transformed by the older women, and at times elite men, with whom they interacted. The second half of the chapter focused on the women affiliated with the post-2009 Hezbollah movement in Iran. The section argued that the state's swift integration of women into Hezbollah cultural institutes was grounded in their pursuit of an anti-feminist movement. Although women volunteered for this opportunity, their exchanges with other women within these spaces, as well as access to the public sphere as community leaders, transformed their visions. The resources and space that cultural institutes provided brought like-minded, pious women together and enabled them to gain insights into one another's social lives.

While Hezbollahi women could previously turn the other way when Iranian women complained about the state's gender policies, they were more willing to listen to women they viewed as equally pious to themselves. Through a close reading of essays prepared for the commemoration of Marzieh Dabbaq's death, the second section demonstrated that a special issue that was to valorize the ideal revolutionary woman from the 1980s instead challenged the entire notion of a "superwoman" and advocated equality between all Iranian women – and at times even women and men. This chapter serves as a background to the importance of accounting for historical contingencies when discussing women's citizenry struggles in post-1979 Iran, and the chapters that follow delve deeper into the different forms that acts of citizenship have taken in contemporary Iran.

3   Revolutionary Citizens
The Confrontation of Power and Spiritual Acts
of Citizenship from 1980 to 1988[*]

3.1   Introduction

There is a motif in memoirs and interviews with women and men who
were politically active during the 1980–1988 period and those who
identify as a revolutionary in contemporary Iran: the belief that one
individual can take on an entire system without the involvement of
mid-level state agents or collaboration with an organized movement.

How do the women I encountered during my research period individually push back on the state and societal limits that they faced?
Importantly, why do they do so? These questions gain significance when
we account for how this individualistic approach to resistance against
unjust rule continues to be a popular theme in Iranian political history.

This chapter shows that during the 1980–1988 period my interlocutors
in warfronts, prisons, seminaries, and hospitals undermined the state's
gender limitations and discrimination by deploying what I refer to as
spiritual acts of citizenship – acts of citizenship geared toward preserving
one's status as a revolutionary citizen. Spiritual acts of citizenship were
constituted through the broader ethical framework that political spirituality offered during the early days of the revolution (Ghamari-Tabrizi,
2016a). I address the underlying historical contingencies and real-time
creativity that enabled Islamic and leftist women to individually challenge
national and transnational structures of power. Additionally, I show the
different forms that spiritual acts of citizenship took during the
1980–1988 period. What follows offers a dynamic view of revolutionary
citizenship as one interspersed with familial love, erudite poetry, and
literature, significantly dependent on different avenues to self-care and
contrasting approaches to self-preservation.

---

[*] This chapter benefited greatly from the comments of both reviewers. I was able to
visualize it, however, through my friendship with Fatemeh Delavari Parizi, and it is to
her that I dedicate this chapter.

According to Foucault, political spirituality is "becoming something other than what one is" and is grounded in self-transformation by revolt against the state, religion, and other powers with a political will that comes from spirituality (Leezenberg, 2018). In a recent work, Ghamari-Tabrizi (2016a) elaborates on how Foucault understood the notion of political spirituality in relation to the 1979 Iranian revolution. Foucault argued that the 1979 Iranian revolution was significant for how it generated the formation of a "new man" in the post-1979 state. Political spirituality highlights the process of self-construction in the individual's quest for "making history" and posits it as central to the "revolutionary act" (Ghamari-Tabrizi, 2016a, pp. 58, 65). According to Ghamari-Tabrizi (2016a, p. 63; emphasis in the original), transforming the self is a process of self-care for Foucault: "he views the care of the self as an ethical imperative wherein ethics is 'the kind of relationship you ought to have with *yourself* ... how the individual is supposed to constitute himself as a moral subject of *his own actions.*'" It should be noted that Foucault did not delve into the formation of subjectivities in relation to his notion of political spirituality and the Iranian revolution (Ghamari-Tabrizi, 2016a).

Foucault further signifies the relevance of self-care as such: "But national feeling has, in my opinion, been only one of the elements of a still more radical rejection: the rejection by a people, not only of foreigners, but of everything that had constituted, for years, for centuries, its political destiny" (Sheridan, 1988, p. 215). He believed that changing the self through care was integral to the political goal of overthrowing the Pahlavi Monarchy.

Scholarship on Foucault's notion of political spirituality relies on a critique of religion and, in particular, his perspectives on Shi'ism (Afary and Anderson, 2005). More recent writing on the 1980–1988 period, however, has highlighted the urgency in engaging with conceptualizations of martyrdom and sacrifice beyond religion to study women's and men's political participation (Ahmadi, 2018; Bolourchi, 2018). This chapter fleshes out Foucault's notion of political spirituality by exploring the formation of subjectivities among Islamist and leftist women who were politically active during the 1980–1988 period. In what follows, I highlight how contextualized forms of spirituality surfaced in my empirical research and worked to establish what I call spiritual acts of citizenship.

Self-care is indeed a component of political spirituality, as Foucault theorized and as I will show in the sections that follow. However, by examining the formation of subjectivities, or the exercise of self-reflection by individuals, I argue that the backdrop of political spirituality engendered women's spiritual acts of citizenship. Moreover, I illustrate that women's actual interventions in routine political affairs rested on an effort to *preserve* the self they had created with care. By underscoring women's spiritual acts of citizenship, this chapter challenges the claim that Foucault's notion of political spirituality denotes merely a fascination with death (Afary and Anderson, 2005).

Rather, grounded in empirical research on subjectivities, I will show that my interlocutors' spiritual acts of citizenship centered on a desire to live a dignified life and not just a "fascination with fearless self-sacrifice" (Honig, 2008, p. 304) as has been purported by Afary and Anderson's (2005) account of Foucault's conceptualization of political spirituality. For women with different political leanings, political spirituality engendered spiritual acts of citizenship that carried multiple meanings and were heterogeneous. For instance, for supporters of Ayatollah Khomeini, taking care of others was integral to self-preservation, for women saw themselves as propagating revolutionary thought through their spiritual acts of citizenship. For leftist political prisoners, on the other hand, self-care through recollection of memories and literature was understood to be a form of preservation for the person they had worked hard to become and which the state sought to break down with imprisonment and torture.

My interlocutors used the austerity of postrevolutionary life, which included different forms of conflict, as well as togetherness in the family and the circulation of national and international literature, to maintain their status as revolutionaries. The women I encountered not only felt that they deserved a more dignified life, but they also actually brought down to earth this ideal through a confrontation of power and undermining of hierarchies in the different spaces they occupied. Spiritual acts of citizenship can help scholars understand how these diverse women informally claimed rights and citizenry statuses in the unstable post-1979 environment by using the revolutionary backdrop to their advantage. Hence, the findings in this chapter contribute to a broader understanding of nation-states and the people that challenge them.

Care of others and self-care make acts of self-preservation spiritual acts of citizenship because of the level of concentration, meditation, and self-reflection they required. I understand spiritual acts of citizenship, then, to entail both a personal transformation process rooted in care and visible interventions exerted during routine political procedures set on preserving the revolutionary self that one has carefully created. The transformation of the self through care generated spiritual acts of citizenship that were detectable on warfronts and in prisons and continue to impact how the nation currently grapples with political struggles. Tracing women's spiritual acts of citizenship demonstrates how one can be "a different subject" (Cornell and Seely, 2014, p. 10) in this world through "live thinking" that leads to self-determining the particulars of one's own life in a way that may generate new worldly possibilities (Cohen, 2014, p. 25).

3.2   Being Cared for in Your Neighborhood: Local Contingencies and the Embodiment of Khomeini's Political Thought

This section addresses the familial and community support that engendered spiritual acts of citizenship for pious women. The impact of the revolutionary atmosphere at the time temporarily suspended gender dichotomies and served as a backdrop to spiritual acts of citizenship (Balasingham, 1983). The undermining of the distinction between the public and private spheres by Khomeini's political thought with respect to women's roles in the 1979 revolution and war further contextualized Islamist women's spiritual acts of citizenship (Keddie, 2000). His gendered lens on the war and its ramifications illuminated the grace with which women moved between the public and private boundaries as revolutionary citizens. Khomeini's lectures, statements, and speeches on self-construction were locally contextualized by his female and male followers to forge a caring environment in which women could transform into revolutionary citizens who performed spiritual acts of citizenship.

Khomeini's pious followers, as well as those not politically active but absorbed by his charismatic leadership, argue that they were influenced by his statements on *khod sazi*, or a building of self. His notion of self-construction was addressed in a series of statements beginning in 1344–1346/1963–1965 in Najaf, Iraq (the exact date for these letters is unknown). These statements and letters focused on the importance of refining one's ethics by following the boundaries that the Islamic faith delineates for Muslims. He addressed Muslim youth in Islamic countries broadly:

There will be large responsibilities for you in the future. If you become an "alem"[1] in a city, you are in charge of that city. God willing, if you become an "alem" of a nation, you are in charge of that nation. If you become the "marja"[2] for a people, you are in charge of those people [that nation]. You should set the [moral] foundation now, so that later you can carry out your duties and responsibilities. Some might say that we will now focus on our studies, and

[1] A knowledgeable person on religious interpretation of the holy verses of Quran.
[2] Religious reference.

God Willing once we are old, we will work on cultivating our ethics [there is ample time for that and our studies matter more at this time]. This is not attainable. If you can refine yourself in your youth, then it is done. If refinement is not achieved in your youth, it is unlikely that it will happen when you are old, the time your will power is weak and the enemy [Satan] strong ... Take care of this issue now, think about it while you are still young and willful. Every step you take now is toward your grave. There is no time to waste. (Khomeini, 1385/2006, *Sahifeh-ye Imam*, vol. 2, pp. 40–41)[3]

Khomeini's pious female followers remember being influenced by these statements that circulated in Iran prior to the revolution. Khomeini also spoke about self-construction to Iranian students living abroad when in France. However, once in France and when speaking with students, his tone was more political and focused on revolutionary change in Iran. For instance, during this speech in 1357/1978 from Neauphle-le-Château, France, he again stressed the importance of practicing Islam but this time to prepare for a political revolt:

Many other stages also exist, but if one reaches this stage of humanity whereby one's actions are for God, then one will not suffer defeat, when the action is for God, defeat is not involved. If it pleases God, the Iranians have risen for God, then they will not suffer defeat. In other words, even if this man were to continue with his oppression until the end and we were not successful in disarming him of this unjust weapon, this would still not be a source of anxiety for us, because we were obeying God, obedience was out of obedience to God, so even if we suffer defeat it will have been brought about through obedience to God. The Prophet suffered defeat in some of his battles, Hadrat Amir was defeated in his battle with MuAwiyah, the Doyen of the Martyrs was killed, but it was out of obedience to God, it was for God, all of it was for Him and for this reason defeat did not come into it, they obeyed Him and that was that. MuAwiyah and the others were eventually defeated and their rule destroyed, yet the path of the Prophet and the Imams has continued until the present day. (Khomeini, 1385/2006, *Sahifeh-ye Imam*, vol. 5, p. 169)[4]

Khomeini continued to bring the importance of self-building into his speeches and statements after the 1979 revolution. For instance, in a 1979 speech in Qom, he addressed the Revolutionary Guards thus:

If the guards, whether you who are busy in your duty as guards, or whether the other strata of the people, one of which is the clergy – though this term does not apply to them at present, but in reality, they are the protectors of Islam – fail to observe, as they should, this feature of the Revolution which was the advent of a

---

[3] Translation comes from the institute for compilation and publication of Imam Khomeini's works (international affairs department).

[4] Translation comes from the institute for compilation and publication of Imam Khomeini's works (international affairs department).

just government in the place of a corrupt one, if that revolutionary path is not followed at this time when a regime has supplanted a corrupt one, if they do not observe the Islamic justice that begins with a person and reaches out to everyone – dealing justly with another person; with friends; with fellow citizens; with people of the same province; with countrymen; with the people of neighboring countries that are friendly with us and with all mankind – if such a state is not attained, then neither will the government be Islamic nor will its guards be the guards of Islam. (Khomeini, 1385/2006, *Sahifeh-ye Imam*, vol. 8, p. 318)[5]

Before the revolution, Khomeini's notion of self-construction was addressed to youth in the Islamic world. As the prospect for a revolution in Iran drew closer, self-construction was connected with uprisings. Following the revolution, he relied on this line of thought to address regime agents and guide them toward restraint and kindness as society transitioned.

Khomeini's discussions on self-construction, however, are made to a general audience without reference to women. Surprisingly, then, many women who followed Khomeini and participated in the war mentioned that they were influenced by this idea in particular. The Iranian war expert Mazaheri (1392/2012) asserts that it is common for war memories to be altered, even new memories created, when people narrate the past long after the event has ended. Yet, I am reminded that Khomeini made women's issues *both* a private and public matter. As Osanloo (2014, p. 250) has stated, "the revolutionary aim of improving society through the rehabilitation of women gave women unexpected social and political power, as improvements in the condition of women's lives were indicative of the success and legitimacy of the new state." However, his lectures on self-construction, unlike his discussion of the revolution and war, were not gendered. For instance, when speaking in 1980 before an audience of martyrs' wives whose husbands were in the air force, Khomeini identifies them as the continuation of their husbands' paths and bestows upon them a public role:

There is a verse repeated in two chapters (Surahs) of the Holy Quran: one chapter is with an addendum and the other is without one. In a chapter, it addresses the holy prophet, may God grant peace and honor on him and his family, and commands him to stand firm in his mission: "Therefore stand firm (in the straight Path) as thou art commanded". In the other chapter, named Surah Hud, it is said, "Therefore stand firm (in the straight Path) as thou art commanded, - thou and those who with thee turn unto Allah". Here, God commands the holy prophet to stand firm as he is commanded and those with

[5] Translation comes from the institute for compilation and publication of Imam Khomeini's works (international affairs department).

him who turned to Allah shall stand firm as well ... It is because all Islamic nations and all Muslims are commanded to stand firm, persist and avoid distraction during their mission. Today, may God be praised, generally our nation, and in particular our armed forces, especially our air forces, pass the holy test as they acted upon what was commanded in this holy mission; they have made self-sacrifices and have been devoted. You, venerated women, are the reminder of their memory. Dignity and honor is their reminiscence for you, and as can be seen, your speech manifests your perseverance. (Bani Luhi, 1378/1999, pp. 103–104)

However, such powerful statements that present women as political equals to men were not made directly to women with respect to self-construction. Khomeini never discussed self-construction with explicit reference to women. Instead, the notion of self-construction gained purchase due to the geographical, political, and historical contingencies that from 1980 to 1988 made pious women receptive to Khomeini's notion of self-construction and, in the process, taught them to care for the revolutionary citizens they were becoming.

Khomeini's view of self-construction become palpable for women, then, through the support of family members and pious women's neighborhood community. Family norms were significant in women's initial introduction to self-construction and an appreciation for self-care and preservation. In her memoir *Man Zendeham* (I am Alive), Masumeh Abad (1395/2016), who was a prisoner of war in Iraq for nearly three-and-a-half years, recognizes her family's decision to distance her from traditional gender roles (such as employment in a beauty salon, which she initially wanted to pursue as a young girl) as important to her politicization. As a girl in her early teens, her family instead suggested she take sewing classes, where she met Christian families that were skilled seamstresses. She reflects on how she grew in comparison to her friend Zari, who stayed in beauty salon training:

Although I had learned the skills of a seamstress, from within I was completely coming undone. This is because all of this was happening as I was going through puberty, and making new discoveries. Something had been found within me that Zari would never understand. Zari constantly talked about eyeliners that lined almond shaped eyes, lips made like flower buds, laces that are now in fashion, and those out of style. She discussed which fabrics matched, and how we could become worthy women. I wanted to talk about things that she did not know about, but which did exist. Zari and I were slowly growing apart, and this made me silent. The distance that had emerged between our spirits was a ramification of the different spaces we had experienced. It was these new spaces that had peaked my intellectual curiosity and pushed Zari toward eyebrows, fashion, and distinguishing what makes a woman worthy. (Abad, 1395/2016, p. 61)

Abad credits her family's decision to prevent her from working in a beauty salon and push her toward sewing classes with having shaped her dedication to education and the pursuit of what she saw as the truth. After this specific familial intervention, the ethnic and religious landscape of Abad's neighborhood in Abadan connected her to Khomeini's notion of self-construction. Abad remembers that the questions asked by her sewing instructor, a Christian Armenian woman named Mrs. Dravansian, greatly influenced her interest in religion and ethics:

She asked why we wear a chador when going to the masjid but are without hijab in other spaces. She wondered why Muslims saw them [Christians] as unclean, but some of them drank alcohol themselves. She wanted to know if I believed Christ had been put on the cross. She asked: did news of the Muslim Prophet's coming not appear in the Bible? Will Jesus come with Mahdi? And many other questions. She had turned my entire being into a question without an answer. In response to all of her questions, I would say: I only know math, and that is even limited to the fifth grade. You have to ask these questions from a scholar of religion. Her questions had ignited my thirst for knowledge.

Inspired by the questions Mrs. Dravansian asked about the Islamic faith, Abad sought answers from the religious authority in her community:

To find answers for her questions and to satisfy my thirst, I went to the masjid every day and returned to sewing class the next day with information. There were few books that could provide responses to my questions and few people that had the patience to deal with a child, although my questions were not that complicated. Mrs. Haseli was another one of my teachers. I sought refuge in Mrs. Haseli to contemplate Mrs. Dravansian's questions. She was the Quran teacher for a masjid near our home. Mrs. Haseli in effect debated Mrs. Dravansian, and I along with Harachek [a Christian friend from sewing class] witnessed this back-and-forth. What I learned from this process is that we were both in the same path, and religion is nothing more than instructions for bringing to fruition human beings. (Abad, 1395/2016, pp. 58–59)

Abad's family controlled her activities as a young teen, and her participation in a sewing class became an opportunity to think more deeply about ethics, religion, and the embodiment of faith. Mrs. Dravansian's questions regarding the performance of Islam and the difficulties in measuring faith frame Abad's interest in Khomeini's notion of self-construction that was facilitated by people in her community.

There is an otherworldly dimension to Khomeini's notion of self-construction that highlights self-care's importance. His discourse on state construction as a dual struggle of building the self and the country remakes the women and men following this path in the image of God:

When you build yourself, all of your work becomes holy work. For you have moved out of the sphere of tyrannies. You have entered the light. All of your actions shine. When you speak, it's light. Even when you listen with your ears, it's light. When you sympathize with your hearts, you are expressing your knowledge through light. In fact, you have become light. (Khomeini, 1385/2006, *Sahifeh-ye Imam*, vol. 11, p. 383)

The connection made between building the self and becoming light destabilizes the boundaries between the private and public spheres. And, perhaps more importantly, it highlights the noncorporeal dimensions of self-construction and the implications they carry for self-care. The person who worked toward justice and endured hardship elevated in the amount of power and influence they held by the grace of God. Such a person goes through a physical transformation, and even their listening is filled with light. As the physical loses its significance, caring for the self one has created with the love of many people becomes an almost sacred task.

Khomeini's emphasis on *erfan* (or mysticism) gained currency on the ground level to support women's movement between the public and private spheres. Abad recalls taking ethics classes in a community center in Abadan in the months leading up to the revolution. In these classes, Hossein Motahar – a local revolutionary activist – further broached self-construction. In one class, Motahar emphasized the connection between knowing the self and knowing God:

The first step toward knowing God is believing in one's self. Ask the first question of yourself. Ask yourself who am I? Become familiar with the real you for you are a part of God. Reach the whole from its parts. Know yourself as a part of God, and by understanding yourself you can access God. Become acquainted with yourself. (Abad, 1395/2016, p. 101)

The subjectivity that Motahar encourages is based on the writing of Khomeini and other revolutionaries, such as Ali Shariati, where there exists "mediated subjectivity" and human progress is reliant on God's subjectivity (Vahdat, 2003). In the process of learning more about herself by relying on these directives, Abad volunteered at a child orphanage, experimented with extreme forms of piety such as minimal eating, and withdrew from interactions with other adults. Motahar intervened and criticized these tactics as too extreme and invited her toward more practical approaches to spiritual life:

The path to balance and moderation is dependent on reason and capacity-building. You have to become familiar with yourself and your environment. In order to increase your piety, you must practice tolerance. Is it possible to fall into water and not get wet? Why are you sitting on the shorelines? Why are you afraid of the waves? Do you think that you can become entangled with your ego and not take a bullet? When a person is born, it means that God has formally invited you into the world. Removing yourself from the world, then, is a great sin. Sometimes human beings reach a point where even faith and devotion mislead them. The path to being at peace with the world and its people is outlined by the prophets and the Quran. Be careful as this path is narrow and has many twists and turns. (Abad, 1395, p. 115)

Motahar invites Abad to remain open to the public sphere and broaden her spatial movements by shifting between different spaces instead of removing herself from the public.

Khomeini's theoretical discussion of self-building and grace came alive during everyday life through the interventions of his supporters on the ground. The rhythm of movement between theory and practice made societal participation and self-care central to women's political participation. The enchanting realms of human subjectivity come to the forefront as the self progresses toward a higher power or the "light" in the dual process of making the self and political participation, and this physical yet risky movement makes the stakes even higher for self-preservation.

Moreover, Khomeini's ideas intersected with the writing of other revolutionary leaders and entered homes in a manner that pushed women's souls (and bodies) across public and private boundaries (Reeves, 1989). Shariati's *Fatima is Fatima* was intended to mobilize Iranian women for participation in transforming Iranian state and society. In this book, which was initially a 1971 lecture Shariati gave describing Fatemeh Zahra – the daughter of Prophet Mohammad, wife of Imam Ali, and mother to Imam Hassan and Hossein – as the ideal role model for Iranian women due to her "devotion, courage, and steadfastness" (Dabashi, 1993, p. 125). Abad recounts how she felt the first time she read Shariati's *Fatima is Fatima* as a high school student:

The words touched me in such a way that I did not notice the passage of time. As I read each page of the book, my temperature increased. Indeed, the book was setting fire to my soul. Each cell in my body was awakened, and this alertness was accompanied by pain, heat, and light. (Abad, 1395, p. 85)

Abad's brother gave her *Fatima is Fatima* while she was suspended from school for distributing leaflets on Islamist thought. At first, she told her family she was ill but felt that she could be honest about her suspension once she overheard her brother discussing the nation's revolutionary fervor. Once she admitted to her family that she was suspended because of her activism, and that she was in fact not ill, her brother expressed his support by giving her reading to do at home. He responded to her circumstance by stressing that learning can take place outside the classroom.

Abad's refusal to abide by the school's anti-Islamic and anti-revolutionary boundaries, in addition to her brother's love, made it possible for her to read Shariati's book that day. As Ebtekar (2000) has discussed in relation to her own experience, it was common for many female supporters of Khomeini to be politicized by Shariati's thoughts on Muslim women's rights and responsibilities. What is left out of these discussions are the sinews that brought apolitical women closer to Shariati, ultimately sparked their devotion to Khomeini, and supported their movement between public and private boundaries. In Abad's story we see the self-construction process hinging on the person's ability to forge the revolutionary citizen through care. Whether it was that of her family or her community or that present in the writing of revolutionary leaders other than Khomeini, Abad's political development was paved with care.

Maryam Farhanian is also purported to have been influenced by the lectures of Motahar on self-construction in Abadan. In particular, she learned from the mountain climbing trips that he organized for students:

Mr. Motahar's goal with these trips was for us to reach the top of the mountain. In our bags we only carried dates, canned beans, and dry bread. We felt like people that had become disconnected from the world during the 3–4 days that we were there. Once we reached the top of the mountain, we put up a God is Great flag. It usually took us three days to reach the top of the mountain and half a day to come back down. One of Mr. Motahar's goals was to show us how difficult it is to climb, and how easy it is to crash, and this law applies to life as well. Because our bags were more than 10–12 kilograms, some of our peers pretended to have leg or stomach pain so someone else could carry their bag. Mr. Motahar made a note of all of these behaviors. He constantly reminded us that if you do not do right during this trip, it is all over. But if you are successful now, you can be sure that you will also be on the right path in life. He wanted us to get to know ourselves. (Saalmee nejad, 1391, pp. 63–64)

The self constructed person held the capacity to create large-scale change through a dynamic private and collective body that fused women to their families and communities but also guided their understanding of self. The intimate origins of Islamist women's connections with Khomeini enhanced the sense of urgency to protect the person that they had become. These origins also added meaning to these women's emphasis on preserving their revolutionary disposition from a society and state that may not have consistently supported them.

Women's connection to Khomeini's message of building a new self was forged through neighborhood relationships and, to some extent, by chance (Jafarian, 1381/2002). Khosravi (2008) argues that the connection between neighborhoods and morality is notable in Iran even to date and that the cultural norms of neighborhoods differ, with this distinction in reputation carrying significant political ramifications. Each neighborhood has a sense of "self-esteem" that relates to economic, educational, or moral standing (Khosravi, 2008, p. 64). As Torab (1996, p. 235) has shown, for some pious women, the neighborhood is their "entire world" and a place from which they expand their moral visions.

Masumeh Mirza-Ali (Mohammadi, 1381/2002b), a medical assistant during the war, remembers picking her daughter up from school in the months prior to the revolution and encountering a woman wearing a black chador. Mirza-Ali saw this hijab as more complete than the colorful chador that she wore, and she decided to emulate the woman's tendency to hold the chador close to her face. That evening she informed her husband that she too wanted to wear a black chador, and she remembers this as her first visible show of solidarity with the 1979 revolution. At the same time, she informs us earlier in the memoir that an elderly physician, Dr. Behroozi, had encouraged her father to allow her to work as an assistant at a medical clinic where her father received treatment during Mirza-Ali's youth. Her father had instructed her to "keep her head down" as she walked home to and from the clinic, even going as far as stressing that she should not say hello even to him should they encounter one another on the street. Mirza-Ali had experienced challenging gender norms from a young age.

Mina Kamaii, also from Abadan, was introduced to Khomeini's notion of self-making through several neighborhood encounters as her family was not particularly religious. In the first instance, she remembers studying the Quran with a religiously devout girl from her neighborhood before the 1979 revolution:

I became acquainted with Aghdas Karimi who lived across from our home. We were around the same age. They had put up thick curtains in front of their door so that when the door opened you could not see inside their home. Aghdas's older sister, Zahra, taught courses on Islamic legal rulings to the girls in the neighborhood. During the month of Ramadan, she lectured us on the Quran. My sisters and I would go to her classes regularly. She asked us to select a treatise from a source of emulation to better understand Quranic rulings. With much fear and hesitation, I went to the bookstore and asked for a treatise.

Kamaii explains how her immediate family was impacted by her decision to learn about Islam from her neighbor Aghdas:

My mom encouraged me in this path. Whenever I went to the Karimi home, I had on hijab and would be surrounded by all the girls in the neighborhood. Miss Karimi also taught us how to prepare for prayers and perform prayers. Mitra [Mina's sister] was friends with Nargis, Aghdas's younger sister. Most of the time Mitra would go to grandma's house because it was easier to fast and do her prayers there. Mitra started wearing the hijab in the fifth grade even though the other kids made fun of her. (Mohammadi, 1381/2002a, p. 14)

Although Kamaii does not describe her family as one steeped in religious traditions, her mother's religiosity piqued her interest in Khomeini's political thought (Mohammadi, 1381/2002a). Living across the street from a family that opened their home to those interested in learning about the Quran is integral to her political transformation as well. Like other women from Abadan, she also remembers being influenced by Motahar's lectures on self-construction:

Professor Motahar taught us a course on ethics. He was small in stature, a young man with a thick beard from Shushtar, Khuzestan. He was well versed in religion. He was the one that introduced us for the first time to the notion of self-construction [khod sazi]. He told us, "limit your speaking, limit your food consumption, and read ten verses from the Quran every day. After your morning prayers, do not go back to sleep and watch the sky." In our class, there were only 10–15 girls, but we later learned that classes were being held in places other than our school. Once he asked us to write down what we wished for before the revolution. At first I wanted to talk a bit about myself and my spiritual needs. Then I thought why should I tell him about myself? On my essay he wrote, "this is one of your strong points, that you realized I'm not someone you need to explain yourself to." He marked our essays with a red pen. He did not know our names. He would put our papers on the desk, and we would pick them up ourselves. Sometimes he would give me the papers to pass back. I was the class leader. Although we went to class with blouses, skirts, and head scarves, he never once said don't come to class dressed this way. He did not ask us to put on a chador. He always said, "do your prayers in a secluded place." By the way he spoke, I could tell that he practiced what he preached. Whatever I learned during this period in my life was first and foremost due to Professor Motahar's teaching and then my own studying. After his classes, I slowly began to wear the chador. The day that his class ended, we cried a lot. (Mohammadi, 1381/2002a, pp. 22–23)

The solidarity that Kamaii sensed from Motahar empowered her to remain on the radical spiritual path that Khomeini's notion of self-construction offered. For women like Abad, Mirza-Ali, and Kamaii, the love they had experienced at home and navigated in neighborhoods and communities prior to and after the revolution prepared them for enacting

Khomeini's thoughts on self-construction. The thoughtfulness embed-ded in the political spirituality that engulfed the atmosphere at this time enhanced a desire to preserve the revolutionary citizens they had become. This section has demonstrated that although Khomeini's idea of self-construction encouraged women to cross the boundary between the public and private, it was the contextualized indoctrination of Khomeini's thought that made self-care central to Islamist women's spiritual acts of citizenship. Supportive families and community leaders gave pious women the confidence to expand their worldview by reflecting on what their movement between the public and private spheres meant in political terms.

3.3   Spiritual Acts of Citizenship and the Followers of Khomeini

For female supporters of Khomeini, caring behavior toward others became the path through which one could preserve the self created with care. Given that an exaggerated sense of self-confidence was central to Khomeini's notion of self-construction (Adib-Moghaddam, 2018), his supporters thus *felt* they upheld their own revolutionary status by caring for others.

Serving others was understood as central to one's revolutionary sub-jectivity for Islamist women, but it was also where spiritual acts of citizenship became most visible (Kohan-rooz, 1391/2012). As Dr. Zarin Taj Keyhani, who was one of the estimated 2,276 female doctors that served in various warfronts during the early days (Anon., 1390/2011, "Defa-e Moghaddas dar Ayneyeh Amaar"; Ghasami, n.d.), observes,

The presence of women was vital to balancing the morale [on warfronts]. They [men] accepted our sister-like collegiality. Sometimes, however, we were questioned. Yet ultimately, we learned about moderation; we learned how to look at others; we learned not to undermine the rights of others. Women were not overwhelmingly involved in direct warfare, but the effect of their spirit was. I will never forget. An elderly woman had written a letter. She stated, "my son, I have no son. I have no husband to accompany you on the warfront, and I have no money to send you something better. I have sent you a needle with some thread of different colors. I have put them in a bag along with a few buttons and pins. God willing, when you see this, you will know that your elderly mother is also thinking of you." I will never forget that whenever I showed this letter to soldiers, they would first cry, and then they would take the letter as an object of great value. Do you think this was not a role? (Aneesi, 1377d, pp. 14–15)

Elderly women are often remembered in documentations on the Iran–Iraq war as citizens whose affective labors enhanced men's sense of security on warfronts. Younger women also participated in uplifting men's spirits. For example, when Saham Taghati and her friends realized that some of the men in Khorramshahr were pulling back from warfronts as Iran began to lose the city, they did the following:

Mahdi Alboghobeish came in and said: "get into the car, and let's go to the Khorramshahr garrison. The soldiers are in poor spirits. They are leaving the city." We asked them why they are leaving. And someone said, "we only have one G3 rifle. We have no other weapons. We are sitting together, if one mortar bomb hits, we will all become martyrs. Give us weapons, and we will resist." The Khorramshahr garrison was located in Ghabristan Street known as Janat Abad. I think today it is called the Persian Gulf. We [all the women with Saham who stayed in the city] went to this location.

She goes on to explain what the women did to uplift men's spirits once they arrived in Khorramshahr:

One of the women with us looked toward the soldiers and said: "If you do not have the courage to stay, give us your guns." The soldiers were very offended by this statement. They stayed in the city, but they were still in poor spirits. The next day we went back, and the soldiers were calmed by our presence. One of them came to me and said, "Sister! I want to visit my family, but I will return. You can have my weapon. I will return in two days and I want it back." I said, "Okay, but I'm not keeping it for more than two days." (Soleimani, 1381/2002, pp. 28–29)

The act of caring for others, such as by uplifting male soldiers' spirits, as an indication of one's effort at preserving the self can be detected in other young revolutionary Islamist women's narratives as well.

In this vein, Abad (1395) remembers forgetting about her own reality as a prisoner of war once she set eyes on male Iranian prisoners of war who were injured:

On seeing these two injured brothers, I instantly forgot about my own circumstance. It escaped my mind that I too was a prisoner and that this soldier standing over my head with a gun was the enemy. With my teeth, I opened up the rope around my hands. Then I freed the hands of sister Bahrami as well. No matter how loud the soldier yelled, I did not listen. I opened up some bandage that I had kept around my socks and ankle just in case. I washed the injured man's face with the water that he had with him. The corner of his eye was seriously injured. After washing his eyes, I wrapped up his cuts to stop the bleeding. But I only had enough gauze bandage for one of his eyes. The other brother was fallen a few meters from him. I ran toward him. The Iraqi soldier screamed: not allowed, not allowed (*mamnu, mamnu*). And in response I yelled, injured, injured (*majru, majru*). I told myself whatever happens, happens. Did I not return to Abadan to help the injured? Did I not beg Miss Moghadam to allow me to continue working in the hospital? (Abad, 1395, p. 164)

As she remembered the difficult path she had travelled to be in the warfront as a medical assistant, Abad found the strength to demand the right to meet the needs of injured Iranians even within the context of imprisonment. While male prisoners reminded her not to make demands and that she was in a sensitive situation, Abad managed to gather some basic material from a nearby house to nurse injured prisoners who were scattered around her during her initial imprisonment. Iranian women's decisions to emotionally and physically meet the needs of Iranian soldiers with the hopes of raising their spirits have been documented in other texts as well (Akbari, 1390/2011).

An effort toward preserving the self in the process of constructing a "new man" engendered spiritual acts of citizenship among Iranian men who were also dependent on supporting others (Kashfi, 1387/2008). As a nurse who was active in the warfront for nine months during the early days of the war recalls:

All of war is memorable, but among my memories of war, the most touching one occurred during the operation to liberate Bostan [city in southern Iran bordering Iraq]. We encountered some 14–15-year-old girls that had been badly raped. Several of them were pregnant and had visited the hospital. During their visit to the hospital, some Basiji brothers and soldiers had announced that they would like to marry the girls. Their marriages were made official by the cleric that led Friday prayers right there in the hospital. (Aneesi, 1377a, p. 4)

Iranian cultural norms during this period prioritized virginity in marriage. Additionally, given that the girls were based in a particularly traditional region, they may have also been treated poorly by their own community – and maybe even family members. By marrying girls who had experienced rape at the hand of Iraqi soldiers, these Iranian men were connecting their own spiritual growth to the solace and love of those in need. For the Shi'i, pain is a necessary sensation on the path to becoming "fully human" (Asad, 2000). These men helped young girls process the pain of rape through marriage, but the men may also have felt pain for the inability to protect women and girls in the context of war where their manliness (*gheyrat*) was also compromised. Perhaps the intersections of different manifestations of pain helped these men embody the revolutionary discourse on becoming human through social commitment that Shariati and others propounded (Rahnema, 1998).

During off-the-record discussions, Iranian war experts acknowledge that rapes occurred on the Iran–Iraq border in the South. The reality of rape in the war is also addressed in works of fiction. In *Chai Talkh* (Taghvaei, 2000), a screenplay by Naser Taghvaei, an Iraqi soldier and general enter a home in Khorramshahr to gather information and ask for some water. When a young girl questions their intentions in the war, she is taken into a room and raped by the general as the soldier waits outside with the girl's helpless grandparents. In the screenplay, the girl is impregnated during the rape. Her grandparents conclude that marriage with the rapist is the best option for her because he continually visits their home and professes his love for the woman, whose name is never revealed. The rape of Iranian women and girls during the war has been acknowledged by scholars based in Iran and also documented in both fiction and nonfiction manuscripts.

The trend in doing for others in an effort to construct the self was also notable in Iran's seminaries during the 1980s. As the new state was taking form after the 1979 revolution, so too were its religious centers in vital cities such as Qom. Seminaries in postrevolutionary Iran were becoming redefined and restructured for elites to gain administrative control of both religious teachings and an Islamic state (Shirkhani and Zare, 1384/2005, p. 51).

This transition likely also provided opportunities for challenging established gender norms, as the state needed the integration of women into its apparatuses. Prior to the revolution, seminaries in Qom lacked structural organization and bureaucratic form, and oftentimes administrative powers were in the hands of one, or at most a few, leading male jurists (Shirkhani and Zare, 1384/2005). Additionally, prior to the 1979 revolution, religious seminaries were not extensively tied to the state. While seminaries were then imagined as a foundational realm of the post-1979 state, many remember women's entrance as a point of contention between male elites.

During my meeting with several female religious clerics in Qom at Jami'at al-Zahra, the first official female seminary in postrevolutionary Iran established in 1984, women claimed that through the coordination, reorganization, and support of Ayatollahs Ghoddusi, Khomeini, and Motahhari, among others, centers for religious studies were encouraged to permit an increasingly large number of women into influential seminaries, such as those located in Qom.[6] During the eight-year war with Iraq, five theological schools in Iran were specifically designated for educating female religious clerics, including the *Jam'at al-Zahra*, which became officially active in 1984 (Hoodfar and Sadr, 2009, p. 28). The expansion of seminaries into major cities and rural regions also supported a large number of aspiring female *talabehs* (students) and those who simply wanted to expand their knowledge of Islam. Following the

---

[6] Interview, Qom, Iran, June 2008.

revolution, centers for religious studies sprang up in provinces and cities throughout Iran, even providing flexible hours and childcare for women interested in pursuing theological studies.[7]

During the 1980–1988 period, women were generally unwelcomed into the seminary even for activities that supported the Islamic Republic's citizenship agenda because of the freedom of movement the process entailed. Most who entered seminaries from 1980 to 1988 expressed the need to "prove themselves" and to "know the material more extensively and thoroughly than male colleagues" to gain credibility as scholars and access to different institutional dimensions.

Raheleh A., a religious cleric, identifies teaching courses to first-year students and lecturing at women's religious gatherings in Qom and Tehran while still a third-year student as laying the groundwork for her own intellectual and political growth.[8] Female *talabehs* expanded the platform for state construction and showed their dedication to the Islamic Republic by meeting the material and spiritual needs of a nation at war.[9] Zeinab C. travelled to Khuzestan during the summers to volunteer as a nurse in the hospitals,[10] and another female *talabeh*, Mahdieh L., remembers meeting with families of martyrs to console them with religious teachings.[11]

Furthermore, as female religious clerics demonstrated their ability to collaborate with state initiatives during its formative years, they found themselves in a position to formally express personal demands and grievances before male religious and political elites. Female *talabeh* wrote letters to professors and the president's office and visited those who were sources of emulation (*Marja'e Taqlid*) to clarify for the new political elites women's post-1979 desires and needs.[12] These women could govern local sites by illustrating their abilities to learn and teach religious scripture, as well as their capabilities in serving the state in other capacities during a time of civil war and international siege. A personalized and moralized interpretation of Khomeini's thoughts on self-construction enhanced the struggle for independence by seminary women as they became caregivers to other women whose lives had intersected with the new state's policies.

Once they had secured a considerable presence within religious seminaries, *talabeh* women argued that the instantaneous and concurrent application of knowledge identified them as authorities in directing national politics and religious education and had strengthened their

---

[7] Interview, Tehran, Iran, June 2008.   [8] Interview, Qom, Iran, June 2008.
[9] Interview, Qom, Iran, June 2008.   [10] Interview, Qom, Iran, June 2008.
[11] Interview, Qom, Iran, June 2008.   [12] Interview, Qom, Iran, June 2008.

concept of self. This also won them the right to independence through
movement into new spaces. Paradoxically, therefore, the political authority given to individuals to act in accordance with Islamic teachings
allowed women to challenge traditional and emergent gender limitations, as well as political and religious hierarchies. This act in turn
supported women's efforts at claiming new rights and allowed them to
self-determine their position toward state structures. The knowledge
that they were not taken seriously pushed some female seminary
students to pursue religious studies aggressively and through
independent study.

I witnessed how this privately accumulated knowledge is then applied
to the different spaces that these women occupy to contest the state's
citizenry boundaries for women. During interviews with female adminis-
trators at Jami'at al-Zahra and younger students, I was told that mandatory hijab and discrimination against women in the workplace lack
religious basis. These conversations took place openly among the women
in the seminary and also among female religious jurists during several
high-level meetings to which I was invited at the Council for Cultural
Revolution.

For men in warfronts, piety meant following the directions given by
wartime commanders on the local terrain (Hosseinipour, 1391/2012).
Seyyed Nasser Hosseinipour (1391/2012) remembers Iranian soldiers
followed commanders' orders to pursue martyrdom during the sensitive
Pad Khandogh operation in southern Iran (1367/1987), where soldiers
were surrounded by Iraqis and expected to quickly surrender. After
sixteen hours of resistance, most of the fighters reached martyrdom,
some became prisoners of war, and those who could have turned back
refused to do so. This obedient behavior was also based on Khomeini's
directive, which identified following commanders' orders as mandatory
(Aneesi, 1377b).

During real-time conversations and in memoirs, however, I readily
encountered discussions where female interlocutors recounted undermining the norms on local terrain as an indication of their piousness.
Some women used their religiously sanctioned right to challenge the
authority of postrevolutionary state security forces when they deemed
appropriate, and in the process they also legitimized women's right to
independence. Prior to the 1982 liberation of Khorramshahr, Zahra
Hosseini (1388/2008) remembers a military commander who asked,
"Have women stayed in this city [Khorramshahr], too?" To which she
recalls that she replied, "Of course they have. We are not a few either.
These women are doing anything that they possibly can to help. I'm
certain that if you provide them with arms, they will have no hesitation in

joining the frontlines" (Hosseini, 1388/2008, p. 437). When another commander asked her to tone it down, she claimed that as long as she was telling the *truth*, she saw no reason to change her discourse (Hosseini, 1388/2008, p. 438). During our conversations in the summer of 2008, Hosseini recounted pridefully:

I was telling the truth and had a right to intervene, and I was one of the first people to call Bani-Sadr [then-president of the Islamic Republic] *khaen* (traitor). I was disappointed with the military's lack of support for Basiji (paramilitary volunteer) forces and locals turned fighters. I viewed my intervention, and consultation later with local authorities on how they could better defend the city, as a contribution to challenging elite misguidance, particularly on behalf of Bani-Sadr. (Interview, Tehran, Iran, June 2008)

As Minoo Moallem (2005, p. 3) has eloquently argued, for many revolutionary women, "oppositional subjectivities" were appealing: They made radical transformation possible by undermining the pressure to submit to preexisting gender identities in society and within the family. For Khomeini supporters, embodiment of oppositional subjectivities in warfronts was understood as an illuminating expression of piety grounded in their care for other women as well as male warriors fighting on warfronts.

In *Didar-e-Zakhmha* (Mohammadi, 1381/2002b), Masoumeh Mirzai's meeting with Khomeini illustrates a notable disruption of gender, socio-political, and religious hierarchies. During the brief encounter, Mirzai, who at the time worked in a Tehran hospital and knew firsthand the shortages soldiers encountered, immediately informed Khomeini of the difficulties wounded soldiers endure at the warfronts and in hospitals. She could have used the few seconds to praise him personally as was customary for his followers:

Reza and others were kissing Imam's hand. I was the last person to see him. They kept telling me to go and speak, but I insisted that I would go after everyone else. When I reached Imam, the yard was vacant and no one was there. I held his hand with a piece of fabric [in order not to touch his hand directly] and I was shaking. I thought Imam would ask me to stop crying and leave. Imam put his hand on the fabric and said, "why are you crying?" I said, "Imam! The injured are very oppressed. They are suffering greatly." Imam shook his head and said, "I know, I know. But don't worry. Please go ..." That was a memorable day for me. I felt satisfied knowing that I had given him a message and had informed him that the injured were suffering greatly. (Mohammadi, 1381/2002b, p. 40)

This decision to give negative news to Khomeini can be interpreted as a subtle but brave form of protest by Mirzai who, in the rest of the passage, stresses her determination to speak with Imam again, even after he asked her to leave. She concludes by expressing her sense of self-satisfaction for taking a stance for injured soldiers while the male soldiers visiting Imam decided to kiss his hand. Mirzai had left her office position at the Martyr Foundation in Tehran where she met the needs of disabled war veterans and entered the front lines of the war as a medical assistant in Khuzestan. She chose the more emotionally and physically difficult route where she decided her services were more useful (Mohammadi, 1381/2002b). The short memoir traces Mirzai's transformation from a girl raised in an illiterate family into a woman who challenges male authority and pursues what she understands to be the most moral path in the ambiguous context of revolution and war.

Similarly embracing spiritual concentration, in the memoir *Az Chande-La ta Jang*, Sobhani, a volunteer on the warfront who was trained as a medical assistant, takes on the more physically strenuous position of head of the laundry room despite her own weak health. She decides her presence is needed more in this new position. As she observes about her work in Shahid Kalantari Hospital in Andimeshk in the Khuzestan Province,

I felt that we needed someone in the laundry room full-time. I went to Mrs. Ghanbari and stated: "the laundry room needs someone there full-time, and if you don't feel this is a problem, I would like to accept this responsibility." At the time, they had brought a few washing machines. Mrs. Ghanbari argued, "you have back pain and are not supposed to do heavy work. Aside from this, you are also experienced as a medical assistant. I think it's best you stay where you are currently. Although I agree, we do need help in the laundry room." She felt it was beneath me to work in the laundry room all day. I told her, "right now we don't need medical assistance or nurses." She said, "okay sister Sobhani! I accept. I will help you too." (Jafarian, 1381/2002, pp. 115–116)

Accepting physically and emotionally difficult tasks appears to be central to some women's efforts at challenging themselves spiritually and caring for those in desperate need. Sobhani's decision to work in the laundry room not only allowed her to care for doctors, nurses, and soldiers, by washing their clothing, but also required an alertness that guided her to the places where her presence was most needed.

The passage above – the conversation between Sobhani and Ghanbari – demonstrates how, while taking care of others, pious women also developed a meaningful bond with one another. While Khomeini argued that the way to heaven for men in an Islamic Republic would be determined by women's roles as dutiful mothers, some of his female followers, through their spiritual acts of citizenship, emphasized their agency to act upon their consciousness as central to their identities as revolutionary women. Civilian women like Hosseini and Mirzai claimed their equality not only to men as warriors by making interventions (*khat shekan*) but also to the most pious and powerful of men who served as leaders on warfronts.

3.4   Contextualizing a Rebellious Life: Critical Thought and Literature for Women of the Left

Similar to Islamist women, leftist women gravitated toward organized political movements. This gravitation was conducive to their experimentation with new subjectivities that undermined the gender inequalities within Iranian society and among leftists. This section illustrates that the emphasis on self-construction in the poetry and novels that inspired Iran's left before and after the revolution engendered women's spiritual acts of citizenship. The Iranian left's intellectual connection to the Russian Revolution and Soviet propaganda has been addressed (Behrooz, 1999). Similar to Khomeini's followers, women affiliated with the Marxist left also further contextualized general ideas to link their resistance to a higher spiritual force. A higher spiritual force for women of the left manifested itself as critical thought and self-reflection that national and international literary work provoked.

Signing renunciation papers was required for release from prison in the Islamic Republic during this political period (Talebi, 2011). This meant that even if prisoners had served their time, they could not leave unless they signed a letter of repent. The interrogators reserved the right to extend the prison sentence or even change the verdict to execution should they feel that the person refused to dismiss their real or imagined political past. However, in many instances, prisoners refused to take part in this last step toward freedom.

Talebi (2011) has eloquently argued that resistance from behind bars had little to do with an innate desire to defend Marxist ideology. In fact, with the passage of time, many of the women no longer identified as Marxists or viewed themselves as members of the political organization with which they were once affiliated. As such, one would assume that they would quickly repent in order to leave prison and regain their freedom. Why, then, did so many leftist women and men refuse to repent?

Talebi (2011, p. 107) contextualizes their refusal thus:

How could I explain to him [her brother-in-law] that my resistance was not so much about an ideology as such as about the kind of subjectivity in which one is forced to bargain that very subjectivity? How was I to elucidate this obscure point that it was not merely about life and death but about the kind of life and death that one has to choose?

Talebi then argues that there was a clear association between the mental breakdown of prisoners and the disintegration of their "dreams and imaginations" (2011, p. 162).

What came to define the context, opportunities, and limits for women's spiritual acts of citizenship was in fact the poetry and literature they oftentimes knew by heart. Similar to Sohrabi (2016), I noticed that interviewees wanted to discuss "subversive books," and the title of the same books and poetry would come up often during interviews. However, while former leftist political prisoners showed little interest in or mastery of Marxist thought or even communist literature more broadly, they attributed their resistance behind bars to the novels and literature that they were inspired by at the time and which in many ways served as a backdrop to their grand visions of political change both before and after the 1979 revolution (Abdolah, 2011; Farzaneh, 2005).

Hillmann (1982) suggests that modernist Persian poetry was a social movement on its own, having voiced political dissent against state and social authoritarianism since the 1960s. The poet whose name recurred repeatedly in interviews with women of the left was Forugh Farrokhzad. In addition to refocusing her reader's attention to everyday social problems, and notwithstanding traditionalist conventions, Farrokhzad and her contemporaries incited individuals to assert their identity – even against the backdrop of uneasiness with acts that complicated one's own presence before spectators. The work of Iranian poets Nima Yushij, Forugh Farrokhzad, and Ahmad Shamlu fostered women's hidden sensibilities to construct a collective political consciousness that nevertheless identified the *individual* as the voice of her own tale. As such, within this body of national poetry, self-care as a dynamic of political spirituality takes on the form of celebrating the individual's right to shape and remake her own identity.

On the life and legacies of Farrokhzad, Hillmann (1987, p. 3) states: "… I interpret her life and art as one woman's poetic struggle within a pervasively patriarchal society and culture to become the individual of her own definition." Importantly, Farrokhzad's poetry invited readers to watch her progression in self-discovery. This understanding of self, however, was grounded not only in her everyday life experiences but also in her use of poetry to legitimize women as desiring subjects (Brookshaw and Rahimieh, 2010). Through this technique, she created an alternative political narrative to the one offered during the modernity struggles of the Pahlavi Monarchy (Brookshaw and Rahimieh, 2010). The pursuit of legitimizing one's subjectivity for leftist women makes sense as many of them recall feeling like "exiles" while living in Iran (Shahidian, 1996). In one of the last poems of her life, entitled "Let Us Believe in the Beginning of the Cold Season," Farrokhzad expresses her new sense of identity and perspective on the disappointing realities of her life, including her divorce, the loss of her son, and societal judgment. Similar to Islamist women, for women of the left, the unification between personal and political is notable, as well as the limits that exist in individual decision-making:

> And this is I
> A woman alone
> At the threshold of a cold season
> At the beginning of understanding
> The polluted existence of the earth
> And the simple and sad pessimism of the sky
> And the incapacity of these concrete hands. (Hillmann, 1982, p. 125)

In effect, Farrokhzad recognizes both the real-time boundaries and possibilities of self-construction. She refuses to lose herself in "illusions," the fruits of passage (Katouzian, 2010, p. 11). Similarly, Milani (1982, p. 121) states:

But though the earlier Forugh [Farrokhzad] evaluates herself mainly as a function of the needs, desires and values of men, in her later writing she sees herself as a human being in her own right, with commitments and goals of her own, truly self-determining.

In an interview shortly before her death, Farrokhzad explains this idea more directly:

Poetry is a serious business for me. It is a responsibility I feel vis-a-vis my own being. It is a sort of answer I feel compelled to give to my own life ... I do not search for anything in my poems. Rather, in my own poems I discover myself. (Hillmann, 1982, p. 142)

For female revolutionaries who wanted to express their selfhood as women with a radical new social vision fueled by both "pleasure" and "submission" (Katouzian, 2010, p. 17), Farrokhzad's voice was the perfect place to sense this wholeness and launch a critique of gender roles. Farrokhzad did not intend to become a revolutionary. She did not write her poetry to support her time's oppositional movements (Dabashi, 1985). Rather, she understood her work to be a reflection of her time. Through this temporal consciousness, she shares another characteristic with the women who politicized her words. Her entire career lasted a short fifteen years, yet Farrokhzad's honesty and public transformations legitimized and rejuvenated Iranian women's political desires before she ever heard a Marxist organization's platform or witnessed a male com-rade's solidarity. Farrokhzad was the private leader for women's most daring public acts during this time, and the courage with which she constructed her own identity became a source of inspiration for women of the left.

Reciting, remembering, and writing poetry in prison was a source of inspiration and solace for Iranian political prisoners (Mesdaghi, 1383/2004). Many former political prisoners cherished Ahmad Shamlu's poems during their detention (Talebi, 2011). Sousan Mehr (2007, pp. 31–32) recalls reading one of his poems, "Fish," on a prison wall in Evin. "Fish" emphasizes the importance of remaining committed to oneself and not losing the sense of conviction that permits the formation and transformation of identities:

> I don't suppose
> my heart was ever
> warm and red
> like this before.
> I sense that
> in the worst moments of this black, death-feeding repast
> a thousand thousand well-springs of sunlight,
> stemming from certitude,
> well up in my heart.
> I sense, further, that
> in every nook and cranny of this salt barrenness of despair
> a thousand thousand joy forests,
> stemming from the soil,
> are suddenly springing.
> Oh, lost certitude, oh, sea-creature
> fleeing in the concentric,
> shivering,
> mirroring pools,
> I am the clear pool:
> mesmerized by love,
> search out a path for me
> among the mirror pools...

The poem reassures political prisoners that their resistance has long-term ramifications that will open new possibilities for others. Perhaps it is for this reason that this poem is the one that was often written on prison walls.

Modern Persian poetry and literature have extensively discussed the challenging experiences of villagers, the marginalized, and the oppressed (Shams, 2018). The women I interviewed and whose memoirs I read, however, remember also being inspired by non-Iranian novels to reconfirm their dedication to the poor. For many, remembering these stories that arise from outside Iran while in prison generated a sense of solidarity to undermine their bleak circumstances. As each woman took turns retelling parts of novels she remembered, the utopian society that was yet to come became tangible for everyone present (Ardavan, 1382/2003).

A reliance on non-Iranian literature can be analyzed as leftist inability to connect with Iranian society. Indeed, the Islamic Republic has often depicted leftists as disconnected from Iran, even identifying them as communist spies or agents (Talebi, 2011). However, following Mirsepassi (1396/2018), this sense of empowerment through a reading of nonnational literature was possibly rooted in the progressive and cosmopolitan essence of the Iranian left, and not an indication of a lack of care for Iranian society. Indeed, another interpretation of non-Iranian literature's centrality to women's sense of self could be their desire to transcend provincial activism and to view themselves as part of a larger global struggle for justice, solidarity, and revolutionary subjectivities. As Bauböck (2010) has argued, citizenship is demarcated nationally, but that does not safeguard the practice of citizenship from multiple dimensions of influence, including the international.

For women of the left in Iran, non-Iranian novels fused different interpretations of self-care and religion in a manner that resonated with the sensibilities of my interviewees. *Bread and Wine* by Ignazio Silone, for instance, was one of the most widely read novels by leftist women within Iran's revolutionary context. Written in the 1930s and considered a twentieth-century masterpiece, the novel traces the emotional and political dimensions of resistance through the story of Pietro Spina who returned to Italy to organize peasants during the fascist era. The novel centers on the relationship between spirituality and the struggle for justice and in important ways undermines the Islamic Republic's depiction of leftist political prisoners as Godless. One character, Don Benedetto, who is a priest that supports socialist views, states the following to a critical former student: "he who does not live according to expediency or convention or convenience or for material things, he who lives for justice and truth, without caring for the consequences, is not an atheist, but he is in the Lord and the Lord is in him" (Silone, 2005, p. 21). The novel critiques superstitious beliefs and a materialistic account of a relationship with God. While hiding as a priest in a village Pietro Spina, the protagonist, encounters a woman who tries to give him a hen in exchange for healing what she believed to be her blind unborn baby. Pietro Spina declined arguing that "grace was free." However, the woman stated, "there's no such thing as free grace," signifying the materialism the author sees in religion (Silone, 2005, p. 73).

Throughout the novel, Silone's tone is sarcastic in regarding the superstitious, disingenuous, and consumerist approach that the religious hold toward pleasing God. Pietro Spina remembers leaving the church "not because he doubted the correctness of its dogmas or the efficacy of the sacraments, but because it seemed to him to identify itself with a corrupt, petty, and cruel society that it should have combated" (Silone, 2005, pp. 87–88). Yet Pietro Spina's sense of suspicion is not limited to the church. During a moment of reflection, he asks:

Is it possible to take part in political life, to put oneself in the service of a party and remain sincere? Has not truth for me become party truth and justice party justice? … Have I, then, escaped from the opportunism of a decadent Church only to end up in the Machiavellianism of a political sect? If these are dangerous cracks in the revolutionary consciousness, if they are ideas that must be banished from it, how is one to confront in good faith the risks of the conspiratorial struggle? (Silone, 2005, p. 88)

One of the limits on leftist women's spiritual acts of citizenship, it seems, was a refusal to become indifferent to suffering and integrate into a materialist understanding of life and death – be it defined by clergymen or the political group they were associated with. The emphasis on maintaining the self through acts that move beyond self-identification is another important theme of *Bread and Wine* that resonates with my interlocutors' spiritual acts of citizenship in prison. The plot includes interactions between revolutionaries and various segments of society, such as peasants, women, reformists, and the marginalized. *Bread and Wine* thus poses questions about what one does in relation to others, in addition to who he or she is becoming, which highlights the importance of thinking about women's citizenship in terms of acts and not only the cultural implications of belonging.

A theme that runs through most of the literature that interviewees recall reading is that of remaining critical toward organized religion and rituals but open to the remaking of the self through critical reflection. The Russian novel *Mother* by Maxim Gorky (2018) was published in Russian in 1907. The main protagonist is Pelagueya Nilovna Vlasov, an illiterate and religiously devout mother, who decides to help her son in his revolutionary activism after the death of her abusive husband. The son, Pavel, had become a heavy drinker and smoker after his father's death. However, revolutionary politics becomes the framework through which both mother and son find salvation. Pavel stops drinking and wasting his life with late-night partying, and his mother gains a higher social status by supporting her son's activism.

The novel mentions Christ but disconnects him from the church, and at times even God, to highlight the possibility of a moral life without organized religion. The character of Christ symbolizes the importance of self-construction, and perhaps love, to the revolutionary project. Early in the novel, Pavel stresses to his mother that he is reading "forbidden books" that address the lives of "working men" and which may ultimately place him in prison. While God is often present in the novel, the relationship between religion and the state is scrutinized.

The hero of this novel is Pavel's mother who, through interactions with her son and his comrades, changes her austere religious views to acknowledge the sacredness of resistive subjectivities struggling for the collective good. For instance, when her son is arrested during a protest at a factory, she tells the following to the crowd: "Our children are going in the world toward happiness. They went for the sake of all, and for Christ's truth – against all with which our malicious, false, avaricious ones have captured, tied, and crushed us" (Gorky, 2018, p. 104).

No longer only the mother that brought her guests tea, Pelagueya transforms into a comrade by secretly distributing leaflets in factories and creating a space in her home for young rebels to meet. By placing herself in danger and being mentally prepared for sacrifice, she creates a Christian utopia. The determination to reclaim the sacredness of man from a God distorted by the state and church, and imagining this process as entangled with the formation of a new and independent self, is a notable theme in several international novels my interviewees recall having influenced their activism in prison.

The novel also maintains a notable gender dimension, as Pelagueya's move toward activism is instigated by her maternal feelings. However, Efat Mahbaz (2008), who spent seven years in prison and was a member of the communist group aksariyyat observes about her reading of *Mother* as a teenager: "I was in the sixth grade when I read *Mother* by Maxim Gorky, and I fell in love with Pavel, the hero of this story. I was into the character of Pavel and began to identify as a communist. I no longer believed in God, and I appreciated the struggles that mother endured for Pavel. However, I never did connect with the mother." As an advanced student who began to read Farrokhzad's poetry at the age of ten, Mahbaz was unable to relate to a character that had spent most of her life in ignorance – however unfortunate she may have been. Depending on their lived experiences, then, different women developed their own understandings of the international novels they read.

Similar to the novels discussed above, *The Gadfly* by E. L. Voynich also maintains the strong theme of separating Christ from organized religious practice and positing thoughtfulness as central to revolutionary change. Set in 1840s Italy, the novel explores the transformation of Arthur Burton, a British man who is initially studying in an Italian seminary but develops an interest in resisting the Austrian occupation of Italy. In *The Gadfly*, Arthur becomes critical of the intersect between national politics and organized religion once he is introduced to radical thought in university reading groups. However, he continues to view Christ and Christianity as central to his revolutionary activism. When a friend asks him what religion has to do with political work, he states: "A priest is a teacher of Christianity, and the greatest of all revolutionists was Christ" (Voynich, 2018, p. 16). Priest Montanelli, who is a mentor to Arthur but also secretly his father, disagrees with Arthur's radical activism. However, he too is depicted as an honest and fair person. As he states about the rights of prisoners, even the most violent ones: "there is no case which calls for injustice; and to condemn a civilian by the judgment of a secret military tribunal is both unjust and illegal" (Voynich, 2018, p. 139). By closely examining the reading material that Iranian leftists were engaged with at the time, it seems that an unequivocal opposition to God or even religion was not central to how this faction understood their politics inside and outside prison. Instead, various depictions of self-awareness framed their spiritual acts of citizenship.

3.5   Spiritual Acts of Citizenship and Women of the Left

Given the large numbers of women who walked to their death because they refused to collaborate with the regime by turning on their friends, self-care was clearly connected to caring for others for leftist female (or male) political prisoners. As I discuss further in Chapter 4, togetherness was also an empowering sentiment that reformulated nationalism and gender dynamics during wartime. In many ways, before leftist women could be there for other prisoners, they had to first cultivate a heightened level of concentration within themselves. Based on my conversations with former political prisoners, as well as a close reading of their written documents, it seems that self-preservation is central to their contextualized response to extensive endurance under pressure.

This section, then, addresses the different forms that spiritual acts of citizenship took for women associated with the left. Due to the Islamic Republic's emphasis on creating "new citizens" within prisons through the enforcement of religious practices and collaboration with the regime, the spiritual acts of citizenship take on a stronger theme of self-preservation as protection of one's own boundaries of self. Additionally, the prison system sought to separate prisoners to break down their sense of solidarity and, hence, resistance. Leftist prisoners in particular further separated from one another by mostly associating with only a few people from their organization who they trusted. In this precarious environment, caring for others was readily prohibited and not a feasible survival tactic in many cases.

Prisoners exploited moments of execution to reconnect with themselves in the face of fear. *How* the final moments prior to execution are remembered by former political prisoners is instructive of spiritual acts of citizenship. As Nasrin Parvaz's poem "Dear Fahimeh" illustrates:

> That day,
> that hot day in July,
> when the Evin loudspeakers
> called out your beautiful name and your lips
> smiled, your eyes said to your friends,
> 'So today is the day.'
>
> You went and your walk
> was a perfume filling the corridor.
> Everyone gasped, everyone asked with their eyes,
> 'Is today then the day?' The Pasdar
> flung back an answer: 'Where is her bag?
> Where are her veil, her socks, her money?'
>
> A rumour went round that you'd given a sign
> that yes, today was the day:
> 'I don't need my food,' you had said.
>
> So tonight is the night.
> A silence hangs in the heart of it.
> Friends look at friends and tell themselves
> that perhaps you'll come back.
>
> Fahimeh dear, tell us, spare
> a word for your friends. Is
> the sky sad where you are, does it weep?
> And the wind, does it ruffle your veil?
> Back here, the ward sweats for your news.
>
> And a message gets through:
> wind-blown breathless dandelion
> comes from the mountains to say that clouds
> are massing up there and they're big with child.
> Head held high, you are standing and waiting for this,
> for the clouds to open, for you
> to be mother of change.
>
> Rifles crack.
> The moorland holds its breath
> at a star shooting across it.

It would be good to sing and go with friends
to face the firing squad, to dance,
to float in the rain.

In the long sea-silence,
a wave lifts, oars clip at the water.
A young fisherman bringing his boat to land,
rice-growers trudging home,
they shape their lips to your name.

Your name is beautiful for young girls born in July.[13]

The poem ends with the thought of new women being born out of the struggle of an executed friend. While the poem could be read as a celebration of self-sacrifice, suggesting that from the blood of martyrs others will rise, the final verse falls short of imposing a resistive identity onto the girls that are to come. While the poem expresses a sadness for the friend's death, up until the last moments of her life, there is an effort to live as the verse to "float in the rain" would suggest. The rhythm and style with which Fahimeh walks toward her imminent death exudes self-preservation or a holding onto her revolutionary subjectivity: "You went and your walk was a perfume filling the corridor."

We are led to believe that Fahimeh walked toward death with her head held high, and therefore her scent would stay long after she departed. Interviewees often recalled singing revolutionary songs as some walked into the moment of execution, an act that brings together voice, memory, and rhythm as a defiant remembrance of the continuation of life in spite of an untimely death. Fahimeh here offers her food to others stating that she would not be needing it, and here digestion and nutrition point us toward the continuation of life. Both male and female interviewees remember executed cellmates giving their clothes and belongings to their friends before leaving the cell one last time.

Each time I heard these accounts, I was touched by the level of planning and composure – concentration – that this ritual necessitated. Additionally, the rituals that accompanied the moments of execution also illustrate how spiritual acts of citizenship centered on practices of self-preservation that readily crossed the boundaries between the self and others for leftist women as well. Spiritual acts of citizenship here entail a level of solace in the idea that life continues anew after one is gone. With this mindset, the threat of execution did not prevent at least some women from continuing their resistance.

---

[13] Accessed February 12, 2018: www.nasrinparvaz.org/web/2016/09/10/dear-fahimeh/ #more-173.

For leftist women, spiritual acts of citizenship also included maintaining control over their own bodies and lifestyle. A dedication to egalitarian gender relations and women's rights was notable among women of the left, which is why both the postrevolutionary state and society accused them of crossing sexual boundaries (Jahangiri, 2003; Parvaz and Namazie, 2003). Within studies of gender and violent conflict in the Middle East, "crossing the boundaries of the collective" is directly associated with "crossing the boundaries of gendered morality" (Kanaaneh, 2005, p. 262). Within the Iranian context, even prior to the 1979 revolution, female political prisoners were referred to as "prostitutes" (*fahesheh*) by prison guards and security elites (Hadjebi-Tabrizi, 1383/2004). Using the notion of prostitution helped the Pahlavi regime to discredit women's political participation and visions, but it also helped undermine women's accusations of rape in prison (Hadjebi-Tabrizi, 1383/2004). Indeed, *fahesheh* deserves its own genealogy in investigations of Iran's political history. However, Talebi (2011) suggests that sexual propriety was understood to be central to spiritual acts of citizenship among women of the left before and after the revolution.

Golrokh Jahangiri (2003) has also argued that women associated with leftist organizations were self-conscious about their interactions with men because undermining conservative sexual norms was understood to be an indication of a weak political character. Indeed, Hammed Shahidian (1994) asserts that traditional conservatism was one reason the left never captured the popular imagination during the 1979 revolution. He claims that while the Islamists were prepared to discuss sex, sexuality, and their understanding of revolutionary gender relations, the left failed to take up this conversation.

Similar to Islamist women, the leftist women I interviewed also challenged the limits male members placed on female affiliates. One woman from aqaliyyat, Maryam Nouri, continued to ride her bike and "take the punishment for it," even though male members labelled the activity as inappropriate and ordered her, even physically threatened her, to stop.[14] Sanaz L., another female member of aqaliyyat, wore make-up and dressed femininely, despite organizational demands for uniformity of style. Bahareh C., with the organization Paykar, however, reinterpreted the organization's simple regulated style as charming because it was "their identity"; it was not Islamic or Western, it was creative:

I don't know why people think we dressed terrible: I used to make my own clothes, wear knee length skirts, high boots; it was elegant, I had short hair, always

---

[14] Interview, Cologne, Germany, April 2008.

had my eyebrows done … we did not look like boys but also refused to be sexual objects. (Interview, London, April 2008)

Leftist women bemoaned organizational emphases on conformity in behavior and thought as well as the lack of support provided for lower ranking members. Some leftist women defined their own identities regardless of organizational decree by reminding male comrades that they were *women* political activists as opposed to "genderless" entities.

Through their activism, nevertheless, women were challenging the traditional links between their gender roles and sexuality. The harder women tried to demonstrate their commitment to sexuality within marriage, the more they seemed to be under surveillance by family and friends. Women had to distribute political flyers in the middle of the night, be present at organizational headquarters from early in the morning until late in the evening, and live in collective homes to prevent themselves from being identified by the state. Due to the spatial movement these activities entailed, many in Iranian society, including female activists' own families, viewed them as "morally loose" women.[15] It is often reported by men and women who were part of the Islamic Republic's governing apparatus that upon arrest of "anti-revolutionaries" birth control pills from unmarried women were confiscated.[16]

In one publication by the state based on interviews with imprisoned members of Mojahedin, female Mojahedin detainees were depicted as gullible victims who were deceived by men to lead demonstrations and carry out violent acts such as tossing "Molotov cocktails" into the crowds.[17] Such narratives highlight the fierce competition that existed between state agents and wider society to define and designate a sexual identity for this group of women in an effort to cast doubt over their politics. Additionally, despite the significant number of young women associated with leftist organizations in post-1979 Iran, leadership positions were dominated by prerevolutionary male activists who also enforced a dismissive attitude toward sex and sexuality (Shahidian, 1996).

Spiritual acts of citizenship become most visible as leftist women discuss physical pressure and pain. Similar to Islamist women, leftist women's demonstration of their ability to endure under physical pressure was a tactic against the state's efforts at disciplining their bodies into the ideal postrevolutionary female subject. Golrokh Jahangiri (2003) states

---

[15] This point is also made by Shahidian (1997, p. 17) and Talebi (2011).
[16] Shahidian (1996, p. 49) also notes that the Islamic Republic often accused the left of sexual indecency.
[17] Anon., 1985, *Confessions*, pp. 112–114.

that "revolutionary patience" (*sabre enghelabi*) was a phrase readily referenced right after the revolution. A high tolerance for hardship was understood to be necessary for undermining the Shah's regime, and this dedication to endurance was carried over into the postrevolutionary environment for many associated with the left. Nooshabeh Amiri (2013) remembers reading poetry as she tried to come to terms with her husband's arrest:

I took refuge in the poetry of Hafez and Rumi. I had read the letters of Imam Ali to his governor Malik al-Ashtar so often that I knew them by heart. This I thought was necessary, because in official communications quoting from these letters could prove pivotal when attempting to gain ground with pious officials. But still no one was willing to do anything. Our little house was quiet. Lifeless. (Amiri, 2013, p. 19)

Nooshabeh's end goal was not to "return to self." Instead, she relied on the utopian and democratic elements of Shi'i political history to push her socialist agenda. From the poetry of Hafez and Rumi she sought comfort and patience, which were vital for everyday life in a precarious condition. Likewise, Fariba Sabet (1383) remembers her daughter while dealing with the anxiety that comes with relocation, and she also shows the centrality of self-preservation for leftist women's survival in prison:

I imagine Sahar's face, and I laugh aloud. While in good spirits, I take out a pin that I had hidden on the back of my shirt. I begin to write on the wall: "My daughter, the fruit of my devotion, I love you. Your mom, May 1365." Finally, I get up from my spot. I recall an excerpt from Jean-Christophe: "I have no need to see you, your love keeps me warm." I walk and walk in my cell. There are several knocks, but I pay no attention. All of a sudden the door of the cell opens and Akbari the Pasdar gives me a plate of food. The call for prayers can be heard from the speakers. The call for prayer, the sound of the food cart, the opening and closing of cell doors, all return me to the environment of the damn prison. (Sabet, 1383, p. 10)

By remembering her daughter's love, and probably her own affection for Sahar, Fariba was "kept warm" and found solace, at least momentarily. She does not view the separation from her child as an opportunity for self-construction or a "return to self." She also does not focus on the urge to take care of her daughter, which is a real sentiment she embodies. Instead, daydreaming is a tactic for escaping the exhaustion of prison life. Given her situation, with her family residing in another part of the country while she was in Tehran, Fariba needed to reach a state that many prisoners call "maintaining the self."

Maintaining the self was a struggle geared toward prevention of mental breakdowns. If a prisoner experienced psychological problems that required medical attention, rarely would they receive this care. In turn, experiencing psychological problems could result in more collaboration with the state than was necessary for getting by – and ultimately being consumed by hidden shame and anger might end with suicide. The act of writing on the wall and pacing back and forth allowed Fariba to transcend her prison reality by remembering the warmth that flourished between Sahar and her. The intersection of literature, love, and imagination was a common theme in leftist women's tactics for self-preservation from behind bars.

Leftist female political prisoners understood endurance under torture as an instructive moment for self-preservation. The Islamic Republic relied on physical force to strip political prisoners of their identities and rebuild them according to its own interpretation of what constitutes being an Islamic subject of the state (Sanadjian, 1996). The actual processes that brought women into torture chambers, which were hidden from public view sometimes and adapted from the disciplinary practices of the previous regime, were diverse (Rejali, 1994). For some it was the desire to protect others and not to give the names of friends to the state. In other moments, women's demands in the prison and refusal to abide by the social order prison guards demanded from prisoners resulted in their punishment.

The state's use of repressive measures and propaganda in prisons was connected to its inability to enforce political control through other mechanisms (Bakhash, 1985). Regardless of the reasons that brought women under torture, it was described in meditational terms. As Nazli Partovi states:

They gave me a piece of paper and asked me to write down my information. Because I did not give them any details, they decided to move me down one floor, which was the torture chamber. I took a deep breath and thought to myself that I should be prepared for all sorts of responses from them. In order to release myself from anything that could disrupt my ability to concentrate under torture, I asked to go to the restroom so that I could take out my contact lenses. (*Zendan: Goft-o-Gu ba Nazli Partovi*, 1377/1999, p. 22)

Each time I read this excerpt, I am moved by this: Despite knowing that she was most likely about to encounter serious physical pain, Partovi was still mindful to take care of her eyes through the mundane practice of removing her contact lenses. This ability to prioritize and remain calm under pressure was a quality that Partovi continued to embody during our face-to-face meeting in Sweden.

The skills that she developed in prison, such as taking care of her body, spirit, and health, guided her transition as a refugee in Europe and later responsibilities as a single mother. During a gathering with other former political prisoners in Sweden, Partovi scolded everyone for smoking, arguing that instead of turning to unhealthy habits they should try to resolve the problems that occupy their minds and push them toward poor health practices. She reminded us that many were in prison during the Shah's regime and in the postrevolutionary period and never touched a cigarette. As Shahidian (1996) has argued, leftist women's experiences in Iran, and the subsequent skills they developed, were instructive for their survival once they left the country and began a life as refugees.

A heightened level of individual concentration was necessary during spiritual acts of citizenship under torture. Political prisoners conceptualized torture to be the closest moment between prisoner's bodies and the state. Torture in the Islamic Republic was then grounded in the state's effort to reconstruct the prisoner into a "normal human being" and was only rarely connected to the extraction of information (Rejali, 1994, p. 113). Shahnaz L., loosely affiliated with the organization aksariyyat, narrated the following struggle with maintaining the self during torture and how she cherished her right to be continue living as a dissident:

Everyone has a substance; aspects of it are genetic, and others are your lived experiences. In prison, we did not have an opportunity to contemplate. Events poured on our heads like rocks; in those moments that substance, the essence of who you are, all of your life accumulated into a moment; that is what comes forth, and it is what develops. Are you going to drown others to save yourself? Or will you take the hits directly? You never know what you will do. No one can predict, not from one interrogation to the next, from one lash to the next, or from one execution to the next. I saw many men and women break down and bow out. But sometimes I look back and think, wow! That was me. I did that. I was able to continue. (Interview, Malmö, Sweden, March 2009)

Shahnaz's referral to genetics and experience emphasizes the importance of independence for her even while enduring violence. Furthermore, she imagines her failure to hold on to her independence to be destructive to the lives of others. During torture, her existence means that she is resisting subjecthood, and, as such, she claims the right to demand rights and the right to be an active dissident for herself and others.

Similarly, physically taking on the social responsibility to challenge the state's attempt to undermine leftist women's insistence on being politically active dissidents, a supporter of the leftist group aksariyyat, Vida M. highlights the centrality of self-directing one's subject formation, even under the stress of torture:

In that moment it is just you, the bed and the whip; Marx is not there; Lenin is not there; your friends are not there, you are a woman alone with your beliefs … it is you and your body with all its capacities, against a state with all of its capacities, the whole moment comes down to that ... and after the first lash, it becomes much easier because you know you are not armed and they are so afraid of you. (Interview, Cologne, Germany, April 2008)

She takes power away from elites such as Marx and Lenin while delineating her independence. She even dislocates her friends from this moment. Rather, she places herself and her dedication to demarcating her right to object at center stage, viewing this struggle as interconnected to her sense of self. While anyone who has experienced lashing will assert that the pain never becomes bearable, for Vida M. the idea that her body symbolized the form of dissent the state sought to eliminate brought her solace under extreme duress. With each lash, she understood *herself* as being in control of space, not the state officials disciplining her body.

In Persian, being lashed translates into "eating lashes" (*shalagh khordan*), which also highlights lashing as a process to be taken in. For instance, Mahbaz (2008) remembers asking her husband, Shapour, who was also in prison and later executed, if he remained committed to their political group, aksariyyat. In response he stated if not, "then what was I doing?" (Mahbaz, 2008, p. 175). After his execution, Mahbaz learned from her husband's cellmates that he was believed by his peers to be one of the most tortured male prisoners in Evin. In retrospect, she understands his awkward retort to center on his body's absorption of many different forms of physical attacks.

Others highlight the unpredictability of humans, the complete breakdown of individual and collective unity, under the extraordinary and unfair pressures of torture (Mesdaghi, 1383/2004). In an interview, Partovi states:

The complexity of human beings is directly related to a person's capacity to resist under torture. With respect to this issue, a person will see the behaviors of others – both positive and negative – and her own behavior. She may be surprised by herself and those around her. When a person resists under the pressure of torture, and looks back on her own resistance, she may be surprised by her own power. This is because when the moment of confrontation comes, it occurs so suddenly that there is no time to consider such matters. The opposite can also be true. It could be that despite one's own claims, past experience, or the experiences of those around her, she gives into the pressures of torture quickly and breaks. This moment can be stunning too. The important point is that even if you have conquered the pressures of torture before, perhaps several times, a new experience will bring unexpected elements. You will encounter yourself anew again. Torture is barbaric and used in contexts of inequality. Therefore, it is difficult to predict how a person will react based on previous behavior. (*Zendan: Goft-o-Gu ba Nazli Partovi*, 1377/1999, p. 23)

Not all political prisoners were able or willing to perform such spectacular spiritual acts of citizenship. Parvaneh Alizadeh (2001, p. 48; 1376/1997), for instance, remembers "running around in the room" in an unsuccessful effort to get away, after the first cable wire hit the bottom of her foot. After the lashing, Alizadeh recalls laughing when she looked at her bloody feet, and she attributes this odd reaction to the shock and extensive pain she was in. Another interviewee, Haleh B., affiliated with the Islamic Mojahedin, answered thus when I asked how she dealt with torture as victim *or* witness:

I guess there are two ways to think about your question, worrying about what would happen to me and worrying about what would happen to others. For me, I felt like nothing really bad would happen because I wasn't that important. I didn't have that deep commitment to the cause and was not that involved when they took me. I could understand a lot of different causes. And I didn't feel like they would kill me because I had not done much. I trusted that they weren't that crazy, even though crazy things did happen. In other words, I never lost hope but I also didn't think I would be free tomorrow.

What happens to others was like any terrible thing that could happen in life, like an accident or earthquake. I tried to accept it, tried to do my best for the situation. I didn't resort to prayer and I wasn't celebrating their death as a great thing for the cause. Mostly, I stuck with my friends and tried to find a mechanism to survive probably the way a prisoner does. If there were ten books we could read, I would ration myself and read them in a way that there will be something for tomorrow. I accepted this as a new way of life with its own challenges that I had to cope with. (Personal interview, Germany, 2008)

Haleh's relatively low-level affiliation with the Mojahedin reassured her that death was not immediate for her, although she also prepared herself emotionally for the unexpected. Her relatively safe position in prison made it possible to take the conditions of others into consideration. Furthermore, she scheduled the activities that she could participate in, such as reading books, to structure her day. Establishing balance in her everyday life as a prisoner was a spiritual act of citizenship that guided Haleh's ability to maintain her sense of self despite the challenging circumstances that accompany prison life.

Spiritual acts of citizenship focus on maintaining the self under enormous pressure for the sake of both the greater good and creating a new resilient citizen in a postrevolutionary context. Whether through accusations of sexual misconduct or physical torture, leftist women's bodies, gender identities, and political agency were to be reconfigured to create subjects for the new regime. One former prisoner, Leila L., affiliated with the organization aqaliyyat, recalls that during *tabut* (coffin) tortures, the prison warden presiding over the torture said, "This will be like judgment day. Do you know why? Because no one will hear your voice."[18] Through their spiritual acts of citizenship within political organizations and then in prison, women themselves largely undermined this effort: They simultaneously demanded the right to have rights and the right to be dissidents while becoming claimants through spiritual acts of citizenship.

3.6 Conclusion

This chapter demonstrates the enactment of spiritual acts of citizenship and how care intersects with self-preservation to produce a revolutionary citizen. I argue that self-care was forged during the prerevolutionary period within families but also through the circulation of poetry and literature. The chapter then shows how different approaches for self-preservation were relied upon to protect the personhood that interlocutors had created with care. The heightened level of concentration, meditation, and contemplation that self-preservation required – as well as the love and thoughtfulness that undergirded the effort – makes women's interventions spiritual acts of citizenship.

On the one hand, the move toward self-preservation at times meant that women cared for others while creating a new identity and spaces for the self. This trend was most strongly visible in the narratives of women involved in the war, perhaps because of their closer relationship with the newly founded Islamic Republic in Iran. For leftist women, on the other hand, due to the state's pressure on this social group for conforming to an ideal post-1979 citizen model from behind bars, self-preservation took on a more individualistic form. What emerged from both Islamist and leftist women's experiences was a rebellious citizenship or acts borne out of lived experiences with revolution and war that enabled more egalitarian relationships between the state and society. While these case studies may not speak for all Iranians, I also do not find them to be isolated occurrences; the next chapter will continue to highlight the gender transgressions that took place as individual forms of empowerment coexisted with a dedication to communal survival.

---

[18] Interview, Malmö, Sweden, March 2009.

4   The Body in Isolation
Morality and the Reconstruction of the Nation in Wartime

4.1   Introduction

How did women's nation-building efforts interfere with what feminist scholars have rightly identified as the heteronormativity embedded in the official state-building agenda in wartime (Alessio, 1997; Kanafani, 2008)?

Moreover, what ramifications does this contention hold for feminist assumptions of a "masculinist" state (Hooper, 2001; Sjoberg and Gentry, 2007)? Classic feminist studies have highlighted that nationalism and feminism are oftentimes antithetical (Enloe, 1989; McClintock 1993; Parker et al., 1992). Other investigations have instead focused on the importance of paying close attention to historical contingencies when addressing the so-called opposing relationship between nationalism and feminism (Enloe, 1998; Jayawardena, 1986; Waetjen, 2001). This chapter postulates nationalism as a tool that political elites use to construct the nation-state in wartime and, at the same time, as a mechanism that can be reconfigured through "politics of the governed" to contest the nation-state's formal narratives (Chatterjee, 2004; Closs Stephens, 2013; Shapiro, 2000). In this chapter I contribute to feminist studies of conflict by arguing that when we account for women's and men's moral assessments of nation-building during the 1980–1988 period, the self and community are constructed in ways that (at least sometimes) contest the state's gendered nation-building efforts.

As True (1996) has argued, the intent here is to highlight the interworkings of structures and agents within specific historical contexts. This chapter addresses the remaking of communities and family norms during the 1980–1988 period. It connects to the reminder of the book, which highlights the legacies of these sporadic, short-term, but nevertheless contestations of the Islamic Republic's nation-building efforts in particular moments and spaces. This chapter aims to capture what non-elite Iranians did within a context that was filled with limitations that separated bodies from one another, as opposed to merely dwelling on that isolation.

Expressions of a relational understanding of the self and other were dominant during this time. In discussions of citizenship in Iran and the broader Middle East, "the politics of citizenship are often eclipsed by the politics of community" (Zubaida, 2001b, p. 21). For some of the women I interviewed or encountered in memoirs, acts of citizenship were under-girded by moral assessments to enliven interventions (Englund 2000, 2004). "Assessing the world in moral terms" should not be surprising; the 1979 revolution was also a reimagining of a more pious nation-state, understood in diverse and complex ways (Abdolah, 2011; Lamont, 2000, p. 9; Mottahedeh, 2000; Swidler, 2001).[1]

In short, individual morality, behavior, decisions, and internal thinking patterns were under great scrutiny from 1980 to 1988 – and upheld by a desire to forge a more pious nation-state. The moral calculations women made as they performed acts of citizenship, I argue, entailed a desire for different kinds of "recognition" but cannot be surmised in a rights framework alone (Sayer, 2005).

Closely related to the centrality of moral assessments during this time is the use of the body in constructing a society concerned with others' needs. Abu-Lughod's (1990) critique of how resistance functions in most social science research, illustrated through Egyptian case studies, argues that "power operates on bodies and in doing so generates modes of corporeal resistance" (Jabri, 2013, p. 110). Jabri (2006) and Masters (2008) have argued that in international studies, which has its roots in war studies, explorations of the body are oddly missing in mainstream literature. Existing examinations of the body can mostly be found within security studies with a perspective on surveillance and policing of bodies (Masters, 2008). Without being dismissive of how violence pulls bodies and communities apart, I demonstrate that the decision to work toward reconfiguration of the notion of community through moral calculations can also be an outcome of modern-day warfare.

If, as scholars of affect, we want to stress the importance of the body to social experience, we must remain cognizant of the interplay between affective contexts and an individual's emotive connections to others (Hemmings, 2005, pp. 548–567). When we study human agents who embody the capacity to act as individuals, it is vital to account for emotions. Subject positionings are informed by self-reflection, and the interplay between affect and emotions is connected to a person's moral worldview (Sayer, 2005). Moral assessments may at times be the cause for political action and not only a demand for rights.

---

[1] Many thanks to Manata Hashemi for helping me think about the interplay between morality and political action.

The various violent conflicts that Iranians experienced from 1980 to 1988, including the war with Iraq and the state's execution and imprisonment of opponents, resulted in sociopolitical separations between families, friends, and partners. This was coupled with the internal cultural changes that the establishment of an Islamic state produced. Interviewees frequently located their struggles for survival within the broader context of isolation, loneliness, or "darkness." Massumi (2002, p. 35) describes these *intensities* or affects as "autonomous" from feelings that develop within individual bodies. On the other hand, helping us to imagine intersubjectivities within discussions of affect, Fanon (1970, pp. 77–99), Lorde (2007, pp. 145–175), and Ahmed (2004) have all asserted that, depending on the racial and gendered position one has in society, affective contexts speak to people's individual and collective histories to generate feelings about the self and one's communities. Affect may be an emotive backdrop, or that "feeling in the air" that we sense, but it also interfaces with emotive connections between people.

A person's location within multiple communities and identities is in constant interplay with their affective environment (Dissanayake, 1996, pp. ix–xxi). As such, one's engagement with the affective context is embedded in the identity formation process, an event that is at once profoundly intimate yet always intersubjective (Mookherjee, 2005, pp. 31–50). This interplay between the collective and individual in subject formation makes it difficult to overlook the intersections between moral assessments, bodies, and individuated emotive histories during wartime *and* women's acts of citizenship. Iranians' gendered subjectivities suggest that affect and emotions, however distinct, can overlap during violent conflict. These included suffering, anger, desire, compassion, love, and other intimate feelings that overlapped with one another *and* the affective experience of isolation. Women's and men's gendered and affective subjectivities in this chapter indicate that not only did affect and emotions amalgamate to enliven bodies but they also drove some Iranians to act and create ethically committed ways of belonging that reconstitute the self and community during a time of war and revolutionary zeal.

In what follows I highlight how gender was rethought and reworked and how gender roles were remade during the 1980–1988 period to contest the established idea in political science that feminism and nationalism are incompatible. In turn, this finding also suggests that national governance from 1980 to 1988 was not as rigid and authoritarian as we previously had assumed it to be during this period.

4.2   The Islamic Republic of Iran at War: Nation-Building, Heteronormativity, and War Tactics

The imagery that the state uses to delineate identities during conflict has implications for "who belongs" and who can be understood as a citizen of the nation-state (Kaufman and Williams, 2004). At the same time, women have shown to be human agents during conflict (Ali, 2006); as such, we should not falsely assume them to be solely its victims, even though this is how they are oftentimes represented by states during wartime.

Acts of citizenship in postrevolutionary Iran began to develop between 1980 and 1988 with Islamists solidifying their grip over institutions and national culture as the state was in a process of political transition and involved in an international war. Recoding citizenship and maintaining popular support for the war were tangled enterprises in the Islamic Republic's state-building efforts. These long- and short-term endeavors were pursued through the formation of an Islamist public sphere. More specifically, the state enforced its social regulations through the Quranic verse *amr-e be ma'ruf va nahy-e az monkar* ("commanding what is just and forbidding what is wrong") (Khatam, 2010, pp. 210–221).

This civic nationalistic legislation intended to distinguish postrevolu-tionary citizens through the extent to which they propagated state-sponsored morality, identities, rituals, and cultural revisions. Obedience to wartime ethics and implementation of the state's citizenry ideals were vital to engendering this emergent "political creed" of governance in post-1979 Iran (Ignatieff, 1994, p. 3). Yet, the state endorsed its version of ethnic nationalism. The Islamic Republic officially described Saddam Hussein and the West, not the Iraqi people, as perpetuators of the war. However, state and societal forces also viewed Iraqi soldiers as cowards and the Iranian soldier as a historically recognized Persian warrior. In some instances, the use of two different moralities in this formulation distinguished the cultural boundaries between the Iranian nation and the Iraqi nation.

Furthermore, the delineation of space that upholds both state-endorsed citizenship and nationalism propels heteronormativity within the nation-state: the spatial monitoring of bodies through the so-called natural grounds and attributes in which men and women are supposed to interact and also via institutionalized forms of public and intimate culture. I understand heteronormativity to be the structures, social organizations, cultures, and ways of thinking that give heterosexuality a dominant and privileged status in everyday life. Thus, I imagine heterosexuality to be about more than sexuality or the erotic (Berlant and Warner, 1998). I conceptualize gender and sexuality as interconnected yet distinct dynamics that are negotiated between people. Heterosexuality is experienced through this vibrant engagement. Importantly, different formulations of gender and sexuality as social categories can result in destabilizing heteronormativity (Jackson, 2006).

Because of this agenda for nation-state building and its diffused heteronormative underpinnings, the Islamic Republic attempted to define the uses of various spaces and demarcate social distinctions based on subjection of its citizenry and nationalist constructs (Moallem, 2005). An array of wartime tactics on the local terrain created normative individual and collective subjecthoods. To interrogate the state's wartime tactics, a struggle central to living independently in a conflict zone, Iranians used their bodies to galvanize polities that supported their individual aspirations. While the body has been central to Western feminist thought, its flesh and material capacities have commonly been sidestepped for its metaphorical usages, and this trend exists in feminist studies of conflict and citizenship as well (Beasley and Bacchi, 2000; Davis, 1997, pp. 1–23).

Women's embodied subjectivities either intentionally or unintentionally undermined the heteronormativity of state-endorsed citizenship and nationalism. Importantly, this process hinged on Iranians' self-mediating the state's segregation and gendering of the public and private spheres in daily life (Paidar, 1995). The nonlinear operation of feelings, time, and space in this physical form of community-making by the activist citizen falls outside the state's citizenry and nationalist systems of regulation, all of which relied on the making of polities based on bounded, hierarchal, and temporally systematized notions of self and other.

4.3   The Body and Polity Formation: Physically Contesting State and Societal Nation-Building Projects

Similar to European and North American experiences during the Second World War, the fiscal demands of the Iran–Iraq war created conditions that undermined the segregation of the spheres (Bahramitash and Esfahani, 2011). The cultural norms that governed society and the family still placed women in the private realm, causing a significant decline in women's employment (Alaedini and Razavi, 2005). The state continued to depict motherhood as women's most important contribution as citizens to the country during wartime (Paidar, 1995). Often colleagues, supervisors, husbands, and fathers were less than supportive when women joined the workforce.[2] Some non-elite women, nevertheless, heeded wartime demands and built polities that were receptive to their controversial location in the nation's postrevolutionary economy.

Some nurses established an imaginary repertoire with the heteronormative pace of life while at work. Their relations to the spatial and temporal dimensions of heterosexuality are imaginative: These women were unable and unwilling to fulfill their gendered responsibilities as, Iranian culture at the time dictated. They instead blended the spheres to support the construction of communities that recognized them as female participants in the labor market. Pari Y., a nurse and mother of four from Ahvaz, remembers all the patients as her "children" while her own kids were sent to nearby Masjid-e Soleiman (a historical city in southern Iran) and stayed with family due to her husband's refusal to help.[3] She immediately goes on to state: "My nation was being attacked, I worked as many hours a day as my body would allow ... I felt successful because I had entered the workforce. I was very proud of myself; no one was allowed to take this away from me. I wanted to have my own income."[4] By quickly remembering that her body had the capacity not only to produce children but also to save the nation, her presence in the workplace was legitimized to lessen the effect of her husband's disapproval and lack of support.

During the war, 23,000 female medical assistants and 2,300 female doctors actively participated in the conflict. Medical assistants often moved around warfronts ("Besh az 25,000 Emdadgar va Zan-e Pezeshk darh Jang-e Tahmele Hozur Dasht," 1397). Contrary to some feminists' assertions that motherhood routinely limits women's citizenship possibilities at wartime (Enloe, 1998), Pari, self-reflecting on her identity as a mother, reconfirmed her physical strength to stand in the face of oppression, identified in this instance through a remembrance of the war. Reconstituting her identity strengthened her ability to achieve two interrelated personal projects: economic independence for herself and national independence for her country. Indeed, Iranian nurses and *emdadgar* (volunteer medical staff at warfronts) have been identified as remarkable civilian agents that saved many lives, including chemical weapons victims (Firouzkouhi et al., 2012; Keyani, 1388/2009).

---

[2] Soheila Farjamfar, a nurse during the war, recounts how one husband divorced his wife who was working long hours as a nurse. Another woman's husband took a second wife (Farjamfar, 1381/2002). However, husbands are not always less than supportive of their wives' roles in the workforce in post-1979 Iran. See for example Hoodfar's (1998) study of female medical volunteers.

[3] Personal interview, Tehran, Iran, May 2008.

[4] Personal interview, Tehran, Iran, May 2008.

Farzaneh G., another nurse from Ahvaz, recalls an experience that similarly made her body crucial to the construction of an additional polity and sustained her despite her husband's lack of support. She remembered how her children played with injured soldiers scattered around the hospital as she worked around the clock. She elaborated: "My milk would run as I attended to the injured, and I watched my son from a distance passed around in the arms of waiting patients, and this energized me; I never got tired."[5] Because her milk was flowing as she simultaneously nursed the wounded and watched her child from a distance, it materialized her body's malleability. The extension of her body through her flowing milk connects these two different social groups by mediating the public and private spheres to construct a space for her in the workforce. Perhaps most importantly, the sensations that this imagery generated throughout her body and mind revived her resolve to continue working.

As citizens who self-mediated the state's segregation of the public and private spheres, women used their bodies to imagine associations that recognized virtue in their dual identities as mothers and professionals taking part in the formal economy. By reimagining the national culture of employment, these nurses built polities that undermined the heteronormativity of state-endorsed citizenship and civic nationalism that discouraged women from participating in the labor market.

Meanwhile, in Iran's prisons, physical connections between prisoners were disrupted by prison officials. Closeness between female political prisoners, in particular, undermines the state's heteronormative wartime tactics, for it can serve as an alternative to male domination and permits women to "synthesize information" and become independent from male-distributed resources for survival (Hoagland, 1988, p. 34). Prior to her execution in 1988, Fatemeh Zarei, a member of the Islamic Mojahedin, recalled that officials at a Sepah prison in Shiraz woke her in the middle of the night in October 1982 to inform her that her sister, Fataneh, had been executed in a prison at Bandar-Abbas (Makaremi, 2013). They then proceeded to watch her until the morning to make sure she did not cry (Makaremi, 2013). If she cried, she would have faced punishment for physical solidarity with her executed sister, who was also a member of the Mojahedin – and eight months pregnant.

There were also moments of unexpected togetherness between prisoners that undermined the state's effort at isolating them from one another as deviant women, prisoners, and vocal political beings.

[5] Personal interview, Tehran, Iran, June 2008.

Soudabeh Ardavan remembers moments of forbidden social interaction as a defining feature of prisoners' capacity to maintain mental balance despite the violence inflicted on them by the prison guards and *tavvabs*. She describes one scene in Ghezel Hesar prison after the hiring of a new warden who temporarily stopped the use of *tavvabs*:

All of us decided that once a week we would do a deep cleaning of the cell. On our cleaning days, we would take all of our belongings to the yard and wash them off. That week we decided to also wash all of our blankets. As we worked, Parvin Goli, who was one of the most beloved prisoners, decided to start playing. She splashed water on a few of her friends. In return, they started to splash water on each other. Water started to reach people that were standing on the opposite side, and they also joined the fun. Slowly, we noticed that no one was washing the blankets anymore. Everyone was screaming and chasing one another. They would laugh and pour the water in their buckets onto one another. Those that were dry would run inside, and those that were drenched in water would follow them and splash water on them. Screams and yelling had filled the entire yard … The men's ward was adjacent to our ward. All the men had gathered around their windows concerned that an uprising had taken place in the women's wing. (Ardavan, 1382/2003, pp. 98–99)

Ardavan stresses how moments of pleasure created through conversations, relaxation, or acts of playfulness discussed above undermined the state's effort at separating female bodies from one another and preventing the formation of a private sphere. In another place she discusses a special friendship:

I had a friend who was younger and physically shorter than me. However, in terms of knowledge and insight, not only was she not lacking, in many instances, she gave better analyses than I did. We always used to walk and chat during the time we were allowed outside. Our conversations were vital. By speaking with one another, we could lessen the pain and pressure we were enduring. Just like me, she was always being harassed. The *tavvabs* always gave reports that I guided her thinking. This actually was never a dynamic in our relationship. My friend would become angry and say, "now tell me, why is it that you are influencing my thoughts and not the other way around?" And I would jokingly say to her, "because I'm taller than you." (Ardavan, 1382/2003, p. 83)

Forbidden relationships and feelings of closeness between political prisoners managed to offset the atmosphere of hopelessness and physical pain that they endured. As prisoners' bodies connected, they enforced an alternative moral view where joy and pleasure were central to their being as well.

Ardavan explains the reading groups that prisoners had created to forge a mental and physical escape for themselves, which also served as a kind of physical healing between women guided by intellectual thought and the warmth of another woman's touch:

Usually in the evening, after the beatings and insults were finished, Haji [prison warden] would leave. We would get together in small groups and talk. I connected with some of the active and unruly prisoners, and we sat together and sang revolutionary songs. We decided to recite a novel that most of us had read. We decided on *Nina* by Sabet Rahman, which addressed the experiences of revolutionary figures involved in the October Revolution. Each one of us remembered sections of this book and added new details to what was recalled. Slowly, a collective memory was created. It was exciting to retell the revolution of the working class and to reconsider the love, tribulation, losses and victories of people in a different time and place, but with the same desires to achieve freedom and social justice that we embodied. As we grew tired, each person would place their head on a friend's legs, and at the same time, their legs would become a pillow for another person. (1382/2003, p. 65)

Ardavan's memory points to the significance of a unification of bodies to prisoners' capacity to live through difficult days. The element of fantasy in the retelling of novels, and the collaboration that this process entailed, created a sense of oneness among female prisoners that the state sought to disrupt. The actual coming together of their bodies at bedtime added to this sense of togetherness layered with physical support after a day of violent beatings.

Self-mediating the experience of motherhood, then, was also central to the formation of polities for political prisoners, for whom imprisonment oftentimes meant that their political identities were pinned against their other desires as young women. Nazli Partovi recalls her longing to have at least one child; spending close to nine years behind bars, she often discussed motherhood with prisoners who had already experienced it.[6] She remembers that prison officials monitored conversations between prisoners through *tavvabs*. Reports from *tavvabs* to prison officials often resulted in lashings or separation of prisoners who knew each other, who had become friends behind bars (Talebi, 2011).

A significant part of a *tavvab*'s show of support to the regime was the reports they wrote against their cellmates regarding the conversations they were having in the cell and their activities (Mesdaghi, 1383/2004). The conversations between women regarding motherhood cultivated "outlawed emotions" of togetherness and joy, in a public place where they were supposed to be isolated and submit to state power (Jaggar, 1989). Discussions of motherhood dismissed the state's material control over their reproductive rights as enemy citizens of a state at war. These deviant talks, which established new connections between women, blurred the boundaries between the state's segregation of the spheres.

---

[6] Personal interview, Malmö, Sweden, March 2009.

Female political prisoners' conversations regarding children and fantasies of motherhood were acts of citizenship that did not just physically fuse a community together but recreated spaces to undermine the state's monopoly over the reproductive rights of enemy citizens. The underlying motivation for these outlawed conversations was not necessarily a demand for rights but a moral assessment regarding the importance of motherhood for women.

Regardless of whether the regime decided to use children as a tactic for control or if they were there merely due to their parents' circumstances, the presence of children in prison wards influenced women's resistance (Talebi, 2014). During our 2008 conversations in Germany, Maryam Nouri emphasizes how seeing children in prison empowered her to continue her resistance. As she exited the hospital without her family or husband nearby, she sensed her nation's solidarity as people shouted at the Revolutionary Guardsmen who had forced her to carry her own luggage and a newborn only a few hours after giving birth. The visual display of solidarity from strangers inspired her to transcend the isolation of prison life and resist the establishment of an Islamic Republic in Iran. The show of support from other Iranians encouraged Nouri to identify as a *sar mozeh* – or someone that intended to continue resisting the Islamic Republic from behind bars.

Shortly after having her son and returning to prison, officials offered Nouri's son baby food but suddenly discontinued serving meals especially made for all other children in the ward. Cherishing the solidarity she felt from her nation months earlier, she refused food for her baby, arguing "either all the babies get food or mine will not have any either."[7] By envisaging the authoritarian nature of the Islamic Republic and its effects on Iranian society, she could deprive her child of food in exchange for an alternative political order. Multiple extensions of her body across spheres took place for this decision to be formulated. Reconceiving her positionality within an imagined polity meant that the state could not manipulate her identity as a mother to construct a subject for its rule. Her identity as a mother embedded within a nation permitted her to take a moral stance against the living conditions for babies in prison with their mothers.

In other cases, the child's body becomes a powerful connection and source of stabilization. Nasrin Parvaz discusses the presence of a four-year-old boy, Arash, in her cell:

Arash had found some peace and he began to play with us. I enjoyed playing with him, and I had made him some toys from bread dough. Every day the prison

---

[7] Personal interview, Cologne, Germany, April 2008.

guards banged on the door to tell us to be quiet, and every day it was Arash that was terrified and jumped from his seat. I took him to the bathroom, and once a week I gave him a bath. Soraya's feet [Arash's mother] had infections, and she was unable to walk. Everyday a prison guard changed the dressing and bandages on her feet, but this did not do much good. She had extreme pain because of the infections in her feet, but she never said a word. What can she say? Who can she say it to? (Parvaz, 2002, p. 41)

Soraya could not express the pain that came from being lashed on her feet due to the fear that it might upset her son. Parvaz took care of Arash but evidently was not left untouched by the entire situation. The notion that children's presence in prison brought pain to other prisoners has been expressed by male prisoners such as Iraj Mesdaghi (1383/2004). Mesdaghi, who spent ten years in different prisons and was affiliated with the Islamic Mojahedin, recalls feeling tormented as he watched a fearful eleven-year-old girl in Evin prison with her newly arrested father in the early 1980s. The presence of children in prison at times created physical connections that were nevertheless fragile and damaged.

At times, having children in prison challenged the state's nationalist discourses that were sought to unify the nation against the invading enemy. Leftist political prisoners were accused of being collaborators with Iraq's Baath Party due to their opposition to the establishment of an Islamic Republic. Monireh Baradaran remembers being in prison with an Iraqi woman and her baby. The Iraqi woman was arrested along with her husband on charges of espionage. Baradaran remembers young Iranian prisoners jokingly stating "[L]ook everyone, here comes our enemy!" when the little girl started walking.[8] By using humor to visualize the state's discourses of a national enemy through the body of an Iraqi child, these women identified the inconsistencies embedded in the abstract narrative that ethnic nationalism imposes. As such, for at least a few moments, these Iranian prisoners welcomed Iraqis into their national body.

The boundaries between enemies were at times disrupted as women extended their bodies and hearts to include the "other" and challenge the state's civic nationalism. Iranian nurses remembered their professional and intimate identities to physically connect with Iraqis despite a similar nationalistic wartime discourse. Soheila Farjamfar was employed in numerous hospitals in Khuzestan during the war. In her memoir, *Kafsh-ha-ye Sargardan* (Wandering Shoes), and during our conversations, she described a scene where an ambulance arrived containing the bodies of dead Iraqi soldiers. While male doctors and medical assistants

---

[8] Personal interview, Frankfurt, Germany, April 2008.

cheered and celebrated, Farjamfar and the other female nurses could only think of the Iraqi women who had become widows that night.[9] Holding back tears, Roya, one of the nurses, stated: "Tonight the light in the home of an Iraqi woman has been turned off."[10] In her memoir and during our discussion, Farjamfar immediately followed this scene by reminiscing about how as a child from Khuzestan she viewed Iraqis as her neighbors "across the water".[11] She reconnected with her childhood memory of watching Iraqis wave and smile at her as she stood near the Shatt al-Arab waterway with her binoculars. With this memory relived, Farjamfar stood in solidarity with Iraqi women during this moment despite the nationalist pressures exerted by male colleagues.

Signifying perhaps the scope of Farjamfar's view, Ehsani (2009) has estimated that between 1980 and 1982 almost 10,000 refugees entered Ramhormoz, nearly doubling the population of this border town near Iraq. Although most of the refugees were ethnically Arab, there were surprisingly few clashes between the residents of Ramhormoz. This is indeed remarkable given the anti-Persian propaganda of the Iraqi state and the reality that Arabs were viewed as potential spies for Iraq by Iranian society. Importantly, the Iranian state's "pan-Islamic ideology" supported the integration of Arabs into Iranian society (Ehsani, 2009, p. 52).[12]

We should remember the fluidity of acts of solidarity between two sides that are at war. There were also instances where emotional connection did not exist due to a nurse's direct presence in a warfront. Maryam Kaatabi was a medical assistant in different warfronts for eight years; she lost many close friends in different operations, including Mohammad Tavasoli, a revered wartime commander. She states the following upon seeing the dead bodies of Komoleh fighters during an operation that resulted in the death of people she worked closely with, including Tavasoli. When the Komoleh attack on the hospital came to a halt and Kaatabi went to the hospital yard, she states: "by seeing the dirty corpses of the Komoleh fighters, I felt a unique sense of sweetness" (Aneesi, 1377b). Depending on their specific location within Iran's prewar and postwar geography, and the private intimate connections they shared with the dead, Iranian wartime nurses experienced different forms of connections with the enemy.

---

[9] Personal interview, Tehran, Iran, May 2008. See also Farjamfar (1381/2002).
[10] Farjamfar (1381/2002, p. 103).
[11] Personal interview, Tehran, Iran, May 2008. Also, Farjamfar (1381/2002, p. 104).
[12] This point can be noted in Iranian memoirs and novels on the Iran–Iraq war, especially those addressing the character of warfront commanders. See, for instance, Arfani (1389).

As Iranians self-determined their positionality in relation to the specific wartime tactics they encountered in daily life, they disrupted the heteronormativities upholding state-endorsed citizenship and nationalism by using their bodies to connect with people they were to be separated from. Due to the sociopolitical context of isolation, these women used their bodies to physically rebuild polities by oscillating between the public and private spheres. Through this complex process they delineated their independence and demonstrated their moral commitments during a period of austere conformity.

4.4   Politics of Local Masculinities: Unmaking the Protector Identity of the Male Warrior

The Islamic Republic's gendered depictions of ideal citizens during the Iran–Iraq war were similar to those in other states at wartime. The Islamic Republic depicted the ideal male citizen as a warrior and the ideal female citizen as a wife or a mother who willingly sent her loved ones to war (Moallem, 2005). Iranian women were officially not permitted to be at warfronts or in cities that had turned into warzones if the possibility of rape existed (Sarhangi, 1385/2006, pp. 13–14). The allegory of the male warrior as the protector of the nation was interrogated through the presence of local women in Khuzestan who refused to leave their cities when Iraqi forces invaded (Kazruneyan, 1382/2003).

Women's contributions at warfronts, however, were not simply another case of militant women taking on symbolized masculinities to wrest new gender rights for themselves. It was often motivated by a desire to support the state at war, and, as can be noted throughout the modern history of the Middle East, Iranian women did not see their political ambitions to be in conflict with Islamic precepts. Parvin Daepour, for instance, had some military training before the 1979 revolution, as did many women active in revolutionary politics. She recalls that when the war began she saw men who did not even know how to use a gun. When she discussed this with local military leaders in Ahvaz, they disapproved of her involvement in the war. She was finally given permission by Mohammad Hossein Alm Alhaadi, the Commander of the Revolutionary Guards in Ahvaz during the early days of the war, to write an announcement regarding her training course to be read on the radio. The Commander of the Revolutionary Guards argued that women participated in wars during the early rise of Islam and thus their participation should have been permissible. Daepour gave basic training to young men and women, and she is credited with preparing 1,000 women for war (Zahidi and Shariflu, 1391/2012, p. 71).

Furthermore, as Jacoby (1999) has argued, women's collaborations within an Islamic framework should not be dismissed as simply co-option. While co-option is the first explanation that comes to mind when studying the participation of pious women in support of the Islamic Republic, it does not capture the numerous reasons why women take part in nationalist projects. During the Iran–Iraq war, there was a tension between how state and societal forces wanted these women to function in this public site and how they wanted to participate at warfronts. These women were often not even supported by state military agents on the ground in warzones. This was despite how political elites continued to praise women's support of the revolution and war from Tehran. More specifically, by physically engaging with this tension, the local Islamist women of Khuzestan unsettled the oppositional subjectivities of genders that underpin the male-warrior-as-protector construct. Through their acts of citizenship, the heteronormativity that underlaid the official state-building agenda during the war was further destabilized.

Women from Khuzestan objected to the wartime tactic of conflating man, warfront, and protection and placing this formulation in opposition to women's subjectivities by highlighting its inability to withstand realities on the local terrain. They made this point by challenging the decisions of the state's highest officials. Zahra Hosseini, a female war volunteer in Khorramshahr, was delivering food to fighters when a male colleague told her to move back due to the possibility of rape as Iraqis were dispersed across the area.

She responded: "I am here until the end … if there is danger, it is for everyone, not only me" (Hosseini, 1388/2008, p. 425). She dismissed her male colleague's attempt at placing her under his protection. Indeed, she claims his protection to be a myth and rape as a mutual concern. Her intervention suggests that there was little difference between their circumstances and options as individuals who had decided to stay and defend their city. Some men supported women's interventions in the state's wartime tactics. During our conversations, Hosseini recalled that a local religious leader, Sheikh Sharif, negotiated with the Revolutionary Guards for women to stay in Khorramshahr after their evacuation had been formally announced by the Revolutionary Guards.[13] Hosseini never disassociated from her identity as a female civilian. Simultaneously, she dismantled the gender binaries that legitimized the allegory of men as protectors of the nation, going as far as resituating her subjectivity in light of even military defense strategizing.

---

[13] Personal interview, Tehran, Iran, June 2008.

It was not acceptable for Iranian women to live away from their parents prior to marriage. Saham Taghati stayed and volunteered in hospitals even though her family had left Khorramshahr. Once Khorramshahr was liberated in 1982, she decided to live in Ahvaz, which was still under attack, to complete her high school diploma. When her father asked her to stay at a family friend's home in Ahvaz, she refused. Her father finally accepted her decision: "Stay wherever you like, just make sure you continue your education" (Soleimani, 1381/2001, p. 101). She rented a home with a few girlfriends and completed her high school diploma in Ahvaz while her parents lived in Qom.

A female high school student having this level of independence in Iran during the 1980s is astonishing. With the male protector being absent from both her warfront and adolescent experiences during the war, an underlying belief in gender equality on behalf of father and daughter seeps through this story. It suggests that the oppositional construct of genders was unsettled as young girls and women decided to take part in defending their city. The unconventional collaboration seen on the part of Taghati's father illustrates that the male protector discourse became less compelling for Khuzestani families whose female relatives were active in the war as fighters or merely as residents of a region under siege.

Some pious women complicated the conceptualization of their heroism within Shi'i-Persian culture through acts of citizenship at warfronts including their deaths in combat. Nevertheless, for Shi'i Iranians, martyrdom is generally associated with men (Gerami, 2003). Shahnaz Haji-Shah, a teen who was part of a first aid unit at a hospital in Khorramshahr, died in 1980 as she tried to rescue potential survivors following an air raid. Her mother remembers her: "The first person to reach martyrdom in our family was Shahnaz. She went and opened the path of martyrdom for her two brothers Hossein and Nasser" (Valadi, 1386/2007, p. 11). Shahnaz is recognized as both an individual martyr and a relative of male martyrs.[14] This undermines the oppositional subjectivities of men and women in understandings of martyrdom for Shi'i Iranians, where women are recognized mostly through familial connections to martyrs. Similar to male martyrs, she creates a path or a background with her death, so her identity is not domesticated through appropriations of the female body. Gender, thus far, does not emerge as a particularly salient category in comparisons between male and female Iranian war martyrs. However, Shahnaz's mother goes on to say:

---

[14] The recognition of women as both martyrs and relatives of male martyrs is also made by Kamari (1385/2006).

She had an awareness of issues that was beyond her age. She understood better than others. She was ahead of her time … At the time of the revolution, saying one's prayers on time was not that common in our society. However, Shahnaz was always very particular about saying her prayers on time. (Valadi, 1386/2007, pp. 2, 7)

As this second narrative shows, her life is depicted through a discourse of symbolized masculinities that connect her to male martyrs through characteristics such as extraordinary levels of insight and piety. These symbolized masculinities are equally attributed to male martyrs. Nevertheless, her death made her an equal to the male martyr. The legacy of her death leads one to question contemporary gender inequalities. The potential outcomes of this scrutiny are so threatening that in Iran only a few streets are named after female martyrs, whereas the names of male martyrs have been used since the early days of the 1979 revolution to name public spaces (Moallem, 2005, p. 109). There have been debates as to why the state has made this differentiation (Saeidi, 2008). As such, in their deaths, Iran's female martyrs disrupt the oppositional subjectivities of genders that reinforce popular imaginings of the male protector during their lifetimes.

Memoirs recount many illustrations of how women's acts of citizenship destabilized this form of masculinity. In 1983 Ameneh Vahabzaadeh was a volunteer medical assistant originally from the Ardabil province working at warfronts along with male war heroes such as Dr. Chamran and Ibrahim Haj Hemat. During Operation Valfajr-1 in Fakkeh, Vahabzaadeh gave her gas mask to a uniformed male fighter who was in grave danger from the chemical bombs Iraq had used against Iranian forces. She became an injured veteran because of this decision, leaving her with just 30 percent of her body's normal function (Dashti, 1390/2011, p. 23).[15] Vahabzaadeh also states the following about her work as a medical assistant, highlighting the transformation of gender roles: "After my time at the warfront, I worked as a medical assistant in the Petroshimi hospital [a hospital in southern Iran]. During those moments, we were not only nursing the injured. We were therapists, we were patient with soldiers that were suffering, we were writers that prepared last wills, and we even helped injured soldiers with their prayers by locating the appropriate soil."[16]

More recent memoirs address the sacrifices of women who did not voluntarily participate in the war but whose deaths equally undermined

[15] During an interview with an Iranian news agency, Ameneh Vahabzaadeh confirms this information. See: www.mehrnews.com/news/2075161/آخرين-شد-شيميايي-جانباز-كه-امدادگري بيرون-آمنه-پاي-از-تركش

[16] www.mehrnews.com/news/2075161/آخرين-شد-شيميايي-جانباز-كه-امدادگري بيرون-آمنه-پاي-از-تركش-از-پاي-آمنه-بيرون.

the myth of the omnipresent male warrior protector and nation-builder. When their house was bombed in the Ardabil province in 1987, Dr. Yousuf Pour-Abulghaasm, his wife, and children were home. What he remembers next from those days is his colleagues coming into his hospital room with medical equipment in case it was needed for his weak heart. They were there to inform him that his stay-at-home wife, Aazam Jamali, and daughters, Parisa and Soolmaz, all died in the bombing (Dashti, 1390/2011, pp. 39–40). He had been asking about his family for three days, but no one knew how to break the news to him, especially given his heart condition. Acts of citizenship of Iranian women and men undermined the symbolism of the male warrior as protector of the nation by fragmenting the oppositional constructs of gender subjectivities that propagated discrimination and prejudice against women. State-sponsored citizenship and nationalism, and the heteronormativity that underpinned them, were destabilized through moral assessments that centered on gender equality on the local terrain.

4.5   Politics of Local Femininities: Nationhood, Gender, and Eroticism

The heteronormative state-endorsed connections between women, the private, and the erotic, employed in other contexts, were also enforced in Iran through the regulation of some women's behavior during periods of public mourning (Paidar, 1995, p. 340). The widows of martyrs were under more public scrutiny during funerals than other grieving women due to their symbolic and material associations with the nation-state in post-1979 Iran. Many interviewees remember sensing social pressure to desist from mourning in public, for as martyrs' wives they were expected to uphold wartime morale more acutely than others.

In *Dokhtare Shina* (Zarabizadeh, 1396) Ghadam Kheyr remembers the role of other men in her husband's family during his burial: "I wanted to ride in the ambulance with him, they did not let me. I insisted that they allow me to sit with him during the ride to the cemetery. I wanted to speak privately with him, but they did not allow this. They forced me into another car. The ambulance [with her husband's body] began to move, and we followed it" (Zarabizadeh, 1396, p. 246). Nevertheless, some martyrs' wives interrogated this wartime tactic by expressing their emotions at funerals and other periods of emotional distress. These women confronted this state-building strategy, which identified them as the "beloved" and pushed them into the private realm to further locate sexuality within the domains of state control.

Not only was this wartime tactic challenged but also at times male representatives of the state supported women's confrontations. Habibeh R., a veteran of war herself and whose first husband was killed in the war, depicted this surprising association. She described the liberation she felt during her husband's funeral because of the support from another member of the Revolutionary Guards:

> During my husband's burial, I don't know why – I am usually very reserved and modest – but I stated aloud, "I want to kiss him," and my brother yelled at me and told me to stop, but *shahid's* [referring to her martyred husband] friend, who was later martyred, stated, "Kiss him, kiss him, do whatever you like … there is nothing wrong with this."

She then proceeded to explain: "So I kissed him and told him how much I loved him right there in front of men from the Revolutionary Guards, my family and his. I still can't believe I did that".[17] In *An Su-ye Devar-e Del* (The Other Side of the Heart), a woman describes her control over, and intimate yearning for, her husband's body while she stood alone, newly widowed at his funeral:

> I closed Asghar's eyes and hands with a white band. I did not allow nurses or his friends from the warfront to touch him. When we were putting his body in the coffin, his friends were hysterical. I told them to be quiet. My effort in calming them was fruitless, they continued. When his corpse was placed in an ambulance, I jumped into the front seat. While washing Asghar's face, I kissed him. I washed his forehead, head and face myself. When they prepared him for burial, I wrote verses from the Quran on his shroud. When everyone gathered around Asghar's grave, I was worried. My heart desired to bury him myself. But a walkway opened. How, I don't know. I only saw that a path opened. I went forward. I took off my shoes. I entered the grave, and was handed the rocks one by one by his friends, and I placed them on his corpse. (Zaghyan, 1386/2007, pp. 112–113)

In this narrative, the male warriors' incapacity creates an opportunity for this martyr's wife to renegotiate the state's segregation of the spheres and mourn publicly as she pleased. With an equal amount of longing, Habibeh recalled the last day with her husband before his death:

> I just watched him sleep; I moved my hands slowly through his hair [*navazesh-esh me kardam*] – this always eased his migraines – I asked him to unbutton his shirt so I could feel his presence by seeing his body. There was a heat which came from him, not because of the weather, but because of his internal worries. There was also a glow; this was not the same body I had seen before.[18]

---

[17] Personal interview, Tehran, Iran, June 2008.
[18] Personal interview, Tehran, Iran, June 2008.

The sensuality with which Habibeh describes her husband's final living day undermined the social norms through which martyrs' wives are to discuss their marital experiences in public. Ghadeh Jaber also challenged the appropriate place and way a woman was to show affection for her husband. She forced Mostafa Chamran's family and the state to bring his body into a mosque the night before his burial, placed her head on his chest, and spoke to him until the morning (Jafarian, 1386/2007, p. 50). Typically, the body would be kept in a mortuary until the funeral.

During her husband's funeral, another interviewee, Leila P., broke tradition through her insistence that she be allowed to ride in the vehicle carrying his body so that her children could sense up close that their father was gone and have an opportunity to say a final goodbye.[19] Golnar W., from Ahvaz, who did not have a chance to see her husband's body prior to burial, stated: "I wanted to kiss his forehead and place him on my heart."[20]

Some women made their presence felt as female lovers in the public sphere. For other women, acts of citizenship and a display of love and physical connection took place in hospitals. For instance, during the last few minutes of his life, as Manouchehr Moddeq lay dying in a hospital bed from injuries sustained from chemical weapons, Fereshteh Malaki proceeded to kiss her husband "from head to toe" (Baradaran, 1386/2007, p. 76). Some women expressed their love in public sites and undermined the state's actual and metaphorical control over sexuality during the war.

It was not only families of war martyrs that interfered in the state's gendering of space. In the summer of 1988, the Islamic Republic executed many political prisoners. Most of the executed were members of the Mojahedin. A human rights organization in the West estimates that up to 1,000 prisoners in Tehran's Evin prison, and many more in Karaj's Gohardasht prison, were executed (Robertson, 2011, p. 5). For families whose loved ones were executed in late July 1988, public mourning of their deaths was strictly banned. Nevertheless, an executed prisoner's wife remembers that she dug through the mass graves of the Khavaran cemetery with her bare hands: "The stench of the corpses was appalling but I started digging with my hands because it was important for me and my two little children that I locate my husband's grave" (Amnesty International, 1990, p. 12). Later, when the authorities began referring to the cemetery as *Kaferestan*, the "land of the unbelievers," and *Lanatabad*, the "land of the damned," families of the executed renamed

---

[19] Personal interview, Tehran, Iran, June 2008.
[20] Personal interview, Ahvaz, Iran, July 2008.

the final resting location of their loved ones *Golzar-e Khaveran*, "Eastern flower fields" (Abrahamian, 1999, p. 217).

The place where mostly male leftists were buried was reclaimed as a flower palace, and women dug their way through the land and labored to identify their loved ones' graves. In the most immediate sense, state-endorsed femininity and its conflation with the private sphere was spatially dislocated through the erotics of forbidden and public mourning. Families of the executed associated a terrain of "soil," silence, and flowers with martyred husbands, while the physical and public work of "bringing into existence" their bodies was left to the hands of women who yearned for them the most (Delaney, 1991, p. 12). During particular moments, the land was no longer symbolic of a woman in need of protection, nor was it a male terrain for enacting this struggle. As women morally assessed public mourning to be permissible, they also challenged the heteronormative state-endorsed connections between women, the private, and the erotic.

4.6   Love at a Time of War: Reconstructing Women's Role in the Family

During the 1980–1988 period, the Islamic Republic promoted marriage and dichotomous gender roles as a part of its citizenship regime from above (Afshar, 1998; Moallem, 2005). What is less often addressed is that Iranian women and men creatively engaged with what heterosexual relations meant in their marriages. Moral assessments not only impacted politics in the public sphere but also entered into the postrevolutionary citizens' remaking of family life. Importantly, this effort was exerted using the notion of gender solidarity in marriage. Both women and men worked toward greater egalitarian relations within the family. They came to see each other as not only partners in politics but also partners in love and life.

This notable trend should be contextualized within the larger gender transformations that took place in the prerevolutionary era. *Behind the Tall Walls: From Palace to Prison* by Azar Aryanpour (2000) is one of the few memoirs written by an elite woman connected to the Pahlavi Monarchy. The memoir depicts the changes that occurred in marital norms during the Pahlavi Monarchy for upper-middle class women. Aryanpour recounts proposing to Shoja, a man that she fell in love with as a teenager, and who would later become her husband. He was a ranking member of the Pahlavi Monarchy, a prisoner during the prerevolutionary period, as well as a prisoner after the 1979 uprising. She states:

I decided to take the initiative and talk with Shoja. I had to know his true feelings. My future depended on it. Against all conventions, I went to the rental apartment that Shoja shared with a few classmates – something that a "decent" girl would never have done! Shoja was stupefied to see an unattended young female standing at his door. Stuttering, yet determined, I told him that I had something very important to discuss. Reluctantly, he let me into the all-male apartment, and then to his room. Every word was a struggle to utter, but I managed to tell Shoja about my marriage proposal [from another man that she was not interested in]. "Is he a good man?" he asked casually. "Yes!" Shoja seemed puzzled. "Then what is the problem?" The problem? Uh-eh-well, I love someone else! I confessed shyly … "So, who is the lucky guy?" he pried. I blushed till my skull tingled. You know him, I said quietly. (Aryanpour, 2000, p. 80)

The "women and development" framework that was popular with authoritarian governments during the modern era in the Middle East (Sika and Khodary, 2012) was also relied upon by Mohammad Reza Shah in the years leading up to the 1979 revolution with the establishment of state-controlled women's organizations. The state's co-option of middle-class and upper-middle class women appears to have had the unintended consequence of also enhancing these women's cultivation of their desires and moral worldview.

Readjustments in familial relations often occur during periods of violent conflict, but rarely is the change transformative of the cultural contents and structural basis of intimate relationships. Using Palestinian women's political participation in the Palestinian Territories as a case study, Abdo-Zubi (1987, p. 52) argues that while local and global isolation can lead to women's increased political activism, it does not necessarily destabilize patriarchal familial structures. However, an unsettling of familial norms occurred in the Iranian experience with political violence from 1980 to 1988 due to the connections the postrevolutionary state made between the politicization of women and the new state's legitimacy (Shaditalab, 2005).

Moreover, for leftist women, the pursuit of freedom in marriage was central to their decisions on love, and *feeling* free was more a sentiment than a clear demarcation of rights (Shahidian, 1996). As such, institutional ramifications existed for how the nation imagined and enacted family life in a time of revolution and war. Marital norms, importantly, did not change in support of women's statuses during this time, but women became more accustomed to divorce in the aftermath of the 1980–1988 period because of how traditional norms were destabilized (Shaditalab, 2005). The moral calculations that women made in relation to their personal lives entail a desire for equality but cannot be surmised in a rights framework alone.

Women involved in various leftist movements defied families and moved into communal homes, or they chose to live alone with their partners and rejected the importance of formal marriage altogether. Following the revolution, leftists either did not get married out of fear of being identified, or they pursued marriage to remain anonymous before the state. For some women, however, the institution of marriage was used to challenge unjust organizational orders. For members of the Mojahedin, Rajavi's decision to divorce her husband for ideological reasons became a platform for women involved in the organization to challenge forced marriages following the 1985 ideological revolution. Many argued that if Rajavi had the choice to marry who she saw as her political equal, then they should be given the same opportunity. For other political factions as well, marriage was viewed as a personal decision and was reclaimed from larger organs such as the family. Much to her family's dismay, one former aksariyyat member, Mitra P., remembers being disenchanted with her wedding celebrations because as a Marxist she did not believe in extravagance. She wore an old white dress and took a single photograph only to not fully disappoint her parents. A passion for the political could be noted in post-1979 street protests and debates, but it was also connected to women's lives behind closed doors.

Non-elite women in remote cities and provinces of Iran who became Khomeini followers also used marriage to assert their love for a political vision and their independence. They understood marriage with soldiers as an act of citizenship that declared their solidarity with the Islamic Republic before international and local aggression; this is while many were members of restrictive and apolitical families where even attending rallies in support of the revolution was deemed inappropriate. One wife of a Revolutionary Guard went against all conventional norms by not even questioning her suitor about a previous marriage that had ended in divorce, already drawn to his strong dedication to social service and to Khomeini (Mirzaeian, n.d.).

Aghajanian (1986, p. 751) notes that divorce rates increased during the Iran–Iraq war. First, the revolutionary and religious atmosphere encouraged many young couples to rush into marriages to which they were not prepared to fully commit. Second, the social, political, and economic disruptions caused by the Iran–Iraq war and the institutionalization of Islamic practices also increased marital conflicts. Ameneh K., another wife of a martyr from Tehran, states: "[W]e all wanted to marry *Pasdars* [Revolutionary Guardsmen] at that time; I would not marry someone who was not directly supporting the Islamic Republic; for me it was either a cleric or a *Pasdar*" (Interview, Tehran, Iran, May 2008).[21]

---

[21] Marriage with men understood to be defending Islam was common during the 1980s for supporters of Ayatollah Khomeini. See also Judaki (1385).

These women, often from the most traditional and religious families of Iranian society, for whom even participation in the revolution's street protests was not permitted, were catapulted into leadership positions within their homes and neighborhoods with the onset of the war. In addition to taking care of their small children, many volunteered in local mosques and homes of other pious women to prepare meals for frontline troops (Akbari, 1390/2011). The context of war brought a previously sheltered group of women into new spaces and social networks; it also revised the morals connected to intimacy, be it with their partners and/or parents. As dedicated followers of Khomeini, many of these women also encountered familial opposition when they married. With husbands, brothers, and fathers at the front and isolated from extended families, their public and private acts made them the Islamic Republic's most favored citizens. The unintentional result of this intersection between men's and women's acts of citizenship, undergirded with different moral calculations, was a move toward egalitarian marital norms for some.

The reconceptualization of marriage through moral assessments disrupted the traditional norms of relations between a young woman and her parents. During interviews, most women described marriage as one of their initial experiences of "breaking traditions." Akbarnejid, the wife of Jahan Ara, a leading revolutionary and military figure who guided the liberation of Khorramshahr, decided to marry her late husband after witnessing his intellectual and moral integrity during their political activism in the late 1970s; she made her final decision despite disapproval from her family (Sarhangi, 1384/2005, p. 13). Similarly, Amini remembers her parents' disapproval of her marriage to Shahid Avini, an Islamic Revolutionary and war photographer; however, she experienced a connection with him based on his artistic and political edge, coupled with a lifelong commitment to learning (Sarhangi, 1381/2002, p. 9).

As the next chapter details, many of these women – who later became war widows during these years – came to lead a movement for autonomy after marriage, demanding a woman's right to maintain custody of her children with a deceased husband (Paidar, 1997, pp. 294–297). This endeavor was also supported by Islamist women in formal positions of power, such as Marzieh Dabbaq during her tenure as a parliamentary representative. The institution of marriage thus became a field where women could implement and exercise their dedication to the values of the Islamic Republic and in return expect solidarity with their causes and protection of their interests as Islamist women.

For many women in Muslim societies, a man's economic status was an important factor in selecting a partner and a central attribute of male honor. However, this was undermined in women's collective display of ideological zeal. This attribute became overshadowed by an emphasis on morality and intellectual capacity for the common good of the postrevolutionary nation. How loving men and women were, then, determined by their acts of citizenship in the public and private spheres came to identify them as superior partners, not their economic status. Leftist women remember caring little about their partner's economic status and being much more concerned with his political aspirations. Many women describe their marital decisions as a "natural" evolution of their political development. One woman from aqaliyyat, Mitra V., states, "politics was love for me ... he had to be a Marxist ... fierce and dedicated ..."[22]

With a life of luxury having been ruled out as being incompatible with their political visions, leftist women lived with poor men from traditional families. It was not uncommon for female revolutionaries to encourage male participation in what eventually became an armed struggle against the formation of an Islamic Republic in Iran. Similarly, Habibeh, a young Iranian Arab whose husband was at the warfront fighting against the Iraqi invasion, rejected her parents' insistence on helping her financially. She chose instead to live modestly in the controversial marriage she had chosen despite her parents' disapproval, which stemmed from her decision to marry a non-Arab.[23]

The connection between a display of ideological fervor and marital customs took an even more dramatic turn for some women. Many of Khomeini's followers identified their dowry as their husband's martyrdom. They defined monetary value as inapplicable in a state built on the bodies of citizens – citizens who identified the process as one of self-development (Zaghyan, 1386/2007, p. 35). Other women completely rejected traditions that secured women's economic stability in case of unexpected marital troubles.

Dedicated to the importance of a modest lifestyle during the war, Safeeh Modarras, the wife of a martyr, rejected her dowry (*mahreh*) and trousseau (*jahezah*), inciting familial accusations that she was purposefully breaking Islamic requirements (Sarhangi, 1381/2002, p. 13). With this decision, however, Modarras, much like the women who demanded martyrdom as their dowry, articulated marital connection as more than a material exchange. They identified the love of values, best demonstrated through social service to the state at a time of need, to be the vital factor for marital decisions. As such, they also challenged the traditional role of family in young women's lives. Many Islamist women remember overturning marital traditions in their youth by assessing suitors based on

[22] Interview, Cologne, Germany, April 2008.   [23] Interview, Tehran, Iran, June 2008.

their political will and activism, rather than through a display of security in the form of monetary guarantees.

The political often attracted couples to each other, and political connections between men and women helped break down traditional gender roles. Malaki's husband identifies the day he saw her, as a teen without her parents' approval, escaping from SAVAK[24] forces, running across rooftops while transferring guns for Islamist factions, as the day he fell in love with her (Baradaran, 1386/2007). Furthermore, practices that had previously been understood as a woman's "duty" were given new meaning by women themselves. A former political prisoner remembers making breakfast for her husband every morning, not because she felt duty-bound but because she found him worthy of her care. Likewise, decisions that women traditionally were not permitted to make in marriages without familial or male approval were now routinely made independently.

Maryam Nouri fell in love with her husband's humility, which she saw in direct contrast to her own unstable, audacious, and confrontational character. She proposed to and married him without ever consulting her family.[25] Similarly, one martyr's wife remembers her husband's peaceful demeanor and style of speech during their first encounter, which differed from her talkative and energetic presence (Bagheri, 1391/2012). While men's openness to their wives' independence as both activists and partners was by no means uniform or always experienced by married couples,[26] it nevertheless existed as a dominant theme in memoirs and conversations.

The intersection between political objectives, moral calculations, and familial construction also radicalized parenting for some couples (Raissi, 1383/2003). This is a significant finding. As Hoodfar (2008) has argued, for many women the postrevolutionary context destabilized women's reproductive plans. Hoodfar (2008, p. 86) writes that it was common for women who had decided to stop pregnancies before the revolution to have a "second set" of children after 1979. This decision was partly attributed to men's right to more than one wife, as well as other legal insecurities that women experienced in post-1979 Iran. Memoirs and interviews reveal that, for some, national well-being and parents' own political aspirations disrupted the conventional understanding of parents'

---

[24] The acronym for *Sāzemān-e Ettelā'āt va Amniyat-e Keshvar*, the secret police/internal intelligence service during the Pahlavi regime.

[25] Interview, Cologne, Germany, April 2008.

[26] See Mojab (1999), where she discusses the marital experiences of a leftist Kurdish-Iranian woman whose husband saw her as a political partner but not a partner in life and love. See also Bauer (1994), where she interviews former leftist political activists about male–female relations.

responsibilities toward children. When his daughter was gravely ill, one woman's husband chose to stay at the warfront, finally coming home in time for their daughter's fortieth-day death ceremony (Zaghyan, 1386/ 2007, p. 85).[27]

Another woman recalls that her baby's serious health problems and need for immediate medical attention were side-tracked because her husband insisted on being at the front. When a physician finally saw the child he exclaimed, "You brought his corpse for me to give life to?" (Moshtagh, 1385/2006, p. 24). Much like their husbands, women also made independent decisions that placed national *and* personal interests above the responsibilities of motherhood. Women who chose to participate in the war efforts, or were obliged to as nurses, experienced transformations in parenting traditions most intensely. In *Didar-e-Zakhmha,* Masoumeh Mirzai's decision to leave her husband and two children behind to fulfill her commitment to help the wounded was radical, given that national and familial discourse viewed motherhood as a woman's main priority.[28] Although Mirzai's husband did not share her enthusiasm and dedication for social service, he was supportive by taking care of their children, which enabled her to continue working in Tehran and later alone in Khuzestan. Farjamfar also left her children with her family to volunteer at a hospital in Abadan, a risky decision given that Iraqi attacks had just begun in the region and the direction and extent of the war remained unknown (Farjamfar, 1381/2002, p. 23).

Shahid Jahan Ara's wife, perhaps in the most dramatic example of a transformation in familial relations, allowed her husband to take their baby boy to the front line (Anon., n.d., *Khorramshahr: Ku Jahan Ara ...* p. 5). This decision evinced the couple's intent to raise the spirits of young men away from their families through reconstruction of space with their own flesh and blood. Moralized understandings of political thought released men and women from their traditional gendered responsibilities and indicated their desire for gender equality.

For women left alone during their pregnancies for political reasons, childbirth became an extension of partnerships and not only a display of male superiority (Delaney, 1988, p. 86). The birthing process was an important moment to be witnessed by both parents. For example, in *Ghermez, Rang-e Khun-e Baba-m,* after her son's birth Soheilipour

---

[27] In Islam, a ceremony is held on the fortieth day after death.
[28] *Zanan-e Jang,* Mirzai (Masoumi, 1376/1997, pp. 40, 56) also mentions discussions by women who left their children, husbands, or parents behind to participate in the war. In *Az Zaban-e Sabr* (Fazel, 1384/2005, p. 16) the wife of Shahid Kazami remembers her parents' refusal to allow her to participate in the war, leading her to marry Kazami due to his insistence on his wife's engagement with the war.

remembers that her husband visited her first and then their newborn child. This was a memorable moment signifying his heightened level of admiration and respect both for her and for their newborn (Saeidi, 1382/ 2003, p. 20). Similarly, in *Ghessi-e Baray-e Sajjad* (Mortazavi and Safeiyeh, 1382/2003), Taki rejoices that her husband was present during their son's birth, a privilege given that in Iran women are usually only accompanied by other women through the birthing process. Taki's satisfaction in challenging institutional norms is highlighted in her description of the surprise expressed by the nurses at the hospital (Mortazavi and Safeiyeh, 1382/2003, p. 20). Noting the significance of Taki's experience in *Az Zaban-e Sabr*, several women remember that their husbands were not present for the birth of their children; this appears to be a memory that they particularly want to express given the limited space provided within the text (Fazel, 1384/2005, pp. 53, 173). Challenging the culture of parenting as a necessary outcome of marriage, Jaber and Chamran did not have any children, and she does not address this issue in her memoir but made clear her objections to Chamran's austere lifestyle.

Women also remember their husband's joy at the birth of a daughter, in addition to the focus fathers placed on their girls, something that was less likely in prerevolutionary Iran among non-elite families (Zaghyan, 1386/2007, p. 62–63, 66). As Hakmat remembers regarding her daughter's birth:

When the baby was born, my father gave the news to him [her husband] – who was working at the command station in Dezful – over the phone. He did not initially say that the baby was a girl. He thought it may upset him. But when he was told, right there, while still on the phone he prostrated before God in gratefulness. (Anon., 1386/2007, *Hamsardari-e Sardaran-e Shahid*, p. 27)

Hakmat's husband surprised her by expressing his gratefulness for the birth of their daughter, which seems to have been uncommon for perhaps the geographical context in which the couple lived. In another radical revision of birthing tradition, Yousefian, a leftist-turned-martyr's-wife after losing her husband in an Ahvaz city bombing, rejected doctors' suggestions that she have an abortion as a war widow (Yahosseini, 1387/ 2008, p. 163). Several months after his death, she gave birth to their daughter Laleh and proceeded to live alone with their two children. Women's reconnection with, and redefining of, their womanhood during the revolution and war indirectly led to readjustments in childbirth traditions and moral values of parenting.

Living through the hardship of this time had long-term effects on child-rearing traditions as well. Golastaan Jafarian's *Roozhaaye be*

Ayneh (1396) introduces the life story of Maneejeh Lashkari, whose husband (Hossein Lashkari) was a US-trained pilot and prisoner of war in Iraq for eighteen years. For sixteen years, his family did not even know for certain if he was dead or alive, although the air force continually reiterated that they believed he was alive. Aside from such stunning details, the story chronicles the disciplined life of a pilot and his wife. Maneejeh waited for Hossein during the eighteen years he was gone, and she did not listen to family, friends, and even the Martyr's Foundation when they suggested she remarry.

Maneejeh and Hossein had a newborn son, Ali, when Hossein was taken by Iraqi forces after his plane crashed in Iraqi territory. When Hossein was finally released after eighteen years, Ali married and had a son. However, when his wife leaves for Europe to study (and does not seem to return), Hossein and Maneejeh appear to be given custody of Ali's son. In the memoir, Jafarian describes intense scenes where Maneejeh and Hossein disagree about how MohammadReza should be raised. For instance, when MohammadReza gets into a fight at daycare with another boy, Hossein goes directly to the little boy and tells him that MohammadReza will hit him the next time the child attacks MohammadReza. Maneejeh is distraught by Hossein's decision to approach the child directly, and the daycare also expresses dismay at this decision. Maneejeh states: "I wanted MohammadReza to be polite and obedient. Hossein was the opposite. He wanted MohammadReza to be daring and confrontational" (p. 128). Hossein argued that Maneejeh had raised Ali, their son, and he was introverted. However, Hossein disliked this characteristic in his son and wished for his grandson to express how he feels. This episode is a critical juncture not only in the life of this couple but also in Iran's postwar history.

While Maneejeh appears to have left behind the revolutionary and Islamic thought that engendered the 1979 revolution, Hossein was not ready to regret his past. Maneejeh mourns the time she lost and the horrible direction her life took with the revolution and war. She discusses her physical pains and the reality that she must take antidepressants to deal with the burdens of her life. Hossein, on the other hand, never discusses what happened to him in Iraq. He is not willing to repent his past due to the severe consequences his decision to remain loyal to Ayatollah Khomeini and the revolution had on his life.

Additionally, women came to express insecurities with motherhood more readily. In *Dokhtare Shina* (Zarabizadeh, 1396) we are introduced to Ghadam Kheyr, who comes from a small village in the Hamadan province. When she married Samad (Satar) at fourteen, she was considered to be marrying late by her sisters, who married before the age of fourteen. Her father did not allow her to go to school, so she was illiterate. The memoir largely discusses how Ghadam Kheyr gave birth to five children and raised them without her husband's support since he was at the warfront most of the time. The Supreme Leader recognized the book and acknowledged Ghadam Kheyr for her patience and faith.

Fascinatingly, throughout the memoir Ghadam Kheyr regrets her later pregnancies and longs to simply have her husband nearby. She appears to be overcome with the everyday tasks of a housewife, while it remains unclear what her alternative lifestyle could be at that time. *Dokhtare Shina* is an honest tale about the life of a woman that did not fully understand her husband's dedication to the revolution or war but was, at the same time, transformed by promises of egalitarianism that both entailed. In this sense, the book also introduces readers to the "revolution of the provinces" that Ehsani (2009, p. 65) has argued came with the other changes that the revolution engendered, such as Islamization.

A critical stance toward motherhood is a motif in memoirs and interviews. In her memoir *Enak-e Shokaran*, Malaki expresses sadness regarding her pregnancy. Already feeling as if she had lost her husband to the war, the thought of becoming parents seemed like another setback for their marriage (Baradaran, 1386/2007, p. 27). Similarly, Hamrahi, also the wife of a martyr, states that after the birth of her second child, she grew unsatisfied with her one-dimensional identity as a mother and wife. She therefore returned to college with her husband's full support, which required the family to relocate (Marj, 1381/2002, p. 38). Most radically, Fahimeh Babayianpour, a martyr's widow, chose not to have children with her first husband because both were focused on participating in the revolution and war and identified the pursuit of martyrdom as their life's work (Kamari, 1385/2006, p. 24). Women's and men's interpretations of revolutionary ideology and its relevance to social and political life destabilized the centrality of motherhood in women's identities.

4.7   Conclusion

This chapter has illustrated that "the right to demand rights" should not be conflated with acts of citizenship. Other frameworks, such as moral calculations, can be important lenses into the unexpected ways that feminism and nationalism interact during war. Examining women's and men's narration of everyday life during conflict may reveal how gender is reworked and rethought alongside the state's nation-state agenda at wartime. The first half of the chapter demonstrated that women relied on their bodies and sentiments of isolation to build communities with those who were near to them. Next, through discussion on women's use of the body and affect, it was shown that women's independence was indeed interconnected with the bodies of others during this period in Iran. At the same time, relying on the body to build connectivities meant that the heteronormative circulation of masculinities and femininities were destabilized in the construction of the nation-state. Finally, solidarity between married couples was undergirded with moral assessments and worked to counter the tendency of war to reassert traditional gender roles in the family. Chapter 5 begins our examination of the aftermath of the Iran–Iraq war through an investigation of the postwar experiences of wives and daughters of martyrs.

5   The Aftermath of War
Wives and Daughters of Martyrs and the Post-1988 State[1]

5.1   Introduction

In his recent novel on the Iran–Iraq war, Mahmoud Dowlatabadi has a character pose a question to a martyr's wife: "Between two circumstances, two stances, two moments and, so to speak, two points in time, within a short space of each other, for example, between the moment he arrived and the moment he said goodbye and left, which was more pleasant? His coming or his going?" (Dowlatabadi, 2014, p. 45). The question also nicely frames this chapter, which demonstrates how martyrs' wives and daughters navigate the conflicting and dense temporalities of their lives before and after their husband's or father's death.

The legacy of war is a neglected area of research, particularly among political scientists (Noori, 2012). This chapter thus explores the legacies of violence that occurred during the first decade of the Islamic Republic through case studies of wives and daughters of war martyrs. It is believed that there are 56,157 wives and 144,525 children of war martyrs (Anon., 1383/2005a, "Dar Hamayeshe Daneshgah"; Anon., 1383/2005b, *Zanan*). Women who occupy a critical place in Iranian society confronted gender-specific and imposed state narratives and policies on their lives and today's society to construct their own subjectivities in relation to these structures of power. They experience a contentious position in constructing the state's real and imaginative boundaries, as both state and society hold well-defined outlooks on women's moral characteristics and citizenry responsibilities. Female relatives of war martyrs occupy a position in Iranian society that contests and complies with diverse, and simultaneously imposed, narratives on their status.

Importantly, blood relations, who carry extra importance for the Shi'i, significantly intensify and complicate the value of each martyr's legacy as both nation and state impose a particular outlook on their families' lifestyles. As martyrs became supreme architects of a revolutionary state at war

---

[1] I dedicate this chapter to Shohreh Pirani and Seyedeh Azam Hosseini.

through self-sacrifice, relatives – particularly mothers, wives, and daughters – were nationally bequeathed a noble citizenry status and a responsibility to sculpt the state that their loved ones desperately sought to create. For many Iranians, families of martyrs are the economic and political winners of the Iran–Iraq war, endowed with statuses and benefits they have not rightly earned – a social group that symbolizes the ideological biases of the Islamic Republic. For the state, they are the living embodiment of the Islamic Republic's establishment and symbolic figures of its endurance.

At the same time, from the early 1990s, Iran witnessed the development of the reformist movement that sought to legitimize individual rights and autonomy in the Islamic Republic (Holliday, 2011). The country's population had doubled by the 1990s, and the Islamic Republic began to question how it was to address an increasingly interconnected global system. These transformations made the presidential election of Seyyed Mohammad Khatami a reality (Tazmini, 2009). The notion of citizenship was formally used by Khatami, who was committed to enhancing political participation (Ansari, 2000). The first decade's revolutionary zeal had dwindled, and the state moved toward pragmatic approaches for integrating into the global economy (Tazmini, 2009). During Khatami's presidency, the government expanded economic and educational opportunities for women and worked to advance women's rights by building their self-confidence (Tazmini, 2009). The Khatami government enlivened civil society, although this process was heavily controlled and engineered as well (Rivetti, forthcoming). Nevertheless, the larger political environment and the application of additional policy lenses by the Khatami government became important factors in the changes to citizenship from below in the postwar years.

Not only was the larger political environment more responsive to citizenry demands but the personal and collective experiences of families connected to the war also reached a point of crisis. During my travels to Iran and participation in national ceremonies with martyrs' families, I noted that many of them still had strong connections to the Khuzestan province. During the reconstruction and reform era, postwar reconstruction efforts slowed down in the Khuzestan region due to corruption, a lack of expertise, and unrealistic state expectations (Kar, 1379/2000). The people of Ahvaz, Abadan, and Khorramshahr were left to deal with water shortage, water pollution, air pollution, unsanitary hospitals, lack of recreational resources for the youth, and the general feeling that they were forgotten by both the state and nation (Kar, 1379/2000).

Having fought an eight-year war, the citizens of this region believed that they had a right to make demands on the state. A national culture developed where those associated with the war, especially families of martyrs, made claims on the state to the benefit of the nation. Indeed, the postwar governments and what was perceived by some as their poor handling of the reconstruction process catalyzed subjectivity formation among families of martyrs.

Martyrs' wives and daughters have a particularly contentious relationship with the state's identity narratives. As a social group, they are institutionally observed, scrutinized, and instrumentalized more than anyone else in Iranian society. This makes an examination of how they reestablish and remake state–societal relations and identities all the more revealing of the long-term effects of state-building during intense political violence. For instance, a martyr's wife who lived in a housing development for martyrs' families in Tehran recalls:

I had just remarried and had not told the security guards at the building. One day I was home and I noticed that a Revolutionary Guard official was standing at my front door with my husband. With anger he asked me, "who is this man?" I replied, "with your permission, he is my husband!" Such incidents had happened to my brother a lot too. They would walk him up to my door to make sure he was really my brother. They had us under intense surveillance in these housing developments … initially, no men were allowed in the community. There were only women and children. There was also one Revolutionary Guardsman that would ride his motorcycle around the community to make sure no one crossed any redlines. He even told martyrs' wives, "you are not allowed to speak with *namahram*. If you need anything, you should consult with the Martyrs' Foundation. Movement within the community was controlled. Anyone that entered the community had to notify the security upfront and was then escorted by a Revolutionary Guardsman to the door." (Harirchian and Hashemi, 2015/1394)

Following the end of the war, women given the title of martyr's wife faced many challenges relating to the state's gender policies. These limitations included cohabitation in gated communities with other widows that separated them from the protection of their own immediate families.

Problematizing the seemingly integrated position these women occupy within the structures of the Islamic Republic reveals the intellectual transformations that have taken place since the end of the war. The intergenerational perspective on changes in values presented in this chapter serves as another illustration of how women's political leanings and adjustments of governing approaches are spatially interdependent. This transformative opening emerges from both mothers' and daughters' special location within current Iranian society, as well as their understanding of each other's gendered spatial histories. Social engagements accumulate to create a self-determined citizenry status within this social group that reinstates, and at other times renounces, designated participatory boundaries and identities imposed by national structures of power.

Within the scholarship on contemporary Iranian society, the complexities of city life are exposed through the juxtaposition of identities and agencies against characteristics associated with the war era.[2] One daughter of a martyr in Shiraz, Golestan M., argues, "the state was made from our fathers' blood – this is while many others did not participate – our souls burn for this country."[3]

However, theoretically grounded in acts of citizenship and methodologically drawing on a diverse set of narratives and experiences, I show that the interrelational component of acts has resulted in intersections between the political aspirations of families of martyrs and wider Iranian society. In a study of family relations, Friedl (2009) also argues that cultural changes are not only occurring quickly in Iran but they are also ineluctably moving in a similar direction for various social groups. These trends suggest that the analytical approach of dichotomizing identities as an interpretative framework for identifying political interests or understanding claim-making techniques proves inadequate.

Importantly, this chapter suggests – with a focus on daughters of martyrs – that the state's arbitrary political violence in its first decade has not escaped the political identities or consciousness of the youth in this social group. An examination focused on acts of citizenship shows how women socially connected to the Iran–Iraq war are complicating the very meaning of identity categories through a dialogical interplay with multitudes of national and international voices. While the war and taxation model underscores legal inclusion as the dominant form of state-making for participants of war, this chapter demonstrates how women have redeployed personal experiences from the revolutionary and war years, in addition to familial affiliations with war heroes, to administer a political stance that constructs a more pluralistic state.

Lastly, this chapter also engages in a seemingly separate yet interconnected discussion regarding the intersects of gender, memory, martyrdom, and the state. By relying on personal memories and martyred husbands, martyrs' wives view the contributions they made to the war and revolution as equating them with their martyred husbands. That is, female partners of male martyrs have also reached the elevated status of a martyr because it was their partnership that made martyrdom possible in the first place. Here we witness female relatives of war martyrs challenging the gender inequality that exists in the Iranian Shi'i expression of martyrdom, where the noble status is generally associated with men and symbolic masculinities (Gerami, 2003).

---

[2] See Basmenji (2005), Varzi (2006).   [3] Interview, Shiraz, Iran, July 2008.

Shi'i thought and reasoning buttresses the belief that martyrs' wives are central to their husband's martyrdom and, as such, equally pious. This is because martyrdom emerges partly through relations and is based on connectivity with the community. According to Shi'i thought, martyrdom is not solely a personal decision or resultant from a moment; rather, it is a process contingent on an individual's embrace of movement through spiritual phases – one that ultimately will emerge as a divine selection (Abedi and Legenhausen, 1986). Thus, while many choose to become a *mojahed* and participate in *jihad*, and while many killed in conflict zones certainly do not, it is believed that only those who possess and practice the pinnacle of constructive qualities as assessed by God are invited.[4] However, not all martyrs carry the same level of honor, and this process is heavily dependent on the way the individuals *lived*, not the way they died. As Mojtaba F., a religious student (*talabeh*) in Qom, explains:

A person that was immoral his whole life and decides to participate in jihad [internal and external] and reaches martyrdom does not have the same honor as a martyr who was pious his entire life. (Interview, Qom, Iran, June 2008)[5]

The Islamic decree on martyrdom also raises the status of female relatives of martyrs and offers possibilities for multiple ways of understanding this status. The transformative phenomenon of martyrdom does not fully manifest with death alone.

Similar to the responsibility endowed to Zeinab following the martyrdom of her brother Imam Hussein in the battle of Karbala (680 CE), which she witnessed and survived to analyze, female relatives of martyrs become integrated into the national narrative as women who enact a loved one's sacrifice as heroic through remembrance, resistance, and mourning. However, much like Zeinab's enduring status as lead narrator of the tragedies and triumphs of Karbala, the constructive acts spawned by processes of grief and remembrance come to identify female relatives of martyrs as equally autonomous heroes in a nation's struggle for independence.[6] Therefore, while armed conflict and martyrdom in remembrance propel contested commemorations and discourses on behalf of local and international political figures and institutions, and

---

[4] Sciolino (2000, pp. 172–189) recounts the legacies of the war for some Iranian men through the story of Hamid Rahimian, a war veteran who lost most of his friends but never reached martyrdom. While in parts Sciolino's style of prose is demeaning of her interviewee's story, I nevertheless found *his* overall voice to be reminiscent of some in the male war veteran community.

[5] I also conducted a follow-up phone interview in October 2008 for further clarification.

[6] On remembrance of martyrdom as engendering Iranian women's current acts in state construction, see also Flaskerud (2004).

work additionally to integrate women into national narratives, this study further indicates that martyrdom posits women as autonomous citizens acting in accordance with their own visions (Bowman, 2006; McDougall, 2006).

Remembering is not solely a contentious way to assemble a much sought-after community for women amid, or at the end of, military conflict. Remembering can also be a relational and radical contextual tool for situating themselves in the vision as they contest the state's narratives of their location within the nation-state.[7] Women's personal contributions to the revolution and war, as well as repudiation of established gender and marital cultures during the years, accrete to form current encounters with the state and the family.

Here, discussions move beyond the intricate politics that mold and retell memories to construct current identities and examine how acknowledgment and interventions can intersect to make everyday people central to the larger project of the Islamic Republic's state-making enterprise. The analysis reveals women's deployment of the body and exhibit of self as devices that govern personal and national claims toward a self-determined citizenry status. The self-presentation, which appears superficially as an act of solely revelation, is in effect women's collective and individual effort to participate in political processes in which they are not formally acknowledged. The case studies ultimately suggest that the changes the state underwent during the 1980–1988 period were not solely a result of political urgency during wartime. Examining the political lives of a specific social group, this chapter suggests that the gains Iranian women captured through their role in contesting the state's wartime nation-state building projects were hardly lost in the postwar years.

Discord and intersect between the past and present repeatedly emerged as the context for women's acts of citizenship today; therefore, this chapter is organized temporally. With a focus on tensions between the tenses, I begin by illustrating how compliance with the postrevolutionary state's political regime can nevertheless engender acts of citizenship that challenge state narratives from this inaccessible temporal site where the past and present compete and inspirations arise. Next, the chapter demonstrates how individualized memorializations of the past are more explicitly and intentionally deployed by wives and daughters to encounter gender and familial cultures today. This section illustrates the state's transformation through a discussion of how individual memories

---

[7] Hasso (2005, p. xxii) states, "women, like men, are often motivated by nationalist and other desires, although their imaginings of community include themselves."

of the Islamic Republic's first decade are specifically utilized by women to resist and consequently remake contemporary structures of the family. Interviewees identify personal participation during the revolution and war and the death of husbands and fathers as central to shaping their contemporary acts of citizenship. These acts bolster their pursuit of autonomy in thought and action, particularly within and through the family.

5.2   Temporal Tensions and Unpredictable Acts: Institutional Construction

State support of the families of martyrs carries an implicit pledge of political allegiance; deviations from, or ruptures of, established orders can result in monetary or social penalties. Some wives of martyrs nevertheless denote personal autonomy by directly encountering state structures that most immediately affect their lives such as the Martyr Foundation. Soraya B. recalls continually confronting the foundation until she was given the necessary funding to send her three children to an exceptional school outside the permitted zoning regulations – a claim not formally sanctioned by the foundation but one propelled by her new identity as a single mother.

On the other hand, women also independently implement creative measures to redress institutional discrepancies. The collective attempt to establish economic independence lessens the foundation's influence in women's daily lives. Reyhaneh R., a wife of a martyr from Shiraz, set up an NGO in her neighborhood to support women economically through a lending system known as *gharz alhasaneh*. Local women contribute some money monthly to be able to withdraw larger sums several times a year. Similarly, the Martyr Foundation planned to rebuild an area of an apartment complex in Tehran by deducting payment from families' incomes. However, it reconsidered when a few women in the neighborhood mentioned dreaming that the spirit of martyrs engulfed the area. These enactments, which superficially appear as focusing only on economic survival and autonomy, also subtly advocate societal entitlement to institutional accountability. Tensions between durations situate women in the unique position to reconstruct networks of power across conflicting citizenry boundaries.

Tensions between the past and present, which frame acts in specific contexts, can also be seen in daughters' encounters and collaborations with the state. These women claim their right to independent thought and action with acts that demand institutional recognition of youth interests. Importantly, events transpire as daughters remain both theoretically committed to the Islamic agenda of state organs, such as the Martyr Foundation, and economically as well as socially vulnerable, as acts that are seen as disruptive or aggressive could revoke promotions and mark women as social outcasts.

Women involved in paramilitary security forces, for instance, acknowledge their cosmopolitan identity while simultaneously acting as participants in upholding the state security apparatus. In her study of urban youth in Tehran, Sadeghi (2008, p. 257) found the identities of religious young women to be similarly complex. A student activist in Basij, Nazanin L. uses herself as a model for pluralistic administration of the organization by sporting the newly created *chador milli*[8] and wearing a light-colored scarf. This contrasts with the dark and austere attire promoted by commanders and places her in close proximity to the post-1988 generation of which she is also a member.[9] Additionally, the act of (re) presenting an alternative style of Muslim dress also makes her an active participant in transforming the institutionalization of Shi'ism and stretching the limits of national inclusion and preferences in post-1979 Iran. Similarly, Mahbobeh A., a daughter of a martyr who is employed by *harasat* (state-run security force), suggests to older female officers that they depend less on male colleagues during strenuous daily tasks; she is proud of this assertion that she began to consider in women's studies courses at the University of Shiraz. In institutional encounters, even within national security forces, these young women use their physical presence to initiate debates regarding democratic reform and in effect also underscore the national right to self-determination in public domains.

At times, historical and immediate notions of "responsibility and answerability" overlap with, and integrate into, ethical values promoted by official state ideology (Isin, 2008, p. 37). This connection, while obscuring the nuances of disruption, also reveals how self-determined compliance with established routines can function as an act of citizenship. This is due to the intentions hidden, and at times propelled, by the act itself. For example, Mahbobeh A., whose father's corpse was never recovered, discussed years of longing for a body and a gravesite. She considered the pursuit of martyrdom as the best way to remember her father's legacy.

However, while portraying life as largely answerable to a specific historical injustice, in the same breath she discusses familial

---

[8] National Iranian chador.
[9] Khosravi (2008, p. 4) argues "the authorities in Iran suppress young people whether they are from the upper middle or working class. The hegemonic order created by the parental generation has somehow caused a homongenisation of the young people's demands."

mistreatment of her widowed mother and self-identifies as both a *shahi-dist* (martyr) and a feminist. In her pursuit of martyrdom, she proves to be an "activist citizen" (Isin, 2008, p. 38) desperately seeking to create the just world that her father dreamt of while simultaneously responding to a consciousness informed by local and international discourses on human rights. She therefore endorses a noble death as a peoples' entitlement against present and past injustices; she identifies the body as a medium to exert claims of autonomy for a variety of interrelated ethical pursuits. With gender and religious–political identities intersecting, her aspiration toward martyrdom intrinsically undermines and upholds different layers of current political affairs in Iran.

Some daughters, in contrast, encounter social problems that stem from discriminatory gender norms in more conflictual and direct ways. With respect to Islamic and traditional Iranian gender norms, daughters of martyrs are expected to adhere to these standards more stringently than others. Many young women disagree with this national double standard. Here, women intentionally draw upon their fathers' decisions in life to counter traditions harmful to women's lives. During these conversations, women discussed their fathers' *lives* in relation to personal acts of citizenship. They draw similarities between their own acts of courage in rupturing official ethical orders and those of their fathers, who demonstrated similar independence as sole participants in the war – at times while no one else in their immediate family took part in the revolution or the following eight-year conflict. This affects ideas of their affirmative and self-determining actions.

Immediately after praising her father's political will, for example, Hadith S., a daughter from Ahvaz who is a therapist and a member of Basij (state-sponsored paramilitary militia), argues that in sessions with young women she emphasizes the importance of acquiring detailed knowledge regarding a suitor's character prior to marriage. She also encourages women not to fear declining proposals, using her own marriage as an example, having repeatedly rejected offers before finally accepting to marry on her own terms. Non-elite Iranian women's willingness to discuss issues pertaining to gender equality and the status of Muslim women in marriage, as opposed to only a desire for economic opportunities, reveals their new women-centered perspective on intimate relationships since the war's end. Daughters almost unanimously defend a women's right to matrimony grounded in mutual understanding, autonomy, and individual connections.[10]

---

[10] Kurzman's (2008, pp. 315–319) findings regarding young women in Iran today demonstrate similar gender-conscious attitudes to marriage.

One married daughter from Tehran, Hoda D., confessed: "To be honest, I did not care that much about my husband's level of religiosity or political leanings. As long as he prayed and fasted, I was happy, but my parents were very concerned."[11] Since mothers typically view adherence to state-promoted religious and political orientation as a priority in selecting a partner, their daughters' emphasis on other values disrupts cultural patterns. However, highlighting an intergenerational exchange, one wife of a martyr, Golnaz T., remembers a young woman in the neighborhood who became pregnant prior to marriage: Community women bought her trousseau and quickly prepared her for marriage. Surprisingly, the relationship between mothers and daughters in this social group generally does not reinforce patriarchal norms; rather, it works to challenge them.

Wives and daughters' exchanges during group interviews also reveal generational transformations. Mahbobeh A. argues that she does not accept the concept of impossible and fully believes in her own capabilities. In a separate interview, her mother describes her as the "man of the house," arguing that she could not have raised her three children without her older daughter's presence. During another group interview in Tehran, a mother attempted to overlook harsh familial treatment, but her daughters, Kosar C. and Mahsa C., interrupted – the only time they did so during our two-hour group interview with several other wives and daughters. They bravely shared a memory of a family wedding to which their mother was not invited because many believed she might seduce the young groom.[12]

In addition to ruling the status of those nearby as irrelevant, their act also breaks through social etiquettes imposed on women, which most abide by regardless of private values, to publicly reveal their own assessment of a circumstance revolving around gender and sexuality. Others' gaze and moral judgment did not prevent these sisters from revisiting and voicing objection to the gender discrimination their mother tolerated years ago.

These examples of marriage and gender identity illustrate a more conservative understanding of social relations than those elucidated in Mahdavi's research (2007, p. 451). The political spectrum nonetheless can be shared. Rituals that are individually assessed as restrictive of women's quality of life are reconfigured despite unequivocal moral principles promoted by the state as well as cultural preferences. Importantly, this is while families of martyrs, particularly daughters, are expected by all to authorize the status quo most rigorously.

---

[11] Interview, Tehran, Iran, June 2008.
[12] Interview, Tehran, Iran, June 2008. Touba (1987, p. 124) highlights this as a common societal perception toward widows in Iran.

5.3   Redefining Statuses

Tensions between the past and present can also be seen in women's determinations to (re)direct state discourse on the war and dismiss propaganda regarding participants' identities.[13] For elements within the Islamic Republic, female relatives of martyrs are eternally tamed revolutionaries – in love, willing to lose it all, steadfast sufferers – who, while always on standby, let boys be boys and willingly opt out of real politics. Elshtain's (1987) identification of the "Just Warriors" for males and "Beautiful Souls" for females as the two most recurrent socially constructed images during wars in the West is also seen in the Iranian experience. Dismantling this passive and depoliticized identity is a specific illustration of some women's resistance to local instrumentalization of their status. Struggles on behalf of martyrs' wives with more liberal backgrounds, to present the war as a national experience and not a gauging factor of loyalty and "Iranian-ness," reaffirm their right to construct identities autonomously.

A group of women including several martyrs' wives deliberately started an NGO to rebuild Khorramshahr; they state that the city belongs to "all of the Iranian people" and have chosen to operate as an NGO despite complications in securing funding. The women make explicit a desire to take action for the "common good" (Nielsen, 2008, p. 283) and redeploy experiences with political injustices to current encounters (Isin, 2008, p. 39). Golnaz T. who often lectures in schools and universities, explains:

> I want the youth to know that martyrs were not different from us; they were men living in their history, but they were able to examine current realities with an elevated view. This notion that they were of another creed is incomplete in my view. For example, my husband allowed my daughter to wear nail polish – he supported women's rights – whenever a couple came to our home in need of guidance, he always told me to take the man's side and that he would support the woman. (Interview, Tehran, Iran, June 2008)

Using her *self* to administer a new moral standard following her husband's martyrdom, Golnaz returned, in a public setting with other families present, the few items she had received from the Foundation of Disabled War Veterans to illustrate that "nothing belongs to us; we have to take care of each other."[14]

During the group interview, one conservative woman whom I had interviewed at length previously, Farideh O., insisted on being present

---

[13] On the one-dimensional presentation of the "war generation" in Iran, see Farhi (2004).
[14] Interview, Tehran, Iran, June 2008.

for this focus group's conversation. Throughout the two-hour group interview, she attempted to dominate the discussion, interrupted other women's analyses, and restated ideas that might challenge the current state of political affairs in Iran. Importantly, she superficially unified Khomeini's charismatic influence and political will with that of Khamenei, the current leader of the Islamic Republic. However, another woman from this group of female war veterans, Ziba M., did not permit this perspective alone to shape discussions that tended to oscillate between the tenses. It was important for most of the participants to delineate and sort out differences between the Islamic Republic of 1980–1988 and the governance that has emerged in the post-Khomeini era. At one point, Ziba looked straight and motionless into my eyes and claimed emphatically, "No one – and I mean no one – was ever able to capture the place Imam Khomeini had in our hearts,"[15] to counter her colleague's attempts at blurring this politically significant distinction. The other six women in the room all became silent except for one, keeping quiet as an expression of solidarity with this subtle yet powerful statement. As she verbalized this differentiation, recognized by others living within the country during its postrevolutionary history, her voice of discontent amid political pressures, even within the room and from her closest peers, testifies to the influential and divisive factor that personal autonomy has become in post-1988 Iran. Assertions regarding the war's history constitute the entitlement of martyrs' wives to individually and publicly memorialize the war as well as the present. Additionally, it is also a subconscious acknowledgment of a nation's right to narrate a past currently monopolized by elite discourses and societal guardianship.

Some daughters, particularly those in major cities, discuss the body to acknowledge gender experiences hidden by the dominant hegemonic discourse that infuses their lives. Self-disclosure, a culturally unacceptable form of personal narrative, claims a woman's right to trust *her story* in addition to a nation's entitlement to give public voice to private experiences. The body of Faranak B. was shaped by, and became transformative in, family relations when she was heavily medicated after her mother's accusations that she was dating.[16] Faranak explains:

They told me I have depression and placed me on antidepressants. They did not know what else to do with my unruliness. Today the skin on my body is stretched and loose because of the years on those pills. Naturally this is hard for me because I can see on my body the result of my resistance. (Interview, Tehran, Iran, June 2008)

---

[15] Interview, Tehran, Iran, June 2008.   [16] Interview, Tehran, Iran, June 2008.

With the support of a female employee at the Martyr Foundation, she was finally granted the right to live alone in Tehran. She goes on to decipher how the state's delimited depiction of identities actually restricts daughters' unique expressions of the Shi'i faith and causes social divisions within the group. Paradoxically, this results in the state's suppression of actual overlaps that exist in official and popular values and interests. Faranak elaborates:

No one understands my identity. I dress modern and am very *sheytoon* [mischievous], but I talk to God all the time and cry. I have been to Syria, Karbala, and Mecca; no one understood why I wanted to go to these places. But I have a strong spiritual and religious side. Unfortunately, in my society no one looks at the heart; they look at your body. (Interview, Tehran, Iran, June 2008)

While hoping to relocate to the West to escape from the watchful eye of Iranian society, she was not dismissive of the US role in the war and cherished her father's memory outside both local and international struggles over her identity. Notably, her best friend was a martyr's daughter from a traditional and religious background, but during hours of conversations, their different levels of allegiances to the state and religious observance was not a divisive issue.

Daughters' artwork reconfigures traditional notions of beauty and sexuality through an emphasis on the body as a resistive yet perishable vessel for the spirit. For one professional painter and designer, Taraneh X., it was the image of women, oftentimes in rural and village settings, standing alone or together, that was representative of her imagination. One portrait of a woman in bright-colored and loose-fitting clothing highlights the mores of a tribal identity with a geometrically balanced and refined-featured face, captivating and mesmerizing viewers in search of modern versions of "Persian beauty." However, a disfigured hand resting on her waist upholds the proportional upper torso to cut her body in half, as she silently enumerates with a stare the destructions paralleling her long-term steadfastness. With contestation between flesh and spirit publicized, the portrait also works to complicate, perhaps reject, the way in which beauty and sexual appeal are understood in modern Iran. Additionally, it demonstrates that fragmented and silenced voices can disrupt and manipulate aesthetic eroticism in pursuit of gender interests. The portrayal of a lone woman standing also serves as a graphic expression and protest of heroism in the country today and invites viewers to rethink the people, acts, and bodies that deserve emulation and praise.

For Kosar C., marriage was an option that she had long rejected, having seen her older sister's predicament of living in an abusive marriage and her mother's status as a widow. However, I was surprised to see vast amounts of decorations for Persian weddings on display in the living room, exemplifying elements of traditional and modern attributes, that were her various projects as a full-time wedding decorator. Similarly distancing herself from a traditional lifestyle but finding pleasure in new forms, Tina C., a daughter of a martyr in Sardar village near Khuzestan Province's Shushtar County and whose father was killed in an air raid at his place of work, claims that although she is single she prefers spending her spare time on the internet.[17] Her wish is to connect with the world outside her small town; at the time of our interview she was taking computer courses to develop new skills to facilitate her interests.[18] In the artistic and expressive realm at least, gender issues emerged as being notable to daughters, and not the country's relations with the West – a feature of national politics oftentimes emphasized by wives in poetry, letters, and self-presentations.

The emphasis for daughters was placed on their desire to communicate with peoples outside of their familial, and perhaps national, boundaries. Without comparing or judging their experience in relation to others, it appears that shedding light on international disputes was also not at the forefront of daughters' self-presentations through the arts. Whether the physical is one's own body or an extension of it through portraits and crafts, young women in this social group are using tangible subjects and objects to show and share their lived and imagined realities of life in the Islamic Republic with a wider audience.

During discussions with these daughters, I also encountered examples of when an "act of demonstration" (Walters, 2008, p. 194) against misuse of their identities overlapped with acts of citizenship. At times, daughters who supported the state's Islamization project and privately identified themselves as children of martyrs refused to publicly claim the citizenry status due to the exploitation of their social group. Instead, withdrawal and silence initiate an alternative stance toward both state and societal structures of power – a position that ignores who one's father is for political membership. For many daughters, much like other youths, the flesh has become a political terrain for reexamining principles that shape acts of citizenship, as well as the public and private boundaries associated with them.[19]

---

[17] Interview, Sardar, Shushtar, Iran, July 2008.
[18] On the liberating effect of cyberspace for Iranian women, see Nouraie-Simone (2005).
[19] For an illustration within middle-class secular urban youth communities in Tehran, see Mahdavi (2009).

For wives and daughters of martyrs from more traditional backgrounds, there exists less skepticism regarding state-promoted depictions of martyrs' families and more emphasis on establishing personal autonomy through state support and collaboration. Most women with this perspective live in state-funded housing for families of martyrs; thus, their political evolutions are shaped by a forced communality. Nonetheless, this is another instance where intersections between self-identification and state influence conceal the destabilization of routine governance that takes place. While both state elites and locals view families of martyrs as a homogenous group, women's individual quest for autonomy, as well as the acts of citizenship that facilitate it, results in distinctions within this supposedly uniform social group. As they assert their own right to autonomy, these women simultaneously endorse personal independence as a national entitlement.

The overlap between personal and collective autonomy became evident as my fieldwork in 2008 coincided with the anniversaries of the deaths of both Ayatollah Khomeini and Fatemeh al-Zahra.[20] During the gatherings that I attended in a Tehran neighborhood that mostly housed families of martyrs, women were less engaged with each other and were instead more focused on spiritual enlightenment through meditation and note-taking while the female religious jurists lectured. Following the session, they quickly dissipated with little discussion afterward.

The point of reference and transformation was often the self and not others – a rejuvenation and building of one's relations with the higher power through a thorough contemplation of personal responsibilities. During ceremonies under state guidance, women create a private space away from the home and in the most public of settings, while simultaneously becoming active agents in personal identity formation. Several interviewees, who have remarried since their first husband's death, revealed that they were not permitted to participate in these gatherings. They argued that their second husbands were at times uncomfortable with their emphasis on remaining members of this community and would prefer that the women had as little interaction with other women as possible. Poran D. discussed at length how she managed to plan her day despite the confinements of her second marriage:

I get up really early on Thursday mornings and make lunch, then I leave for *Behesht Zahra* [cemetery] and go to *shahid*'s grave [referencing her martyred husband]. Then, I walk all around the graveyard and say prayers for other

---

[20] The daughter of Prophet Mohammad, wife of Imam Ali, and mother of Imam Hussein. The lineage of all twelve Shi'i Imams traces back to the Prophet through Fatemeh al-Zahra.

shahids, my friends' partners. Then I go and say a prayer for the 72 *tan*, and believe me, this has more spiritual value for me than an entire day at the park … sometimes I even do this twice a day. (Interview, Tehran, Iran, May 2008)

Several other interviewees revealed that their husbands did not permit them to attend these gatherings; however, these women scheduled their time to make a brief absence unnoticeable. Despite this restriction, women from traditional familial backgrounds who remarried argue that they now have more control over their time, an ability to partake in activities of their choosing, and an opportunity to strengthen their character through religious studies and worship.

Another interviewee, Marjan N., explained how she structured her time to attend the religious events she enjoyed: "I make lunch on Friday in a way that I will be able to attend at least half of Friday Prayer at the University of Tehran. If all goes well, I may even attend the entire program."[21] This use of personal autonomy is a further example of growing assertiveness despite normative and assumed restrictions. Through these voluntary gatherings, women give life to the most significant foundational structure of the Islamic Republic, martyrdom and remembrance of its values. As their entitlement to social capital rises as a result of these meetings, distinctions can even separate and elevate women's statuses above those of state elites.

Importantly, prior to and following the gathering, many women spoke to me, often only to reiterate, or from their perspective *expose*, the US role in prolonging the Iran–Iraq war through its support of Saddam Hussein. Marking historical memory both interconnected to, and distinct from, state elites' influence, this social group continues to memorialize the international community's violation and interruption of their lives during the 1980–1988 period. An abstract remembrance of the Iran–Iraq war is synonymous with recollections of US–Iran relations after the fall of the Pahlavi Monarchy for some wives of martyrs. Participation in neighborhood religious events, in addition to accommodating the mainstream state-promoted political–religious agenda, is also a silent acknowledgment before state elites and locals alike of the Islamic Republic's original claimants. With many of the women having lost brothers, fathers, and other relatives and friends, in addition to their husbands, their self-determined presence or *shahadat* becomes citizenship par excellence.

During the gatherings, I also met young women not from martyr families but who had deliberately sought out and married war veterans. Many of these women were too young for marriage during the war.

---

[21] Interview, Tehran, Iran, May 2008.

This act of citizenship in the postwar years signifies how some women have attempted to both demonstrate their political stances and delineate personal autonomy grounded in political identities. For the wives of disabled veterans who married their partners following the end of the war, the institution of marriage was explicitly used to meet the state's needs. Many women decided to marry veterans as an unequivocal expression of support for the post-1979 political establishment. These women's acts of citizenship caused great disruptions in familial norms and preferences, while also placing them in the position of authority in marriages that create what are oftentimes female-centered families. Regardless of their personal backgrounds, most women openly admit to not initially being in love, and they even describe their living arrangements as being structured by a comprehensive sacrifice of worldly pleasures on their behalf. However, these realities do not mar the great respect women feel for their husbands' service to the state. For this group of women, therefore, marriage can be understood as a tool for continued participation in state construction through commitment to those they view as its original architects.

Women in this post-1988 social group encountered conflict within their families due to the socially stigmatized lifestyles they chose through this radical move for personal autonomy. Kobra A. recalls that employees at the Martyr Foundation where she was employed at the time implored her to reject this form of marriage. This event took place after 1988, and she was also much younger than her suitor. Her colleagues argued that a woman who has not had a previous marriage (and was therefore assumed to be a virgin) should not make this grand sacrifice; instead, disabled veterans should marry martyrs' wives.[22]

Nevertheless, they married, and Kobra A. states the following about their relationship: "I don't just tolerate him; I truly enjoy being in his company."[23] Importantly, many of these women do not believe that their radical marital decision overturns the privileges women traditionally have as first-time brides. Susan E., from Tabriz and in her mid-thirties, whose husband is paralyzed from the waist down, expresses that she still expects him to help her raise their son and carry out his share of the housework. She stresses that his physical disabilities have not prevented her from implementing contemporary perspectives on gender roles that other young women from her generation and class background have in their marriages – that her role is not one of a caregiver and sexual object. For this group of women, establishing independence in the institutions of marriage and family has been supported, perhaps even advanced, by their preferences to marry war veterans.

The site that women occupy is just as interconnected to their acts of citizenship as the individuals with whom they live. Wives who reside in designated housing communities independently reinstate "piety" as an act of citizenship (Turner, 2008, p. 123) that parades personal superiority and makes distinctions within, and between, social groups. These women use the extraordinary moral regulations expected of families to become local heroes as exemplary citizens of an Islamic Republic. Women's neighborhood roles present a particular form of citizenship in the post-1979 state where Islamic morality became a necessary component of local and national governance.

Habibeh R. is often visited by other women in the neighborhood who are interested in the Shi'i tradition of connecting with martyrs and seeking salvation through their interceptions in daily life. The ability to connect with martyrs through dreams is believed to be an indicator of a *del-e paak*, or pure heart, which only the most pious can achieve. It brings them closer to God than others and thus distinguishes social excellence. On the other hand, the communal dimensions of the Shi'i faith also propel virtual acts of citizenship and bring women together through collective rituals, such as the interpretation of dreams. A shared reading of the divine, an ancient Shi'i-Persian tradition, balances the exclusionary aspects of neighborhood life for wives and daughters. By acting on Islamic moral teachings and endorsing the state's emphasis on physical embodiment of religious precepts, some women's local status is elevated and their autonomy expanded, oftentimes without ever stepping foot outside their home.

Many wives, particularly those from less affluent backgrounds, shared a spiritual connection with martyred husbands through dreams. Importantly, these women were either in troubled second marriages or had not remarried. Women not permitted to discuss or remember first husbands in a second marriage find the autonomous space in dreams in which to encounter their first husbands and receive lifelong advice, emotional support, and guidance in decision-making (Sameti et al., 1382/2003, p. 40). Dreaming becomes an act of citizenship that forges an arena for implicit and unspoken contestation over patriarchal authority, especially for those unable to independently select partners. Widows in Iran have few opportunities for remarriage due to the cultural importance of virginity. While a higher socioeconomic status can make the cultural bias less definitive, many war widows, particularly those in rural regions, do not have this option.

In contrast, although daughters similarly claimed to feel a spiritual connection with their fathers, they reported feeling this presence while awake. This foregrounds a virtual approach toward state construction as they embark on immediate responsibilities and decipher moral rights. Whether meeting martyred husbands in dreams or sensing a long-lost father's presence while awake, expanding the political field to other worlds forges a link with influential state spokespersons. The act creates a transcendent sense of belonging for female citizens living without their most valued male companions in an Islamic Republic.

5.4   Intersections of Times and Acts of Citizenship Today: "If Shahid Was Chosen, Then So Was I"[24]

Studies of war and state formation in the Middle East focus on the politics of remembering and its significance in constructing a nation. Furthermore, regional studies of the family focus solely on male control, practices, and power; less frequently is the family unit seen as an inter-relational structure.[25] In this section I am interested in understanding the relationship between remembrance of the past and the contemporary state, and I place particular emphasis on exploring how familial structures and relations were revised as wives and daughters came to terms with their postwar identities. Like the previous section, the focus is on disclosing aspects of the war's legacy through an investigation of remembrance and acts of citizenship today. However, whereas in the previous section I examined how tensions between the past and present propel acts of citizenship, this section studies the intersections between virtual acknowledgments of the past and actual reconstructive efforts today. To this end, I show that a lens focused on time periods in isolation may keep hidden the full spectrum or falsely classify the ways that people imagine themselves in the aftermath of war.

Often wives began interviews by clarifying that they were *political* partners with their husbands, and not merely companions in the intimate realms of life. They argue for an understanding of martyrdom as more than an end to a loved one's physical presence. They also view themselves as constructors of the autonomous journey their partnerships cultivated and the self-development they simultaneously endured, and at times initiated, with husbands. Challenging the image of a strong woman standing behind a heroic husband, Golnaz T. noted:

---

[24] An interviewee used this phrase in Tehran in May 2008 and similar phrases abounded among interviewed wives of martyrs.

[25] Joseph (1994) also makes this point in her study of brother–sister relations in the context of upholding patriarchal family structures in Lebanon. Similarly, Sayigh (2002) draws this conclusion regarding mother–daughter relationships in her study of non-elite Palestinian women in Lebanese refugee camps.

I want my society to understand that there would have been no *shahid* without me and me without him: We were partners. The great love he had for this world, humanity and his faith could be seen in our relationship, and this is what is valuable, not simply shouting slogans ... he was *ashegh* [in love] and so was I, and we are all capable of loving this way. It is only love that leads one to sacrifice so much, building in the process, and this is the essence of *shahadat* [martyrdom]. (Interview, Tehran, Iran, June 2008)

For women who understand themselves as having been involved in this type of partnership, activism in their current lives represents a continuation of their own characters, not just a remembrance of their first husbands. Moreover, in their wills, many martyrs described their wives as irreplaceable partners in their growth, without whom they would not have spiritually risen to the levels needed for martyrdom.[26] Memories of these short yet fulfilling partnerships led to an additional cultural transformation, permitting some wives of martyrs to remember their first husbands and previous lives on a temporal continuum. For many, martyred husbands are their partners in the next world, while current husbands are worldly companions; this is a marital reality that coexists with the dominant cultural view that women are to have only one life partner.[27] Through this perspective on their own act in engendering the noble status of martyrdom for their husbands, their capacities as citizens in the post-1979 state are reconstructed as women undertake new roles as war widows.

In discussions of contemporary acts of citizenship that establish or maintain autonomy, women also remember the personal contributions they made to the war. Habibeh recalls helping her soldier husband decipher war plans in Khorramshahr prior to his martyrdom:

The soldiers transferring water to the front continually reached *shahadat* [martyrdom] because their vehicle[s] could be detected by Iraqis and came under fire. I told my husband to dig water wells in the yards of deserted homes and move water to the front from house to house; this way there would be less possibility for injuries and death. And as far as I know, this is the approach implemented in Khorramshahr during those first days. (Interview, Tehran, Iran, June 2008)

She goes on to argue that the prospect of being a "stay-at-home" housewife in a second marriage was unacceptable because she was "too active" during the revolution and war. The reality of this discourse of personal intention became apparent as a result of an unexpected incident that occurred during our interview. I witnessed her heated debate with an

---

[26] This view is also expressed by Kamari (1385/2006, p. 22).
[27] Interview, Tehran, Iran, June 2008.

employee from the Institute for the Art of Resistance, a young freelance writer authoring her upcoming memoir and my companion for the day.

At issue was a private memory of her husband that she had elaborated on during their several months of interviews but had prohibited the institute and the writer from making public. She held the author personally responsible for protecting the confidentiality and integrity of her story. While she attempted to use the time we had together to also emphasize my responsibility to present the Islamic Republic in a "positive" light, she herself was unwilling to permit national history to be undermined for political reasons. She expressed a preference for not disclosing certain memories in her memoir as it might give the Western "enemy" an opportunity to depict inaccurately Iranian men during the war. However, her debate with the young writer was carried out in front of me, intrinsically an "outsider," most notably due to my identity and responsibilities as a researcher. Hence the effectiveness and individual capacity to establish conflictual categories in analyses, representations, and discourse are invalidated through her own enactment and emphasis on self-presentation.

The freelance writer who accompanied me for the day interrupted our interviewee upon this request by stating that *she* plans to write the story of the wife of a martyr and war veteran exactly as she hears and understands it, dismissing any suggestions of self-censorship when writing in Farsi for an Iranian audience. The distinction between her rights as an Iranian author writing in Iran and my rights as an outsider writing in "enemy" territory became clear. Therefore, the author's target readers and location help determine a scholar's permitted agenda, priorities, and voice from the perspective of many living in the Islamic Republic of Iran today.

Similarly, Golnaz T. refused to give permission to the Institute for the Art of Resistance to publish her memoir. She objected to how parts of her narrative had been written by another freelance writer employed by the institute.[28] Publication of the memoir has been delayed for over a year due to this conflict.

Reaffirming personal authority with a similar claim to autonomy, Somayeh R., who defied her family to serve on the front lines of the war, is today reexperiencing similar social alienation as she selects a new career path. She has started an Islamic clothing line, despite former colleagues' dismay at her entrepreneurial spirit, to create fashionable apparel for Iranian women that are both appealing and conform to cultural standards of pudeur. She hopes to counter the current dictate

---

[28] Interview, Tehran, Iran, June 2008.

of Islamic attire by state elites and the diasporic community alike, which leads to fissures between Iranian women "inside and outside of the country."[29] Somayeh volunteers at Imam Musa Sadr's Research Centre and is focused on a project that fosters dialogue to combat the country's increasing factionalism. During our last meeting, after several previous interviews, I was surprised to learn of her deep admiration for Imam Musa Sadr, a leader who for many was the spiritual founder of Hezbollah and a believer in the unification of politics and Shi'i thought; from Sadr's life, this interviewee finds his skills in social relations – bringing together the diverse nation of Lebanon despite important political differences – to be of primary importance. Women's memories of overturning cultural patterns out of a sense of responsibility to state and society during the revolution and war transmute to sanction new sites and identities as accessible for Iranian women today.

For many women, remember, their first encounters with marital and parenting issues were founded in trust and mutual recognition. (See Chapter 4.) As such, the culture of both institutions became more contested and negotiable for women living in the postwar years. Established as irreplaceable partners in marriage and parenthood during the revolutionary and war years, women gained the confidence to reassess and modify child custody customs and gender roles as war widows.

The harmony Somayeh has solidified between remembrance and contemporary acts of citizenship are captured in how she discusses both her daughter and late husband. While most remarried wives of martyrs refer to deceased husbands as *shahid*, she remembers him as Nargis's father, signifying both his continued role in their adult daughter's life and her refusal to view him merely as a part of the past. And this despite her remarrying more than fifteen years ago. Moreover, her decision is a significant cultural transformation: Rarely are women in Iranian marital culture allowed to love two men at once; also, they are often separated even from fathers, brothers, and other male relatives following marriage. She prioritized raising her daughter under routine conditions and opposed the isolation of martyrs' children in particular neighborhoods and schools, as well as their special treatment in society.

Using the refusal of other families to show affection to their children in front of her daughter as an example, Somayeh noted: "I told my relative and friends, no, hug your children in front of my daughter! This is the normal interaction between children and parents; your children have a father and she does not."[30] During our interview, she stressed the natural

---

[29] Interview, Tehran, Iran, May 2008. [30] Interview, Tehran, Iran, August 2008.

rhythm of life and the importance of learning to move with, instead of struggle against, its progression. She allowed her daughter to be the first to propose a discussion about her father, not wanting to bombard her with heroic legacies and instead hoping that Nargis would self-initiate a rediscovery. From a young age, she emphasized to Nargis that she has a physically present father, her second husband, but that her spiritual father is always with her and is irreplaceable. Importantly, she made this reality equally clear to her second husband prior to their marriage.

These difficult negotiations did not go unnoticed by daughters. Highlighting the transmutable quality of inherited memories, while daughters of martyrs tend to abide by religious guidelines more rigorously than others, very few interviewees remembered Fatemeh al-Zahra as their role model. They usually responded to this question by nominating their mothers' bravery as single parents to be a source of desired emulation.[31] This perspective reveals an intergenerational transformation when contrasted with martyrs' wives, who referred to the state-promoted role model for Shi'i women. Mothers' revisions of gender and familial and parenting relations, then, have expanded daughters' conceptualizations of heroism.

When it came to confronting traditions, male veterans often defended their fallen comrades' wives, presenting another dimension of revised marital and parenting approaches. This memory, both for wives and their children who often stood beside them during the initial days of bereavement, shades their support for different segments of the Revolutionary Guards and Basij today. While some wives and daughters of martyrs attend marches in support of the state's military forces, others, often with more liberal backgrounds, support the original ideals of the revolution that led to the formation of organs such as Basij. This group, however, refuses to align itself with current organizational structures, political perspectives, and military organizations' role in Iranian society. As one wife of a martyr, Azadeh Y., stated: "I consider myself a Basiji, although I no longer wish to be a member of Basij."[32] Women's complex relationships with these organs became more apparent during the interviews. In conversation, many wives of martyrs remember their husbands' friends just as fondly as their own partners. These memories influence their analysis of current affairs in Iran. Somayeh recounts:

I did not just lose my husband, I lost a lot of people that I worked with closely and loved dearly; remembering is not just about him and I certainly did not support [the state] because of him. (Interview, Tehran, Iran, August 2008)

---

[31] Sadeghi (2008, p. 253) draws a similar conclusion in her study.
[32] Interview, Tehran, Iran, June 2008.

Hence, remembrance of how the common pursuit of national defense united men and women also complicates women's relations with the new generation of male state elites. Battles over the war's memory are fought by women in this social group, not only in remembrance of deceased husbands but also for living war veterans whose sacrifices and character they know just as well. Veterans link the dead and living war heroes to give heightened meaning to diverse national demands in current Iranian politics.

Daughters of martyrs also remember receiving attention, kindness, and fatherly love from their fathers' warfront friends. Additionally, many daughters remember viewing Khomeini as their surrogate father due to his empathizing with families of martyrs on a level and intensity that others did not demonstrate.[33] Two sisters, Yasamin L. and Yekta L. from Ahvaz, argued that his death was more painful than their father's because he was the strongest and most consistent male ally they had had since childhood.

For some, however, learning to accept that they did not have a father distinguished them from other children of martyrs. Many of the daughters I interviewed view "family" as their siblings and mother and stress that they cannot imagine living with a man or having a father. Daughters who are now married recount the difficulties they had in learning how to live and interact with husbands, having never seen marital life close-up. Often estranged from other family members, the lack of male support was an imminent worry and a reality they knew all too well. Memories spur women's disruptions of current practices in the Islamic Republic, but they can also shield them against disruption of a governing apparatus so closely connected to their intimate lives.

While women's status as partners and parents changed, relations with their own parents and families also transformed in the long term. Homa K., who became a follower of Khomeini and whose husband served in the war, remembers not seeking solace with her parents, who disapproved of her decision to participate in post-1979 Iranian politics. Her notion of family now included those who were dedicated to the notion of Islamic government and Khomeini, and the role of her own parents in her life lost its significance. She instead focused on fostering the relationship with her husband. Their closeness and "solidarity in solitude,"[34]

---

[33] From the establishment of the Islamic Republic up to his death, Khomeini consistently demanded that state elites, particularly those employed by the Martyr Foundation, meet the needs of families of martyrs, prior to and following the 1979 revolution, to the highest of standards; see Khomeini (1385/2006, volume 17, p. 17; volume 18, p.1; volume 19, p. 404; volume 20, p. 422; volume 21, p. 365).

[34] Interview, Ahvaz, Iran, July 2008.

she believed, exemplified the values she most wanted to instill in her four small children. Therefore, materialism was not central to her maternal responsibilities as it may have been for mothers of previous generations. Rather, faithful adherence to principles she believed would benefit her children in the long term were sought, and in the process, her independent identity was also reaffirmed.

I witnessed what this meant, and understood it, through her conversations regarding how "different" they are from others in their close-knit family. While living in the same apartment complex as her brother, his wife, and two children, Homa and her two daughters and sons are alone in their adherence to strict Islamic guidelines in attire and rituals. They describe how isolated and alone they feel, even with their own family, because of their voluntary decision to live in accordance with Islamic values. The daughters described family gatherings and weddings where they could not find modest yet stylish clothing to wear that suited their age. In another example, when their aunt, Sanam B., joined us for tea in colorful and revealing tops and high heels and enquired about my life as a single woman living alone in the West, the young girls and their mother remained silent during this portion of our exchanges. Significantly, while acting on different notions of autonomy, respect of each other's independence demonstrated an overall commitment to the freedom of individual will.

The family's emphasis on personal autonomy, however, does not necessarily result in generational agreement over meanings attached to historical experiences. Interpretations of post-1988 politics and historical analyses are at times generationally situated – and opposed. As a guest in their home for several weeks, and throughout my various trips to Iran for fieldwork, I noticed that Homa continued to maintain her stance as an unwavering supporter of the Islamic Republic's decisions regarding the Iran–Iraq war. And this despite many in her family, including her children, espousing significantly different views and making important temporal distinctions within the eight-year period.

During one family discussion for which I was present, her children questioned the state's decision to continue the war following Khorramshahr's liberation. They argued that from that point onward the "imposed" war served the Islamic Republic's interests in consolidating power. She disagreed and emphasized that at the time her love for Imam Khomeini and the revolution galvanized all of her political decisions and efforts. While she agrees with her children on the sacrifices they too endured because of their parents' implementation of political objectives, and in fact expresses much guilt around this issue, she also reiterated that she would repeat her acts of citizenship in the same fashion if given another opportunity. For her, the political stances she took are interconnected with her delineation of objectives in and readings of current affairs. For her children, on the other hand, the meanings associated with historical events are meticulously distinguished within analyses of current politics and indeed are at times negotiated, as they attempt to rectify contemporary problems in Iranian society.

5.5   Conclusion

Using the experiences of wives and daughters of martyrs from the 1980–1988 Iran–Iraq war, I explored acts of citizenship initiated by tensions between the past, present, and future, as well as intersections among multiple temporalities. Case studies showed how the body and lived experiences contest state and societal narratives on the postrevolutionary state, crossing generational, regime, and social boundaries in the process. This chapter suggested that understandings of citizenship could become more revealing and applicable if focus does not rest only on immediate approaches to "regime change" but is also provided on transformation in the Islamic Republic's state-building enterprise. This chapter considered how women encounter the postwar violence that stems from a competition between different social groups for narrating national history and the contentions over memory this process entails. It was argued that another legacy of war in the Middle East, aside from policies and legal changes, may be the desires negotiated and connections made between past and present work to redefine citizenship. The self-made citizens of the state, in turn, work to unite a politically diverse populace that has undergone much political trauma. This chapter illustrated that the aftermath of war did not result in a centralization of state power through dispersion of rights and privileges. Rather, because of women's reconfiguration of state discourse and established orders, female relatives of martyrs managed to claim and act on their status as state makers in the war's aftermath.

Furthermore, examining citizenship as a relational process, this chapter suggests that martyrs' wives and daughters are not only affected by the country's evolving social context; they are also participants in transforming the state into a more pluralistic one in several important respects. First, changes in concepts of self, reconstruction of state organs, and changes in familial traditions each revise how the state is imagined and subsequently governed. Second, women's silent and voiced claims to a redefined notion of autonomy reveal the Islamic Republic's transformative capacities despite its discriminatory legal-rights structures vis-à-vis state structures. Third, in the Iranian experience, social exchanges have lessened the real and imaginary political distances between and within diverse social groups. Finally, as wives and daughters of martyrs self-identify what it means to act as a citizen in the Islamic Republic, the state loses its monopoly on the classification of political memberships. Chapter 6 will examine acts of citizenship among another group that is positioned by the state as followers of the martyrs' path: Hezbollah's cultural activists.

6 Iran's Hezbollah and Citizenship Politics
The Surprises of Islamization Projects in Post-2009 Iran

6.1   Introduction

This penultimate chapter is based on nearly three years of fieldwork at various Hezbollah cultural institutions in Tehran (2012–2014). Here, I examine acts of citizenship among another group touched by the legacies of the Iran–Iraq war, posing the following questions: (1) How have women's rights been addressed during everyday encounters with the state's violation of civil liberties in post-2009 Iran? (2) Do women's acts of citizenship continue to condition the state formation process during this period as well?

However, these women ascribe to a notion of democratic politics that deviates from the Western sensibilities of popular sovereignty. Contrary to acts of citizenship performed by female relatives of war martyrs, post-2009 Hezbollah-affiliated cultural activists view rights to be only one pillar of the state's structure, and not necessarily the most important element of statecraft to be protected. They engage with the tensions that exist between the state's Islamic and Republic elements, and the entanglement of religion and politics, but without necessarily intending to resolve or undo them in the interest of the people. Instead, they struggle to create a state where sovereignty belongs to God and rights are conceptualized and practiced under that framework.

At the same time, one of the constraints on this political objective is the informality that guides the engagement of affiliates with the guidelines of Hezbollah cultural institutes, the Islamic Republic's foundational theories, and the constitution. This context creates space not only to compensate for the state's inability to articulate formal boundaries on citizenship (Ledeneva, 2006) but also to exploit an inefficient system (Ledeneva, 2001), complete with confusion and experimentation.

An examination of Hezbollahi women's citizenship politics and contribution to state formation after the 2009 presidential conflict helps assess my central claim in this book: Different forms and expressions of citizenship can emerge in hybrid regimes, and this process transforms women's status, rights, roles, and responsibilities in conditioning the state's formation.

Members of the transnational Hezbollah movement are loyal supporters of the Supreme Leader in Iran. Hezbollah activists in Iran are part of a pious social group that acts as state agents in various security, political, and social capacities. They believe state sovereignty belongs only to God, are not interested in democratization, and are the Islamic Republic's dominant support base. The term *Hezbollahi* (followers of the Party of God) was first associated with supporters of Ayatollah Khomeini and vigilantes who were willing to violently confront secular and leftist supporters during the 1979 revolution (Gheissari and Nasr, 2006). However, Hezbollah leaders argue that the movement officially formed at the end of the Iran–Iraq war and was a response to the "growth-oriented planning" Akbar Hashim Rafsanjani promoted, which undermined the revolutionary characteristic of the post-1979 Iranian state (Ghamari-Tabrizi, 2009, p. 110). Moreover, Hezbollah's cultural affiliates today strongly oppose violence as a means of garnering political power. A good Hezbollahi citizen in Iran, similar to their counterparts in Lebanon, is most recognizable through an unwavering support of the Palestinian struggle and piety in everyday life (Shaery-Eisenlohr, 2008).

In this chapter, I move into the ambit of citizenship and politics among pro-state Hezbollah affiliates in post-2009 Iran to make this counter-intuitive argument: The legislation of religion is not necessarily a fruitless effort for the state even when it fails to uniformly produce its ideal religious citizen.

Indeed, hybrid regimes' contradictions and ambiguities work in different ways to produce particular types of citizens. In the Iranian case, there exists a disconnect between how autonomy and equality of Muslim citizens are legislated in Hezbollah's cultural institutions, how autonomy and equality are theorized by the Islamic Republic's founding fathers, and how the Muslim citizen emerged from the post-1979 constitution. Within Hezbollah's cultural institutions, there are contentions over the level of autonomy that activists can exercise, although it is generally agreed that this population is more pious than the rest of Iranian society. Conversely, the formal theorization of citizenship by Iran's revolutionary leaders entails an interdependence between individual autonomy and obedience. Finally, the post-1979 constitution engenders, even more, independence through vague references to Islam and the attribution of sovereignty to God alone. The overlap between these three different interpretations of autonomy and equality, and the unwritten "know-how" (Ledeneva, 2006, p. 6) required to navigate them in various contexts, results in unpredictable citizens in quotidian life.

6.2   Post-2009 Renewal of Hezbollah's Cultural Institutions

The Islamic Republic, similar to other states in the aftermath of the 2011 uprisings, intended to redraw the boundaries of the nation after the 2009 unrest. It did so through a more aggressive promotion of its citizenship framework from within society. Importantly, this framework refuses to acknowledge a discourse of rights or critical thought. This occurs despite a legal framework for rights and a politicized population being central to how citizenship is formally conceptualized by the postrevolutionary state's founding fathers (e.g., Ali Shariati and Ayatollah Khomeini). Instead, a depoliticized, obedient form of citizenship is inculcated within Hezbollah's cultural institutions, which are more aligned with pious Muslim subjectivities and quite distant from the independent character of Hezbollah that these political elites also promote. Nevertheless, affiliates entering into Hezbollah's cultural institutions, and striving toward ideal Muslim subjectivities, are identified by the state as being more pious than the rest of the population.

The 2009 presidential election conflict was initially based on the belief that Mir-Hussein Mousavi, not Mahmood Ahmadinejad (2005–2013), had won. However, the protests erupted into a movement demanding a revised citizenry framework. Against this backdrop of depleting authority, the Islamic Republic's leaders sought to both reassure their support base and redraw national boundaries through various Islamization projects. Newly reconfigured cultural institutions in post-2009 Tehran were funded aggressively by the Revolutionary Guards (*sepah-e pasdaran*), Office of the Leader (*beyt-e rahbari*), and the Intelligence Ministry (*vezarat-e etelaat*). By recruiting students from poor or lower-middle-class backgrounds, the regime hoped to promote various Islamization projects to confront social demands for democratic reform.

The creation of new institutions has been a survival tactic for elite leaders in the Middle East amid social unrest (Lust and Ndegwa, 2010). However, seeking an agenda for cultural domination also defines the modern state (Brubaker and Cooper, 2000). In this fundamental sense, Iran's post-2009 cultural plan is similar to other states in the international system.

Following the 1979 revolution, religious institutes and centers flourished in Iran. Similar to other postrevolutionary regimes (Malarney, 2002) Islamization projects have long been sought after by political elites in the Islamic Republic to sustain the revolutionary culture of 1979 and to continue undermining the Pahlavi Monarchy's cultural norms. Arshin Adib-Moghaddam (2006a) has even suggested that one of the reasons for the Iran–Iraq war was Iran's cultural ambitions in the Persian Gulf and the intent to pursue political projects having to do with Iranian Islamism regionally. From a domestic perspective, Stella Morgana (2018) illustrates that the Islamic Republic Party's Islamization of the labor movement began shortly after the 1979 revolution through a revision of leftist posters with Islamic symbols.

Reading through my interview notes and also memoirs and transcripts of other interviews with women involved in the Iran–Iraq war, I was struck by how often these women were simultaneously involved in warfront activities that they specifically referred to as cultural (Aneesi, 1378). As a medical assistant during the war, Shams Sobhani remembers calming mothers that were looking for their soldier sons in the hospital by reminding them of the story of Karbala and the sacrifices of Hazrat-e Zeinab or gathering intelligence from injured soldiers as they came out of the surgery room (Aneesi, 1377c.). Promoting Islamic culture is grounded in the belief that cultures that stand in opposition to Islam work to destabilize the Islamic Republic from within society. This is understood to be one of the greatest dangers for the postrevolutionary state (Abulghasemi, 1382/2003).

To prevent such occurrences, the postrevolutionary state has relied on cultural organizations throughout the country. For instance, in 2003–2004, 30,000 Islamic associations, cultural centers, and offices connected to mosques registered with the Islamic Development Organization in Iran. This increased to about 45,000 (Noruzi and Nouri, 1386/2007) during Mahmood Ahmadinejad's first term (2005–2013) (Homazadeh, 1382/2003). Citizenship rights are not, however, part of the work that such organizations carry out (Homazadeh, 1382/2003). Instead, volunteers and those who work for little pay within these spaces offer religious education to the communities where they are based (Homazadeh, 1382/2003). Significantly, the Ahmadinejad presidency brought with it an attack on cultural institutes created during the Khatami presidency (1997–2005), and other cultural institutes "were severely restricted; the budgets of cultural centers in Tehran were cut by half, while more funding was provided to religious institutions" (Khatam, 2010, p. 220).

For segments of the Islamic Republic's elite, the activism that they prefer inside and outside Hezbollah's cultural institutions is similar to what O'Neill (2010) has termed "Christian Citizenship" in his study of postwar Guatemala. O'Neill has argued that this form of religious citizenship centers on prayer, weeping, fasting, self-discipline, and other traditions of neo-Pentecostal Christianity. He found that his interviewees work to construct the *City of God* through their volunteer activism and struggle to establish peace and "save" Guatemala by means of "spiritual warfare" (O'Neill, 2010, p. 88).

Segments of the security faction that fund Hezbollah's cultural institutions rely on this understanding of religion to engender "good citizens" who are obedient and focus on both duties and the state's delineation of the "true" path to prosperity in this world and the next. The dutiful citizen who "does not ask what the state can do for him/her but what he/she can do for the state" has been a model for conservative citizenship in democratic contexts as well (Delanty, 1997, p. 290; Selbourne, 1994). Similar to other religious movements in the postcolonial context (Meyer, 2004), Hezbollah leaders broadly promote the notion of citizenship as self-governance to better society through a Muslim framework and to maintain control of the state formation process during a moment of crisis.

In addition to their daily acts of devotion, however, ideal citizens of the Islamic Republic, represented by the Hezbollah, should be prepared to follow political instructions handed down from above. As Delanty (1997, p. 290) observes, "the conservative model of citizenship reduces citizenship to something both active and passive; active in that it implies that citizens must actually do something as opposed to being recipients of the state's services; and passive in that citizens are not supposed to engage in critical discourse." The denial of individual autonomy in the creation of cultural artefacts often becomes the first point of explicit and implicit contention between Hezbollah's cultural affiliates and those organs that fund the cultural institutions.

My three years of work with affiliates of post-2009 Hezbollah's cultural institutions illustrates that many interlocutors consciously and, at times, unintentionally regarded themselves as an extension of God's will on earth. A self-governing citizen, as reformulated by my interlocutors, was not a citizen who only espouses Muslim subjectivities geared toward establishing a utopian city on earth through Islamic ritual practices, the miraculous, divine encounters, proselytizing and a return to self. Instead, such a citizen also viewed themselves to be *special* and closer to God than others due to their efforts to achieve higher levels of piety.

This perspective of the self, which is bolstered by the state's support of Hezbollah affiliates through the distribution of resources and religious interpretation, unintentionally fuses God's sovereignty with people's sovereignty. On the one hand, the women and men who frequent Hezbollah cultural institutes are understood by the state as candidates for obedient citizenship with little individual agency; on the other hand, cultural institute supervisors and those funding the institutes are ambivalent toward Hezbollah affiliates that act as leaders. In this context, the only leaders are the supervisors of cultural institutes who hold close relationships with the Office of the Supreme Leader and/or his representatives. The decision to be flexible with respect to how affiliates engage with Islamization projects may be because an exaggerated sense of self is necessary for intervening in societal norms. Additionally, the inconsistencies between different sites of religious legislation do not go unnoticed by political and cultural elites. It seems that rectifying this messiness is understood to be beyond their control and perhaps even detrimental to their larger goal of remaking national culture.

This process of conflating the imposition of religion with the imposition of the self is not unique to the post-2009 period. As Parsipur (2013, p. 134) has argued, during the 1980s the Hezbollahi citizen also insisted not only on imposing Islam onto wider society "but they wanted to force everyone to believe that they and the religion were one and the same." While this characteristic of the Hezbollahi citizens may have remained the same due to their elevated status as the most pious social group, their position within the state had transformed. Iran's Hezbollah today is both a repressive and oppressed movement. As such, there is an almost unreasonable emphasis on individual supporters' acting power.

Once again, the Iranian nation's writer explains this condition well: "Under duress, you create a great 'I' of fantastical strength. You come to believe that you have the power to damn someone, or that with your glare you can destroy your oppressor's peace of mind" (Parsipur, 2013, p. 151). Hezbollah's cultural institutions create an atmosphere conducive to the exchange of ideas, offer access to resources, and bring young men and women from religious backgrounds into the public sphere. Islamization projects are thus often carried out with little philosophical conversations on God, justice, history, the law, social limits, or the sacred. An environment filled with a loss of information and connections results in inconsistent and unpredictable acts of citizenship.

Through this social process, the distinction between God's sovereignty and people's sovereignty, which remains central to politics in the Islamic Republic, becomes less of an obstacle for change. Yet, it also makes that change more unpredictable in a postrevolutionary context. This political consciousness and social positionality conditions citizenship for Hezbollah affiliates and intersects with the Islamic Republic's state-building efforts after 2009.

6.3   The Contours of Citizenship in the Islamic Republic's Formal Discourse

The aforementioned official citizenry framework that is legislated in cultural institutions is incomplete; it only partially resonates with the state's own formal discourses on citizenship and constitutional text.

Importantly, Hezbollah affiliates are well versed in these formal documents and rely on them extensively to justify and explain their activism. Although thinkers such as Shariati and Khomeini hold complex ideas on state–societal relations, they tend to favor obedient citizenship for the majority of the population and most of the time. According to the theorization of Iran's founding fathers, obedience is not simply a blind following of leadership or pious Muslim behavior. Instead, obedient citizenship has autonomy embedded within it, requires critical thought, and demands self-control and a dedication to the formal discourses of the 1979 revolution. The closer that one becomes to this understanding of obedient citizenship, the higher levels of piety they are believed to embody. In turn, their citizenry status elevates them before the state and allows them more authority to delineate autonomy and equality.

The idea of individual and collective rights and responsibilities is extensively addressed by religious ideologues of the 1979 Iranian Revolution but without using the term *citizen* (*shahrvand*). Ideal citizenry subjectivities were also legislated formally and informally. Anti-colonial and revolutionary movements have historically been sites for rethinking established frameworks for doing politics and not simply reactionary responses to the international governing system (Berger, 2004). However, Iran's Islamist leaders seemingly also saw no need to unify the people and their rights under the rubric of citizenship. This might be because the nation-state, while sought after, did not alone determine how Islamist revolutionaries imagined "solidarities," "political modernity," or their larger projects for freedom (Mantena, 2016, p. 301).

In a series of prerevolution lectures that would later be referenced extensively by the Islamic Republic with respect to its citizenship paradigm (particularly after 2009), Shariati argues that in Islam it is not blood, national borders, or kinship that is utilized to build a community. He discusses a borderless community through the concept of *ommat*. He describes this *ommat* as "a human society where all the individuals who share a common goal come together under the same leadership, to move toward their ideal" (Shariati, 1391/2012, p. 20).[1] He defines the life as a member of an *ommat* as an existence based on responsibility and self-cultivation: "Therefore, the goal is not to be human (*bashar*), but to become a human being (*ensan*). Being a member of an *ommat* is not being free and happy. It is moving correctly and swiftly" (Shariati, 1391/ 2012, p. 27). According to Shariati, Islam is also a social revolution in

---

[1] *Ommat-o-Imammat* is a collection of speeches given at Hosseiniyeh-ye Ershad (a meeting hall in Tehran) by Ali Shariati in 1348/1969. Shariati (1391/2012, p. 20).

how it undermines class and produces individuals who are "conscious, free and responsible" (Shariati, 1391/2012, p. 102).

The *ommat* is led by a leader (*imam*) with insights that will result in the most efficient and direct development (*takamol*) of the people. The leader directs people from what they are to what they should be as revolutionary persons. For Shariati, the human being is inherently incomplete and unable to reach God through their own path. Whether he addresses the character of Shi'i imams, debates on alienation, free-thinkers, freedom of choice, or the history of creation, Shariati insists that national unity and cultural authenticity produce healthy societies and content individuals.[2] He strongly advocates critical thinking. He encourages Iranians to question their own history and to break out of the "prison of society."[3] However, in this effort, submission to a leader becomes necessary to generate a genuine revolutionary process of self-actualization.

Shariati remained ambiguous with regard to the issue of rights. This is not because he refused to recognize individual autonomy. For example, he claimed that "man is capable of working like God" because God's divine spirit rests within human beings and allows them to decide on their path and begin to resemble the divine power in their daily lives (Marjani, 1981, p. 6). However, he does seem uninterested in discussing the law. Although he clearly believes in God-made laws, he also insists that responsibility is central to the human experience (Algar, 1979). He argues that if an individual perceives a leader to be intellectually, morally, practically, or religiously unfit, they have the right to reject that leader-ship – even if it means opposing the rest of the community (Algar, 1979, p. 67): "Even if all the people agree with him, you can condemn the leader, and there is no obligation to commit. The reverse is also true: if all the people view the leader as an infidel (*kafar*), it is the right of the individual to remain a devoted follower" (Algar, 1979, p. 67). In this sense, Shariati supports the notion of citizen as an independent subject who can make claims, even perhaps disruptive ones, against a passive concept of citizenship as a member of a collective obeying a leader who is well versed in Islamic thought. Either way, the individual cannot determine their own path to reach God and must obey a trusted leader. However, Shariati avoided a "literalist reading of either *ummah* [religious community] or *imamat* [leadership]" in these early and significant lectures (Chatterjee, 2011, p. 102). As such, it seems that further details regarding the interaction between these two notions should be decided

---

[2] For online access to Shariati's work see: http://anti666.ir/forum/thread-4324.html.
[3] See, for instance, Shariati's *ensan va Islam*: http://anti666.ir/forum/thread-4324.html.

upon in the context that they emerge and by those who intend to construct this form of social order.

It can be argued, then, Shariati's formulation of community enables an interdependence between individual autonomy and obedience. This individual is, however, bounded by the predefined path of an Islamic revolution that they believe is most authentic for the people of Iran. The revolution, in other words, is a tool for establishing an Islamic order that guides individuals and collectives toward prosperity in this life and the eternal afterlife. As Motahhari (1386/2007, p. 92) stated:

An Islamic Revolution is the path for Islam and Islamic values. Revolution and resistance are for establishing Islamic values. We revolt for Islamic values, and we resist for Islamic values. Therefore, the goal for us is Islam. Resistance and revolution are our tools. However, some have mistaken an Islamic Revolution for revolutionary Islam. For them, resistance and revolution are the end goal ... the outcome of this is that we select from Islam, that which places us on the path of resistance, and that which we think does not place us on the path, we reject from Islam.

When Motahhari was challenged during an interview about the irrefutable place of resistance in Islam, he stated: "The principle of *jihad* and commanding what is just and forbidding what is wrong (*amr-e be ma'ruf va nahy- e az monkar*) must be kept alive and should never be abandoned. But that which we oppose is an understanding of Islam solely through *jihad*, claiming that Islam means *jihad* and *jihad* means Islam. This understanding overlooks other Islamic values" (1386/2007, p. 103). That the revolution must be carried out in the name of Islam was a shared characteristic among many thinkers during this period in Iran.

Ayatollah Khomeini regarded Islam as the framework guiding the nation and determining its rights.[4] The people's priority is to serve Islam, and there is no known instance of him using the term *citizenship*. This is probably because he understood laws in postrevolutionary Iran to be divine laws, not profane state ones (Shahbani, 1386/2007). Abiding by God's law imposes certain limits on individual and collective autonomy that, under a secular legal framework, would be negotiable. Shariati's understanding of leadership and community thus resembles Khomeini's notions of state–societal relations: Both seem to agree on a general framework of obedient citizenship.

Unlike Shariati, however, Khomeini addresses rights in legal terms. For Khomeini, and other revolutionary leaders who supported him after the 1979 revolution, autonomy beyond the boundaries of Islam was

---

[4] Ruhollah Khomeini, *Sahefeye Imam*, speech 1358/1979. No. 6: 436.

recognized as being outside the boundaries of the nation-state. But the notion of legal rights belonging to the individual was central in their conceptualization of the nation-state and the Islamic Republic.[5] They often espoused a democratic understanding of rights that legitimizes an independent citizenry that challenges state authority on the basis of self-governance in the name and path of Islam. Similar to other revolutionary factions at the time, Khomeini readily criticized the Pahlavi state for violating citizens' rights, including those of political prisoners.[6] He seemed particularly concerned about minority rights. He, for instance, believed that Sunnis in Iran should have equal rights: "First of all, our Sunni brothers are never a religious minority. We have said many times that our treatment of religious minorities will be very good. Islam views them [religious minorities] as respectable. We will give them all of their rights. They have the right to hold their ceremonies, and they have the freedom to take part in political activities."[7] During a radio message in 1358/1979, broadcast from Qom, he stated that all religious minorities, and indeed all people, are equal in rights to one another.[8]

Khomeini's discussion of rights posits them as a force that advances national independence. For instance, while in Paris in 1978, he observed about the Pahlavi state: "and it has destroyed all the rights of the Muslim nation, all the freedoms; even the rights of minorities have been violated. The nation's independence has been taken, and they have used the country to advance their own interests and that of their [foreign] masters."[9] The term *masters* suggests that he believed nations should have the right to self-determination and should counter international violation of their rights. In his will, Khomeini advises the people, and Hezbollahi youth in particular, to individually stop media sources that they believe promote corruption. Khomeini stated that this level of individual initiative is permissible when formal state institutions are approached but refrain from enforcing Islamic decree within the media.[10] In defense of Islamic edicts, a citizen's independence extends to the edge of unruliness.

Khomeini's views on rights were not only developed in relation to the Iranian case but included the international system as well. He was not opposed to human rights. Rather, he was critical of the double standards

---

[5] See, for instance, the writing of Motahhari (1386/2007) on human rights.
[6] Ruhollah Khomeini, *Sahefeye Imam*, message 1357/1978. No. 4: 157.
[7] Ruhollah Khomeini, *Sahefeye Imam*, interview 1357/1978. No. 5: 292; see also No. 7: 150 and No. 4: 364 for the rights of minorities.
[8] Ruhollah Khomeini, *Sahefeye Imam*, message 1358/1979. No. 6: 462.
[9] Ruhollah Khomeini, *Sahefeye Imam*, interview 1357/1978. No. 5: 185.
[10] See http://farsi.khamenei.ir/imam-content?id=9447, accessed 20 April 2017.

in how they were enforced. When criticizing human rights in a 1356/ 1977 speech in Najaf, he stated: "And this is America that we see in Israel – they have created that place. Look at what they have done to Muslims and what they are doing to them."[11] During an interview in 1357/1978 in Paris, he addressed the Palestinian struggle as a struggle for rights.[12] Decolonization and independence included for Khomeini citizens' rights to have rights as well as to engage in the international support for human rights. For Khomeini, allegiance to the Islamic Republic is performed through independent and transnational activism. However, claim-making is placed within an undetermined Islamic framework and does not include activism that undermines Islamic edicts.

What is significant about Khomeini's engagement with rights is that religion prevails over citizenship. While citizens are to be equal before the law, everyone will not be treated the same in the Islamic Republic. While people do have the right to dissent, this right is not uniformly applied to all people or in all contexts. The state representative (understood broadly) retains the right to intervene and decide how the rules will be applied *in situ*. This is because Khomeini viewed piety (*taghva*) to be the most significant source of distinction between believers, which is also reflected in their status as citizens.[13]

Like Shariati, Khomeini understood independence as embedded within the obedient citizenship framework. Moreover, placing ad hoc limits on citizens that run counter to parts of the social contract is not unique to nondemocratic regimes, Iran, Islam, or the Middle East (Starr et al., 2011). The advantages of relational autonomy have been emphasized elsewhere as well, including the North American context (Fineman, 2004). There is an interesting connection between an individual's level of autonomy and an ambiguous parameter surrounding Islam. The ambiguity derives from two conflicting sources of legitimacy. While one is based on citizens' rights to revolt, freedom, and equality, the other derives from belief and the distinction in belief. Ultimately, the right to exercise autonomy and delineate equality in the Islamic Republic seems to expand as a person's level of piety increases and when Islamic edicts are being violated.

After Khomeini's death in 1989 and Akbar Hashemi Rafsanjani's presidency came a new era in postrevolutionary Iran. As Chapter 5

---

[11] Ruhollah Khomeini, *Sahefeye Imam*, speech 1356/1977. No. 3: 333. There are many instances where human rights are criticized because of Western foreign policy. See, for instance, *Sahefeye Imam*, No. 4: 39, 399–403.

[12] Ruhollah Khomeini, *Sahefeye Imam*, interview 1357/1978. No. 5: 306.

[13] Ruhollah Khomeini, *Sahefeye Imam*, speech 1357/1978. No. 6: 314; Radio message 1358/1979. No. 6: 462.

demonstrated, with the end of the revolutionary period and the exhausting Iran–Iraq War (1980–1988), notions of citizenship and rights expanded. The emergence of the reform movement at the end of the Iran–Iraq War meant that citizens, and not just the elite, acquired the right to participate in defining what is and is not Islamic. Elements within the Islamic Republic's ruling elite began to explicitly refer to the Iranian people as citizens who have rights based on Iran's legal framework (Arjomand, 2002). Much of this had to do with the new interpretations of Islam. Foody (2015a) has argued that reformist thinkers such as Abdolkarim Soroush and Muhammad Mujtahid Shabestari introduced liberal interpretations of Islam in postrevolutionary Iran. Although they relied on different methods, both scholars point out that the interpretation of religion is an individual right and obligation and should not be legislated by elites alone. While Soroush's work highlights the multiple interpretations of Islam and the relevance of individual experience, Shabestari stresses the limits of religious knowledge in addressing many modern issues (Sadri, 2001). Kadivar's work is also significant in that he relies on Islamic sources to question Khomeini's absolutist authority of the jurist, identifying it as one model of an Islamic state among many (Sadri, 2001). With the new assertion in the 1990s of the individual's right to interpret Islam, early revolutionary leaders lost their cultural monopoly.

6.4   Making It (II) Legal: The Independent Citizen and the Post-1979 Iranian Constitution

While the Islamic Republic's founders preferred the state's citizens obedient, though not devoid of autonomy, the constitution tends to engender independent citizenry practices for those who believe that sovereignty belongs only to God. The post-1979 constitution engenders independent citizenship through the centrality of God's sovereignty. The postrevolutionary Iranian constitution has been studied as a poorly constructed document that deliberately and/or implicitly suppresses citizenship, even though it has a chapter titled "The Rights of the People." This is a common and somewhat persuasive reading of the postrevolutionary Iranian constitution when we consider how ambivalent revolutionary leaders were to use the term *citizenship*. As Brown (2002, p. 89) has argued, constitutions in the Middle East often rely on "techniques to limit freedoms, democracy, and pluralism (without publicly repudiating them)." I am nevertheless more interested in understanding what these constitutional inconsistencies reproduce and less in the sinister intents that may have rested behind the drafting process.

The constitution oscillates between an unequivocally independent citizen and an obedient member of the nation within a vague framework of Islam. For instance, Article 9 states:

In the Islamic Republic of Iran, the freedom, independence, unity, and territorial integrity of the country are inseparable from one another, and their preservation is the duty of the government and all individual citizens. No individual, group, or authority, has the right to infringe in the slightest way upon the political, cultural, economic, and military independence or the territorial integrity of Iran under the pretext of exercising freedom. Similarly, no authority has the right to abrogate legitimate freedoms, not even by enacting laws and regulations for that purpose, under the pretext of preserving the independence and territorial integrity of the country.[14]

The participation of an independent citizen with public awareness and ethical sensibilities is legally permitted. The law suggests that this citizen should intervene when leaders undermine individual rights in the name of security or sovereignty. Yet the spatial and temporal boundaries of this law remain unclear, and the precise moment for acting as an independent citizen is murky at best. Importantly, *who* is to determine when a freedom is legitimate (*mashru*) and Islamically sound and *how* freedoms can be reclaimed by the people are left unmentioned. Indeed, the boundaries on rights are more tangible than the level of autonomy one can exert in exercising rights as a Muslim.

A similar movement between an independent citizen and subdued national can be noted in other parts of the constitution. Article 8, for example, begins boldly: "In the Islamic Republic of Iran, commanding what is just and forbidding what is wrong (*amr-e be ma'ruf va nahy- e az monkar*) is a universal and reciprocal duty that must be fulfilled by the people with respect to one another, by the government with respect to the people, and by the people with respect to the government."[15] This first half of Article 8 seems to legitimize independent citizenship. It suggests that if citizens believe an official policy, an official's actions, or local initiatives carry the potential to do harm or are unjust, they have not only the state-sanctioned right but also the religious responsibility to intervene.

However, in its concluding sentence, Article 8's transformative and performative potentials become potentially criminal instead of inherently supportive of vigilant citizens: "The conditions, limits, and nature of this duty will be specified by law (this is in accordance with the Qur'anic

---

[14] www.iranonline.com/iran/iran-info/government/consitution-1.html, accessed 16 March 2017; www.emdad.ir/central/asnad/files/ghanoonasasi.pdf, accessed 16 March 2017.

[15] www.iranonline.com/iran/iran-info/government/constitution-1.html, accessed 16 March 2017. www.emdad.ir/central/asnad/files/ghanoonasasi.pdf, accessed 16 March 2017.

verse; 'The believers, men, and women, are guardians of one another; they enjoin the good and forbid the evil').[16] What is meant by law, and what law outside the constitution will determine when it is time to mobilize as citizens against injustice (*zolm*), remains unknown. Another illustration is Article 20. It was intended to enforce equality between all citizens and states: "All citizens of the country, both men and women, equally enjoy the protection of the law and enjoy all human, political, economic, social, and cultural rights, in conformity with Islamic criteria."[17] The vague reference to Islam has been interpreted as a deliberate effort to limit women's rights (Hoodfar and Sadr, 2010).

One way to interpret the constitution's vague prose and language with respect to Islam is to recognize how a "subordination of law to the dictates of power politics" is encouraged through it (Brumberg and Farhi, 2016, p. 14). However, an attempt to curtail popular power through constitutional prose has been noted in other experiences with constitutional writing, including the American, French, and Polish (Brown, 2002, p. 89). What makes Iran exemplary is that the centrality of God's sovereignty to the entire enterprise is explicitly recognized in Articles 2 and 56. Article 4 does stipulate that the *fuqaha* (experts in Islamic jurisprudence) of the Guardian Council have the right to judge all facets of social and political life to make certain that "Islamic criteria" are upheld, thereby making the clergy God's representatives on earth. However, this does not resolve the ambiguity surrounding what counts as Islamic. This is because the document also holds that the most constitutionally powerful person in the country, the Supreme Leader, "is equal with the rest of the people of the country" before the law (Article 107).[18] This stipulation in the constitution formally recognizes that the clerical leaders of the Islamic Republic are fallible, and therefore it reasserts God's sovereignty once again through an inability to define Islamic.

The ambiguity that upholds the entrance and exit of Islam in the text can also be read as proof of God's sovereignty and the state as a location for slippage – a place where justice can be undermined. Moreover, the text's intended audience is in key moments the Muslim *Ummah* (*ommat* in Persian) and not only the Iranian nation. This points toward God's elusive sovereignty again. From a Hezbollah affiliate's vantage point, for instance, the ambiguity that surrounds Islam is enabling precisely

---

[16] www.iranonline.com/iran/iran-info/government/constitution-1.html, accessed 16 March 2017. www.emdad.ir/central/asnad/files/ghanoonasasi.pdf, accessed 16 March 2017.
[17] www.iranonline.com/iran/iran-info/government/constitution-3.html, accessed 16 March 2017. www.emdad.ir/central/asnad/files/ghanoonasasi.pdf, accessed 16 March 2017.
[18] www.iranonline.com/iran/iran-info/government/constitution-8.html, accessed 31 March 2017. www.emdad.ir/central/asnad/files/ghanoonasasi.pdf, accessed 31 March 2017.

because it recognizes a modern state's limit to uphold the "sovereignty of truth and Quranic justice."[19] God's sovereignty escapes state jurisdiction and has the unique capacity to redeem independent citizenships through its "promise of space" (Cooper, 2014). This constitutional ethos of space-making ingrains a "constant adaptation and change" (Cooper, 2014, p. 4) into everyday life, which makes establishing a postrevolutionary Thermidor (Brinton, 1938) challenging.

Furthermore, during daily acts of worship the yearning for utopia may intersect with what the individual's heart has come to learn to construct: a revised emancipatory political framework. The heart is another site for knowledge and virtue in Islamic traditions (Gianotti, 2011). The heart could generate political work that those following the state's "good citizen" framework never intended to do. Hence, there are multiple ways to study the postrevolutionary Iranian constitution; one approach is to examine its relevance to social contentions through the lens of a sovereign God that rests within and above the text.

6.5 Case Studies: Islamization of the Social Sciences

The final sections illustrate the erratic movement of Hezbollah affiliates as obedient citizenship in post-2009 through case studies examining two Islamization projects: one regarding social sciences, the other women's rights. Together, these case studies demonstrate that when citizenry categories are established through distinction in beliefs but sovereignty remains in the hands of God, those closest to the state can become its most unpredictable advocates. Ultimately, a hybrid regime's legislation of religion through citizenship moves the state in an unknown direction as agents on the ground continually remake the boundaries of autonomy and equality through different frames of reference.

Like his predecessor, Ayatollah Khamenei's call for Iran's independence from Western social influence also promotes securitization. Khamenei first referred to a cultural invasion (*tahajome farhangi*) during the 1990s when discussing the West's influence on Iran. Senior leaders in cultural institutions remember being encouraged by his lectures on a "software movement" (*jombeshe narmafsari*), which began in 2001, to focus on the Islamization of the social sciences.[20] During these lectures,

---

[19] www.iranonline.com/iran/iran-info/government/constitution-1.html, accessed 17 March 2017. www.emdad.ir/central/asnad/files/ghanoonasasi.pdf, accessed 17 March 2017.

[20] http://farsi.khamenei.ir/speech-content?id=3053. This is the earliest lecture I could find on this topic, but more can be located here: http://farsi.khamenei.ir/tag-content?id= 1014.

the Supreme Leader argued that students should focus on developing the Islamic Republic's theoretical power and ideas to strengthen its structural framework. While both of these paradigms stressed that a foreign attack was underway through the social sciences, only after the 2009 presidential conflict was the phrase "soft war" (*jange narm*) used to refer to Western influence in Iran (Mohseni, 2013). Such terminology set the stage for a confrontation with the West. Unable to tackle the country's cultural transformations, some Islamic Republic elites concluded that they not only needed the formation of new organic paradigms but they also had to unequivocally conceptualize this process as warfare.

Thus, the Islamization of the social sciences is partly dependent on and invested in the securitization of society through a deliberate effort at preventing independent citizenship by monitoring and vetting educational institutions. Yet even in this most conservative context, Hezbollah affiliates incorporate unsanctioned, and potentially risky, criticism toward the Islamic Republic to remake the boundaries on rights and equality. Hezbollah affiliates often work as researchers for various state organizations, producing confidential reports on state and society.

As Bayatrizi (2010) has argued, most sociological research in post-revolutionary Iran is funded by and produced for state organizations in the form of confidential reports. The presence of Hezbollah affiliates in these spaces is not surprising, although certainly an indication of their strong connections with the state as these research opportunities are much sought after. Typically, Hezbollah activists are not even required to have a PhD to conduct research for the state. They are given an opportunity to inform national policy, develop skills, and build social networks. Senior scholars based in universities are readily denied such coveted opportunities due to a lack of personal connections with influential individuals.

Additionally, for most researchers who work for the state, this is typically a second job that supplements their income. According to Bayatrizi (2010), there is the additional reality that most of these reports are confidential, lack scholarly scrutiny, and often are not even read by the organizations that funded the research. As such, rarely do researchers cross the regime's "red-lines" during the write-up phase, although they may further explore their findings in their own research or teaching. One researcher, not affiliated with Hezbollah, stated that he often knows what will go into his reports even before he begins the research. However, during our conversations he shared his critical analysis of a variety of social issues that he had worked on throughout the years.

As Daghagheleh and Salime (2018) have argued, "since 2005 the country's currency has lost 75 percent of its value, unemployment hit twelve percent of the general population, and (according to the Statistical

Center of Iran) more than one fifth of college graduates are unemployed." Within these structural spaces, it is significant that some Hezbollah affiliates, who are mostly young students still searching for permanent employment, decide to take on a critical line of argument in their reports. This suggests that at least some of the younger generation of Hezbollah affiliates have used their privileged citizenry status in post-2009 to defend others' rights. In one project report shared with me, several activists were invited by the Iran Think Tank Network (ITAN) to write a report for the National Foundation for Distinguished Scholars (Bonyad Melli Nokhbegan). ITAN was created over ten years before the 2009 presidential crisis, but many leading cultural activists interested in projects related to Islamization are employed by the expanding network. The report intended to help the state find a way to manage the gifted as claimants in the public sphere. It also offered ideas on how to prevent their ultimate departure from the country.

The almost 200-page report begins by briefly mentioning that without institutional reform it will be difficult to meet the needs of the gifted – an obvious reference to state corruption, among other problems – through an intervention that goes against the state's effort at eliminating rights discourses. It also stresses that the state should refrain from imposing specific cultural directives on individuals as it identifies the social engineering of individuals to be contrary to the human spirit. It references the scholarship of contemporary Shi'i thinkers, such as Bagheri and Tabataba'i, to argue that within the Islamic tradition, humans are recognized as embodying agency and interact with the world through their senses. The report thus establishes the people's right to intervene at the center of the Islamization debate.

While the authors delegitimize efforts toward an extensive social engineering project aimed at individuals, they support cultural engineering by acknowledging the Islamic Republic's right to enforce cultural regimes on institutions. They argue that the Islamization of cultural institutions does not mean that all aspects of culture have to be dictated by Islamic law or norms. Rather, some aspects should be directly influenced and other elements of Iranian culture "that are not in conflict with Islam" should be "directed" more gradually. They suggest that the state should employ indirect approaches for promoting its cultural agenda, along with direct ones such as profiling teachers by their adherence to Islamic rituals and symbols (e.g., prayer and *hijab*).

However, this is the edited version of how many in the cultural wing of Hezbollah think about and address these issues in other moments of their social lives in the education system. For instance, I visited a women's dormitory at the University of Tehran in the spring of 2013 to carry out interviews. I arrived late in the evening, unaware that I would not be allowed to leave the dormitory after 10 p.m. because no woman can exit the premises after that time. To leave, I had to get permission from the head of the dormitory who happened to be present that evening due to a conflict that had taken place. I found her in an auditorium filled with angry female students.

Along with the male director of the University of Tehran's security (*herasat*), she stood front and center. The female students claimed that, a few hours earlier, four men who had taken drugs climbed over the fence and chased down a female student. The student began to scream and had a severe panic attack. She suffered an injury, causing her leg to bleed, and she was given a sedative at the hospital. Female students told me that this was the fourth or fifth time that men had invaded the girl's dormitory. (Others mentioned that in reality a female student was caught with her boyfriend and fabricated this story to eschew disciplinary measures.) At any rate, female students had gathered at the scene and refused to return to their rooms until the head of security met with them. All the female students in the auditorium were shouting, but two had microphones and were directing their complaints to the head of security. I recognized both as Hezbollah affiliates that I had met and interacted with at several cultural institutes. One of the students holding the microphone stated:

We are sick of being treated like children and lied to. The university should either provide better protection for us or tell us not to leave our homes in *shahrestan* ... you are only here having this meeting because you are afraid of unrest (*shuresh*) ... you will do absolutely nothing about this problem again as you have ignored it in the past.[21]

In this instance, then, female Hezbollah affiliates understood public performances of religious piety to include forms of morality that escaped the security forces' preferences but which coincided with the sensibilities of others in Iranian society.

I witnessed similar performances during my fieldwork and time at the university. In the fall of 2012, I attended a conference at the sociology faculty of the University of Tehran that addressed the gender quota system that barred women from many fields and was aggressively pursued after 2009. In the summer of 2012, it was announced that some thirty-six universities in Iran were barring women from seventy-seven fields (Shahrokni and Dokouhaki, 2012). Women's entrance into the university has been on the rise since 1998, reaching a peak in 2008 when women made up 66 percent of the entering class (Shahrokni and

---

[21] May 12, 2013, University of Tehran women's dormitory.

Dokouhaki, 2012). The gender quotas in some instances barred women from fields of study understood to be "masculine" such as the oil industry. In other cases, such as the University of Tehran, the fifty-fifty gender quota was applied as had been the norm since 1980s for disciplines such as philosophy. The motivation behind the quotas was to protect men's prospects for securing jobs and pursuing marriage in a context where women had more of a presence in universities (Shahrokni and Dokouhaki, 2012). While we sat in an auditorium filled with several hundred students, one woman stood up and spoke most eloquently. She argued that although she had passed the national entrance exam with high marks and was accepted into a difficult field of research, she was ultimately not given permission to enter the program that year. She argued that this was unfair to her and many women in her position.

I had met the young woman several times at a cultural institute and even interviewed her. Although she expressed her enthusiasm to participate in cultural projects having to do with the Islamization of women's rights during our group interviews, she clarified before other female Hezbollah cultural activists and me that she was not convinced by the state's moral argumentation regarding gender rights. She discussed how, for example, she had to endure her father's excoriation just for attending activities at cultural institutions. She discussed how stressed she was that her brother-in-law had prevented her sister from pursuing a PhD. Her father and brother-in-law were both clergymen and generally opposed women's presence in the public sphere. In their Islamization efforts, some affiliates give those who embody the ritualistic and symbolic components of religion more political space than others. Nevertheless, developing a normative standard for university administration does not prevent Hezbollah affiliates from pushing the boundaries of autonomy and equality in other spaces of the educational system.

6.6 Islamization of Women's Rights and the Anti-feminist Movement Post-2009

Following the 2009 presidential election, the state tried to integrate women with religious backgrounds into Hezbollah's cultural institutions, albeit in segregated spaces. This was in the context where nearly all independent women's NGOs, which had been established during the Khatami presidency, were shut down (Mouri and Batmanghelichi, 2015). Women affiliated with Hezbollah had been integrated into formal and informal state institutions since the 1979 revolution in Iran (Sedghi, 2007). Prior to the 2009 crisis, however, the limited Hezbollah cultural spaces that did exist were mostly occupied by men. Only after 2012 did female and some male affiliates actively contest this trend. The state claimed that feminist ideology played a central role in politicizing women against it in 2009 (Mouri and Batmanghelichi, 2015). The mere presence of women in these institutions is viewed as a means to keep them away from organized women's rights movements. Since the 2008 economic crisis, anti-feminist movements have become active worldwide and push back on women's individual rights with promises to bring protection for the family unit (Korolczuk and Graff, 2018). Linking anti-genderism to anti-colonial narratives within the broader economic context that exposed the fragility of liberal democracy, these movements promote an illiberal populism by replacing "individual rights with rights of the family as a basic societal unit and depicts religious conservatives as an embattled minority" (Korolczuk and Graff, 2018, p. 798).

Grounding her work in the context of contemporary UK politics, Angela McRobbie has argued that since the gains of feminist activities in the 1970s and 1980s, today

elements of feminism have been taken into account, and have been absolutely incorporated into political and institutional life. Drawing on a vocabulary that includes words like "empowerment" and "choice," these elements are then converted into a much more individualistic discourse, and they are deployed in this new guise, particularly in media and popular culture, but also by agencies of the state, as kind of substitute for feminism. (2009, p. 1)

Yet, few studies have examined how anti-feminist movements operate in real time, particularly in a nondemocratic context. Moreover, the integration of women into Hezbollah's cultural institutions, which includes interactions with male colleagues that cross the boundaries of gendered spaces, is a rather innovative form of governance in Iran. This is a new approach that relies on the creativity, time, and energy of its most sympathetic citizens to better develop the state's legislation of religion.

Islamization of women's rights in post-2009 Iran also differs in form and content from other periods in postrevolutionary history. As Paidar (1995) has argued, from 1979 to 1981, the Islamic Republic focused on pushing women back into the private sphere and transforming gender relations through Islamization of family and sexual relations. The endeavor was rather explicit, including the curtailment of women's public presence and emphasis on the political relevance of religious symbols such as the *hijab* in signifying a new political order in Iran.

Today, the process is more one of co-option carried out through ambiguous politics that seem to legitimize Hezbollahi youths' competing and contradictory interests. During the 2013 Congress on 7,000 Female Martyrs at Tehran's Vahdat Hall, I watched as Major General Hassan

Firouzabadi, then Chief of Staff of the Iranian armed forces, spoke to an all-female audience of Hezbollah affiliates. He brought together several political strands to persuade women to cooperate, albeit through much ambiguity. First, he stated that while some people within the state may want to negotiate with the international system due to sanctions and threats, the 7,000 female martyrs tell us that we have to be active in fully defending an "Islamic Iran." He then spoke for a few minutes on the 2009 *fitna* (sedition), arguing that while those who protested following the 2009 presidential election stated that they wanted freedom, in reality they were backed by American and British media outlets.

Furthermore, he identified Fatemeh al-Zahra, the daughter of Prophet Mohammad and wife of Imam Ali, as a role model for Shi'i and Sunni women. He claimed that any Muslim woman, even if she lived in a small town, should confront anyone who spread rumors that promoted discourses contrary to the official ones promulgated by the Islamic Republic. He had thus far made it clear that he was addressing: (1) women who were opposed to reformists within the ruling elite and who wanted to negotiate with the West; (2) women who resisted opposition movements within society that made demands on the state; and (3) women who during their everyday lives, even at home and within the family, challenged those who criticized the establishment.

He concluded by arguing that there was no reason why women fulfilling all of these criteria could not participate at the highest levels of the state. He asked: "Why don't we have women at the negotiating table for the nuclear crisis when we have female nuclear scientists? Why don't we have women in the highest levels of the military when we had female military leaders in the Iran–Iraq war?" It seems that if Iranian women police the nation, they will be given opportunities to climb the state's power structures because they have exerted a higher level of piety by simply siding with the state's preferred citizenry body.

Due to the historical teleologies in the state's anti-feminist formulation above, female Hezbollah activists rely on their own moral imaginings to connect the spiritual and material to relate to Iran's changing social context. Scholars agree that social militarization through prolonged international conflict is one of the definitive outcomes of revolutions; this character of a postrevolutionary state enhances its survival capacities.[22] State-controlled memorialization of the Iran–Iraq war has a social militarization effect within this social group that results in the unification of the private sphere and the state-building process for many. A female

---

[22] See, for instance, Skocpol (1988).

leader in this newly solidified social group told me that she decided to marry her husband when they went on an *ordu* (camping trip) together to the south of Iran to visit war sites from the Iran–Iraq war. During the trip, an accident occurred in which some students died in full view of the other travelers. When she witnessed his bravery at the scene and his ability to regroup others, she decided to marry him.

During my 2008 field research in Tehran, I heard similar stories of love from wives of Iranian war martyrs. By rehashing this narrative, the state aims to generate the following message: Piety and a dedication to the postrevolutionary state mean that one gives less attention to a suitor's economic status. This narrative positions women who make marital decisions through a social militarization framework as martyrs' wives-in-waiting, and since 1979, this subjectivity has been noble for and sought-after by many who associate with the postrevolutionary state. If my research had ended here, it would seem that political elites had achieved their goal of creating the ideal "good citizen."

As my relationships developed, however, I began to see that many Hezbollahi women switch to modes of statecraft that undermine state-sanctioned discourses on love, marriage, and piety with an underlying motivation for women's rights. While performances of public piety are important for this social group, they intersect with other human achievements such as higher degrees, gender equality in marriage, wealth, and frequent travel abroad that are considered to be equally praiseworthy. It is commonly known that pious Shi'i women view Zeinab, the sister of Imam Hussein, as a role model. This is particularly so for women affiliated with Hezbollah (Deeb, 2009). During interactions with female cultural activists, however, they seemed most inspired by Iran's female leaders in the public sphere, including PhD students, female professors, politicians, parliament members, writers, athletes, and artists.

This was surprising.

During my fieldwork in 2008, daughters of martyrs that supported the Islamic Republic overwhelmingly identified their mothers as their role models. Their mothers, on the other hand, viewed Zeinab as a source of inspiration. This contrast between different generations and factions of pious women affiliated with the Islamic Republic indicate the unpredictability of Islamization projects and how they can remake religious identities in ways that escape the state's citizenship-building efforts.

These young people are influenced by the materialist ambitions that are central to city life in Iran today. Hezbollah affiliates are dedicated to public expressions of piety through marriages based on values, but they also firmly believe in progress (*peshraft*), understood to mean material development. For instance, when I got married in 2014 in Tehran, several leading female members of this social group privately suggested that I demand the right to divorce and request a high *mehrieh* (promissory bride price payable to the bride), arguing that it would protect me from ill-treatment in the marriage – a protection they did not have and continued to regret. They argued that this legal demand was my right because I held a PhD from a prestigious university (Cambridge).

This was an interesting perspective as it reasserted a classification of the population devoid of equality. One Hezbollah affiliate even stopped me on the street one day and told me that she could no longer keep silent and wanted to talk. As we walked, she gently expressed that my marital decision was all wrong because my husband did not have a PhD. She further argued that my husband should not only hold a doctoral degree but preferably hold one from Cambridge; otherwise, she believed I was "selling myself short." Another affiliate remained adamant that I should marry a state elite: "You deserve someone that is high-ranking, you know, like a member of the nuclear negotiation team."[23] Female Hezbollah affiliates strike their own balance between public expressions of piety and material progress, oscillate between individual and collective rights demands, and in the process undermine the state's good citizen framework.

Another point that I found significant was how the women's suggestions divert from an egalitarian agenda based on relationality and mutual respect that has historically been proposed by those committed to gender justice within and outside of an Islamic framework in Iran. Material development here is strikingly different from what Deeb (2006) articulated as an understanding of progress that included the community and others' rights and needs among pious Shi'i Hezbollah supporters in Lebanon. For instance, the legal demands cultural activists suggested I insist upon during negotiations on my marriage contract would in practice mean that I could both divorce my husband and demand a large sum of money from him. This in effect is a contract set on privatized domination and not equality or piety in statecraft.

While this suggestion does not fall outside the boundaries of religion, it does challenge the mode of morality enforced by the state and most Shi'i scholars where a low *mehrieh* and a decision not to include further stipulations of the marriage contract are encouraged. However, because there is room for negotiation on this issue religiously, women draw on their feminist sensibilities to establish a contract that they personally prefer; their preferences do not necessarily feel obliged to engage with

---

[23] Personal conversations, February 2014.

piety at all. When I asked one activist if it was just to create such a contract, she replied:

Look, we cannot run a country based on personal preferences or individual theorizations of justice. Maybe you think this is unfair [referring to the contract suggestion that included both a high *mehrieh* and the right to divorce], maybe you think it is feminism ... but none of this changes the reality that this is a right that Islam gives to women. Therefore, it is Islamic, I love the Supreme Leader, and I am Hezbollahi.[24]

The state's promotion of a heteronormative narrative of marriages during the 1980–1988 period and its subsequent dramatization in the postwar years do not prevent female Hezbollah affiliates from imagining alternative moral futures that include women as citizens who dominate male counterparts in marriage – or even reject the institution of marriage altogether. While Hezbollah affiliates are influenced by the state's rhetoric on the war and current nuclear dispute, they are also employing material lenses geared toward personal and collective development when interacting within their society. Importantly, this conceptualization of rights is not grounded in equality and may not view as equally significant the interests of men or other women. The role of female and male Hezbollah affiliates should be analyzed within this matrix of ambiguity and unpredictability.

In 2014 I attended a conference, The First National Conference for Activists Dedicated to Transformations in the Social Sciences. At one evening session, we were introduced to Mahnaz. She was the head of an organization created in 2011 because, along with a few other women, she wanted to join the fight against feminism. When I asked where I could find their work, she replied that it is mostly confidential reports shared with different state institutions. As we sat in a circle, one woman who joined us from a small village near Mashhad questioned the objectives of the center:

We need a model for living, not just advice given to the government! What will you do with popular culture? How are you going to speak with the everyday woman? Our intellectual investigations of the West are generally weak, we don't have a deep understanding of Western theories, so how are you going to explain what we should and should not be doing in comparison?[25]

Mahnaz became visibly shaken. I asked her why she was against collaboration with feminists. The unrest compelled her to move beyond the promulgation of propaganda when speaking with us. She calmly responded that her work was Islamized because of the emphasis on

---

[24] Personal interview, November 2013.   [25] Personal interview, September 2014.

spreading faith (*iman*) in society, not capitalist culture. She argued that she was not against collaboration with anyone but that international women's rights organizations seek to impose a single narrative on women's lives. She felt this was violent and also characteristic of feminism in capitalist culture. All the women in the room nodded in agreement. However, what she said next was more revealing for it brings women's lived experiences with gender inequality into the debate: "Ultimately, we want to break through these two boundaries: women have to either sit at home, or if they want to join society, to hell with them (*dandeshun narm*), they have to deal with lower income, no daycare, harassment etc. ..." (Personal interview, September 2014).

The unexpected acts of citizenship in the room resulted in the collective decision that faith should be able to meet women's desire to both have a family and be an active and respected member of society. At the same time, I noted during our walk back to the resting area that Mahnaz personally did not identify with traditional gender roles but did not see this as a feminist sentiment. She talked about how her husband is actually more emotional than she is and that he pays more attention to their daughter's transformations and emotional well-being.

Mahnaz, like most of the other female Hezbollah cultural activists that I encountered after 2009, rarely discusses motherhood, unless to acknowledge it as a part of womanhood that does not come naturally to her. I found this to be surprising given that the glorification of motherhood has emerged in my research as a sentiment that tends to cut across the divisions that prevail among Iranian women with conflicting political views. Moreover, while talks of motherhood were nearly nonexistent among the women I encountered, they were a recurring theme in my exchanges with Iranian women I met in other spaces such as gyms, libraries, cabs, and neighborhood mosques. The family is constitutionally identified as a central organizing institution in the Islamic Republic of Iran (Paidar, 1995). Motherhood is elevated in the constitution as the most important aspect of womanhood and a current or future status that legitimizes women's political rights (Paidar, 1995). As such, these women's tepid stance toward motherhood suggests that the Islamic Republic's chief architects are radically conditioning the state by deviating from this Islamization project's emphasis on positing Hezbollahi women as the social guardians of motherhood.

6.7   Conclusion

In post-2009 Iran, the state hoped that Islamization projects would encourage citizens to practice self-governance as obedience through a depoliticized admiration of the divine and the erosion of solidarity between women. However, this formulation of the "good citizen" was ambiguous. These are due to the tensions between the legislation of religion in post-2009 Hezbollah cultural institutions, the state's formal theorization of citizenship, and its constitutional framework.

The conflict between these domains of power over who the ideal Muslim citizen is duly informs acts of citizenship among Hezbollah affiliates on the ground. Hezbollah affiliates oscillate between a desire to create the City of God and being the individual and collective extensions of God on earth because of their exceptional piety, which is augmented through the confirmation of cultural institutions. How they navigate the contrasting boundaries between autonomy and equality in Hezbollah cultural institutes, the state's foundational theories, and the constitution results in unpredictable citizenry interventions. An examination of two Islamization projects invested in reforming the social sciences and women's rights illustrates that the boundaries of autonomy and equality are continually being remade through this empowering yet risky perspective on self-governance. Female Hezbollah activists advance a women's rights agenda that at certain moments intersects with the demands of other women in Iranian society. Despite the Islamic Republic's best efforts, its anti-feminist project seemingly fails to eliminate demands for equality and autonomy among even Hezbollah-affiliated women.

The chapter has suggested that elite support of new societal actors and institutions during moments of revived religious legislation may move the state formation process toward an uncertain path, producing citizens that are continually "on the edge rather than progressing into the mainstream" (Newma, 2013, p. 101). At the same time, the expansions of institutions and empowerment of new social actors may also support state survival, at least in the short term, through the formation of independent citizenship with ambiguous outcomes. Forging solidarity between collectives that share similar commitments is an intended goal of a state's citizenship policies (Faist, 2000). The Islamic Republic has successfully united the younger generation of Hezbollah supporters to embody a revived sense of group solidarity despite significant differences within this social group and between this social group and wider Iranian society. Given the convergences in political culture and governing techniques between democratic and hybrid regimes, as well as how they similarly envision self-discipline as central to freedom, the findings in this chapter may be relevant elsewhere.

7 Conclusion
Gendered Citizenship and Conditioning of the State

7.1 Summary of Chapters

During different moments of conflict, postrevolutionary Iranians' formal and informal legislation ebbs and flows between plans to condition, eliminate, or limit citizenship. This trend in the country's postrevolutionary history also leaves much space for mediation and slippages that reconfigure national governance projects on the local terrain. In postrevolutionary Iran, then, it is not only the state's republican elements that make it unpredictable through elections and the press (Osanloo, 2009).

Women and the Islamic Republic has argued that when we integrate acts of citizenship into the state-building process, we see that the postrevolutionary Iranian state is heavily conditioned by the gendered legacies of the Iran–Iraq war. Moreover, authoritarianism is an ambiguous project when examined from within society. In some instances, such as with the implementation of Islamization projects addressed in Chapter 6, authoritarian state-building tactics – expressed through the state's insistence on obedient subjecthood – become the point of contention themselves. Despite the state's best efforts at directing national resistance toward its feminist opposition, the engendering of Islamization through authoritarianism ends up being another moment where women's rights struggles are amplified.

Yet, *Women and the Islamic Republic* has also shown that in the process of defining their role as state-makers, Iranian women as activist citizens in the postrevolutionary contexts have become subjects of the state. For the women who participated in this study, the competing discourses and visions of the nation-state have been central to how they imagine their rights, how they enact and claim them, and how they develop a sense of belonging through different expressions of acts of citizenship. This study of state formation through acts of citizenship poses many questions regarding how we contemplate Iranian women's role in transforming the postrevolutionary Iranian state, as well as their engagement with authoritarianism more generally.

By illustrating the unfolding of women's lives during different periods of conflict in postrevolutionary Iran, this book illustrates that, despite its authoritarian history, the Islamic Republic is also home to particularly unruly forms of acts of citizenship that construct the state in surprising ways. This becomes evident when we examine the making of postrevolutionary Iran during different moments of conflict. Women's contestation of the nation-state's gender projects is unpredictable but highly dependent on the particular national, international, or local context in which their acts of citizenship are performed.

During the 1980–1988 period, for example, there was little consideration for the rights of those with different political agendas. In the post-1988 period, families of war martyrs held an elevated position in Iranian society due to the Shi'i devotion to martyrdom. Additionally, these families were an important social group to contest the austere and uncompromising position of the state on people's rights because of the reformist movement and the presidency of Mohammad Khatami. Martyrs' wives and daughters were activist citizens that supported the rights of other Iranian women and men while remaining dedicated to the notion of Islamic government themselves.

One of *Women and the Islamic Republic*'s central findings is that while the authoritarian/democracy binary may be useful for understanding general political trends, it tells us less about the direction, texture, and tempo of political change on the ground.

It is surprising to me, for example, that female Hezbollah cultural activists, the social group that the state's security forces sought to make the majority to battle feminism, have occasionally participated in state construction by blending Islamization projects with a highly individualistic brand of citizenship uninterested in community's, men's, or other women's rights. Yet, through their participation in Islamization projects, female Hezbollah activists have played a central role in culturally reproducing the Islamic Republic following the contested 2009 presidential election. At least for some Hezbollah women today, the desire to advance women's individual and collective rights motivates their participation in Islamization of women's rights. I rarely encountered Hezbollah female cultural activists who sought to limit women's lives and rights, which is what the state's original goal was in funding these projects. As they push the boundaries of rights among themselves or wider society, these women too are upholding the state's hybrid form – but not always in ways that are egalitarian.

This book has illustrated how the construction of individual autonomy and collectivities are connected to the state formation process during different moments of conflict in postrevolutionary Iran. As non-elite women engage with the state and society in different spaces, they also condition the formation of the postrevolutionary state by redefining their rights, roles, and responsibilities. By bringing a sociological perspective into studies of state formation, *Women and the Islamic Republic* has highlighted how a citizenry lens on authoritarianism helps us better understand and acknowledge the role of non-elite women in the state construction process.

Chapter 1 laid out the theoretical foundation for this study by situating the investigation at the intersects of several different fields and subfields. The chapter brought together the newer generation of state formation literature with their focus on cultural formation, feminist works that stress the ongoing nature of state configuration, and critical citizenship studies that view citizenship emerging without official permission. It did so to reconceptualize state formation through acts of citizenship and examine Iranian women's contentions on the local terrain as acts of state-building. More precisely, I sought to explore the following questions: How do non-elite women outside of organized women's rights movements act as postrevolutionary citizens in a historically authoritarian state? In turn, how do acts of citizenship affect the state formation process?

Chapter 2 challenged the linear association between women's rights struggles during the 1900s and women's postrevolutionary rights demands. The chapter demonstrated that for women associated with leftist and Islamist organizations during the 1980–1988 period, it was rarely organizational or historical women's rights struggles that engendered women's activism. Instead, my interviewees recounted personal and familial experiences with discrimination and injustice as central to their decision to take a more proactive role in society. Women's activism was also advanced when male relatives and political elites morally supported women in the public and private spheres.

The ensuing chapters examined how non-elite Iranian women, not affiliated with any women's rights movements, undermined and engaged with state-building tactics in various spaces, including prisons, warfronts, seminaries, and hospitals. Chapter 3 examined how spiritual citizenship engendered women's role as claimants during everyday life. I illustrate that the notion of political spirituality, which Foucault identified as the force behind the Iranian struggle for a new subjectivity in revolutionary period, propelled women's spiritual acts of citizenship. The chapter showed that political spirituality meant that women carried out acts of citizenship, which revolved around their efforts of self-care.

Chapter 4 was attentive to the unpredictability of sentiments propelled by political violence, in particular the sense of isolation that interviewees remember feeling. The chapter turned to the nexus between nationalist enactments and nation-building during a time of war. While women self-determined their subjectivities in various spaces (including hospitals, warfronts, and prisons), they were simultaneously conditioning renewed understandings of nationalism by repositioning the interplay between the nation, gender, and sexuality. A look into the construction of polities and the notions of masculinities and femininities that circulate through them showed that sexual dichotomies and the nation's heteronormative form and imaginings were destabilized by some of the Iranians that participated in this study. The disruption of sexual roles and identities illustrated that the "national body" holds no essential position and that the nation-state can be forged without the privileging of masculinity.

Chapters 5 and 6 examined the legacies of the Iran–Iraq war for the state formation process through the experiences of two social groups that participated in the war and became the target of numerous state policies geared toward militarization of everyday life after the war ended. Since the 1979 revolution was proclaimed in the name of the pious, it is important to examine how these privileged social groups engage with the state formation process. While both chapters continue to focus on non-elite women, war martyrs' families and Hezbollah cultural activists symbolize the physical architecture of the Islamic Republic as representatives of the war martyrs' political path. Through case studies of wives and daughters of war martyrs, and with an eye on the legacies of political violence in the first decade of the Islamic Republic and intergenerational transformations, Chapter 5 explored gendered subjectivities for this particular category of women who overwhelmingly ascribe to reformist politics. This is a social group that was both implicated in and the subject of intersections between revolution, war, and narratives of the nation-state in post-1979 Iran.

Simply put, these families stand in the middle of a national conflict over how the Iran–Iraq war will be remembered. Will the war only be remembered in the context of a foreign invasion? Or do the martyrs also have something to say about the local violation of citizenry rights? As such, gendered subjectivities here showed how the Islamic Republic's narrative of the nation-state was contested by families of martyrs to create counternarratives that defended the rights of other Iranian women to demand the right to autonomy, freedom of choice, and freedom of speech, to name just a few. Although these women adhere to the notion of Islamic government, they too are acting as activist citizens who challenge the patriarchal and discriminatory gender norms imposed through state and societal forces.

After 2009, many of these families are no longer given a political platform in the country. Instead, it is families of nuclear energy martyrs and Iranian martyrs on the Syrian warfronts who have taken center stage in Iranian pious politics. The state has pushed families of war martyrs out of the national eye deliberately because of their adherence to an explicitly democratic vision where power rests with the people.

Chapter 6 contrasts well with the previous discussion because we can see how the relationship between the religiously pious population and the state has transformed after the 2009 presidential conflict. The chapter examined female cultural activists' acts of citizenship affiliated with the Hezbollah movement in Iran after the 2009 uprisings. Hezbollah cultural activists are depicted by the state as the rightful owners of the state and representatives of the war martyrs' path and ideology. Hezbollah-affiliated youth also ascribe to an understanding of Islamic government that views people's rights and citizenship as only one pillar of the post-revolutionary state, and striking a balance between the state's power and people's power is not how these young people envision change. I argued that the ambiguities of articulating Islamization projects in a top-down manner led to unexpected acts of citizenship performed with an under-lying motivation for women's rights. This contrasts with the subjecthood agenda the state hopes to pursue through its Islamization projects. Through an investigation of the state's Islamization of the social sciences and women's rights project, the penultimate chapter argued that although they are far from being democrats, for the first time in post-revolutionary Iranian history, women – and at times men – affiliated with Hezbollah cultural activism are relying on normative moral formulations to advance women's interests because of their desire to socialize in a changing Iran.

During my fieldwork in Tehran from 2012 to 2014, I witnessed Hezbollahi couples deciding on their sexual and physical boundaries together, instead of simply assuming men's right to control women's sexuality as is stipulated in Iranian family law. Hezbollah-affiliated women in Iran are also supporting the gender rights struggles of their Lebanese female counterparts. For instance, during one meeting with a researcher who works for a private research firm, I was told that they had spoken privately with the Supreme Leader regarding the negative effects of polygamy on Lebanese families. At times, she argued, men affiliated with Lebanon's Hezbollah bring their second wives into the same home and bed as their first wives. The Iranian researcher found this alarming and claimed that the Supreme Leader had spoken with Hassan Nasrallah, the Secretary General of Lebanese Hezbollah, about this concern. Hezbollah-affiliated Iranian women are also in some instances relying on Islamic texts to dominate men in marriage by insisting on a woman's right to have both a high *mehrieh* and the right to divorce.

In other moments, they protest side by side with other citizens to demand that the state be held accountable, as I witnessed in the women's dormitory at the University of Tehran. While scholars have assumed that Islamization projects would only result in further centralization of state power, it is unclear what direction Islamization projects may take in nondemocratic settings. An investigation into the cultural activism of Hezbollah affiliates in Iran points us toward the reality that acts of citizenship can both support the state's authoritarian politics and advance its survival through unpredictable revisions.

I argued a counterintuitive claim throughout *Women and the Islamic Republic*: despite the Islamic Republic's nondemocratic elements, Shi'i reverence for sacred female figures, the Iran–Iraq war, and the fight over its legacies propelled manifold acts of citizenship. Securing gender equality has become an inescapable battle for both women and men to varying degrees, and the state is often left in a position where it must catch up to societal transformations in the struggle to redefine freedom, morals, rights, belonging, and other attributes of citizenship. Undoubtedly, in whatever direction Iran's struggle for state formation goes, the Iranian nation has its female population to thank for fueling the struggle toward citizenship in the postrevolutionary era.

Bibliography

"Amaar-e Shohada va Esargare-haye Zanan dar Doran-e Defa Moghaddas."
1395. Khabargozare-ye Seda va Sima. www.iribnews.ir/fa/news/1296766/
مقدس-دفاع-دوران-در-زنان-های-ایثارگری-و-شهدا-آمار [Accessed May 2017].

"Az en Nasl Motefaker berun Nmi aayad." 1387/2008. *Habil*, 9, pp. 20–21.

Vaghte hameh chez be khoda khatm meshavad. 1391. In *Vijehnamehye yadvareh zanane shahide Maazandaran*, pp. 24–27.

Markaze motalat va tahgheghate jang. 1378/1999. *Reshehaye Tahajom*. Tehran: Sepahe Pasdarane Enghelabe Islami, Markaze motalat va tahgheghate jang.

Zendan: Goft-o-Gu ba Nazli Partovi. 1377/1999. *Journal of the Centre for Women and Socialism*, 3, pp. 22–26.

"Besh a 25,000 Emdadgar va Zan-e Pezeshk darh Jang-e Tahmele Hozur Dasht."
1397. *Farhang Sadid*. http://farhangesadid.ir/fa/news/443/بیش-از-۲۵-هزار-
انقلاب-به-زن-جانباز-هزار-شهید-و-۵-هزار-۷-داشتند-حضور-تحمیلی-جنگ-در-پزشک-زن-و-امدادگر-
هدیه-شده-است [Accessed March 2018].

"Revayat-e Zan-e Emdadgar-e Abadani az Ruzhaay-e Jang." 1396. *Iranian Students' News Agency*. www.isna.ir/news/96070201124/روایت-زن-امدادگر-آبادانی-از-روزهای-جنگ [Accessed March 2018].

Abad, M. 1395/2016. *Maan Zendeh-am*. Tehran: Boruj Publishers.

Abdelrahman, M. 2013. In Praise of Organization: Egypt between Activism and Revolution. *Development and Change*, 44(3), pp. 569–585.

Abdo-Zubi, N. 1987. *Family, Women and Social Change in the Middle East: The Palestinian Case*. Toronto: Canadian Scholars' Press.

Abdolah, K. 2011. *The House of the Mosque*. London: Canongate.

Abedi, M. and Legenhausen, G. 1986. Jihad and Shahadat. In M. M. Mutahhari and S. Shariati, eds. *Islam/Taleqani*. Houston, TX: The Institute for Research and Islamic Studies, pp. 58–89.

Abrahamian, E. 1999. *Tortured Confessions: Prisons and Public Recantations in Modern Iran*. London and Berkeley: University of California Press.

2008. *A History of Modern Iran*. Cambridge: Cambridge University Press.

Abrams, P. 1988. Notes on the Difficulty of Studying the State. *Journal of Historical Sociology*, 1(1), pp. 58–89.

Abu-Lughod, L. 1990. The Romance of Resistance: Tracing Transformations of Power through Bedouin Women. *American Ethnologist*, 17(1), pp. 41–55.

Abulghasemi, M. J. 1382/2003. Aseb shenase ye farhangi ye enghelabe Islami. *Andesheye Enghelabe Islami*, 7–8, pp. 131–162.

Acharya, A. 2014. Global International Relations (IR) and Regional Worlds. *International Studies Quarterly*, 58(4), pp. 647–659.

Adib-Moghaddam, A. 2006a. *The International Politics of the Persian Gulf: A Cultural Genealogy*. London: Routledge.

2006b. The Pluralistic Momentum in Iran and the Future of the Reform Movement. *Third World Quarterly*, 27(4), pp. 665–674.

2018. *Psycho-nationalism: Global Thought, Iranian Imaginations*. Cambridge: Cambridge University Press.

Afary, J. 1996. *The Iranian Constitutional Revolution, 1906–1911: Grassroots Democracy, Social Democracy, & the Origins of Feminism*. New York: Columbia University Press.

2001. Portraits of Two Islamist Women: Escape from Freedom or from Tradition? *Critique: Journal for Critical Studies of the Middle East*, 19(Fall), pp. 47–77.

Afary, J. and Anderson, K. B. 2005. *Foucault and the Iranian Revolution: Gender and the Seductions of Islamism*. Chicago and London: University of Chicago Press.

Afkhami, M. and Friedl, E., eds. 1994. *In the Eye of the Storm: Women in Post-revolutionary Iran*. London: I. B. Tauris.

Afshar, H. 1998. *Islam and Feminisms: An Iranian Case-Study*. New York: St. Martin's Press.

Afshari, R. 2001. *Human Rights in Iran: The Abuse of Cultural Relativism*. Philadelphia: University of Pennsylvania Press.

Aghajanian, A. 1986. Some Notes on Divorce in Iran. *Journal of Marriage and Family*, 48(4), pp. 749–755.

Ahmadi, S. R. 2018. "In My Eyes He Was a Man": Poor and Working-Class Boy Soldiers in the Iran-Iraq War. *Journal of Middle East Women's Studies*, 14(2), pp. 174–192.

Ahmed, S. 2004. *The Cultural Politics of Emotion*. New York: Routledge.

Akbari, M. 1390/2011. *Hozur-e Zanan-e Ostan-e Elam dar Defa Moghaddas*. Elam: Johar-e Hayat.

Alaedini, P. and Razavi, M. R. 2005. Women's Participation and Employment in Iran: A Critical Examination. *Critique: Critical Middle Eastern Studies*, 14(1), pp. 57–73.

Alessio, D. D. 1997. Domesticating "the Heart of the Wild": Female Personifications of the Colonies, 1886–1940. *Women's History Review*, 6 (2), pp. 239–270.

Algar, H. 1979. *On the Sociology of Islam: Lectures by Ali Shari'ati*. Berkeley: Mizan Press.

Ali, F. 2006. Rocking the Cradle to Rocking the World: The Role of Muslim Female Fighters. *Journal of International Women's Studies*, 8(1), pp. 21–35.

Alizadeh, P. 1376/1997. *Khoob Negah Koned Rastaki hast*. France: Khavaran.

2001. Look Closely, It Is Real. *Iran Bulletin*, pp. 46–53.

Amjadian, M. 1381/2002. *Nameh haye Esaarat*. Tehran: Sureh Mehr.

Amnesty International. 1990. *Iran: Violations of Human Rights 1987–1990*. MDE 13/21/90.

Aneesi, F. 1377a. Nokhosten Hamayesh-e Zanane Hamaseh Afarin-e Defa Moghaddas Gozaresh. *Payam-e Zan*, 81, pp. 1–6.

1377b. Goft-o-Gu ba Fereshtehgane Esar va Parastarane Shahadat. *Payam-e Zan*, 80, pp. 1–20.

1377c. Az Khat-e Kurdistan ta Dashte Nakhlah haaye be Sar. *Payam-e Zan*, 73, pp. 1–13.

1377d. Goft-o-Gu ba khanoome Zarin Taj Keyhani. *Payam-e Zan*, 75, pp. 1–16.

1378. Goft-o-Gu ba Khahar Mina Kamaeei. *Payam-e Zan*, no. 90.

Anon. 1383/2005a. Dar Hamayeshe Daneshgah, Zan va Defa-e Moghadas Amaari az Khanavadehye Shohada Elam Shod. *Payame Zan* [online], 153. Available at: www.hawzah.net/fa/magart.html?MagazineID=0&MagazineNumberID=4163&MagazineArticleID=26026.

1383/2005b. Hamsaran-e Shohada va Mahdodeyathaye Taghdis Shode. *Zanan* [online]. Available at: http://zananmag.org/spip.php?article390.

1386/2007. *Hamsardari-e Sardaran-e Shahid* (The Relationships of Wives of Martyrs). Tehran: Moaasese Farhangi Ghadr-e Velayat.

1390/2011. Defa-e Moghadas dar Ayneyeh Amaar. *Maaref*, 87, pp. 54–57.

Anon. n.d., Khorramshahr: Ku Jahan Ara ... (Khorramshahr: Where is Jahan Ara ...). *Kaman*, 43.

Ansari, A. 2000. *Iran, Islam and Democracy: The Politics of Managing Change*. London: The Royal Institute of International Affairs.

Ardavan, S. 1382/2003. *yadnegarehay-e zendan* (Prison Drawings). Sweden: Trydells Tryckeri AB publishers.

Arfani, S. 1389. *Delavar Mard-e Sistan*. Tehran: Sooremehr.

Arjomand, S. A. 1988. *The Turban for the Crown: The Islamic Revolution in Iran*. New York: Oxford University Press.

2002. The Reform Movement and the Debate on Modernity and Tradition in Contemporary Iran. *International Journal of Middle East Studies*, 34(40), pp. 719–731.

Aryanpour, A. 2000. *Behind the Tall Walls: From Palace to Prison*. USA: Authorhouse.

Asad, T. 2000. Agency and Pain: An Exploration. *Culture & Religion*, 1(1), pp. 29–60.

Auchter, J. 2014. *The Politics of Haunting and Memory in International Relations*. London: Routledge.

Bagheri, L. 1391/2012. *Ghoreshy be Revayate Hamsare Shahid*. Tehran: Ravayat-e Fath.

Bahramitash, R. and Esfahani, H. S. 2011. Modernization, Revolution, and Islamism: Political Economy of Women's Employment. In: R. Bahramitash and H. S. Esfahani, eds. *Veiled Employment: Islamism and the Political Economy of Women's Employment in Iran*. Syracuse: Syracuse University Press, pp. 53–82.

Bakhash, S. 1985. *The Reign of the Ayatollahs: Iran and the Islamic Revolution*. London: I. B. Tauris.

Balasingham, A. 1983. *Women and Revolution: The Role of Women in Tamil Eelam National Liberation Struggle*. Released by the Political Committee Liberation Tigers of Tamil Eelam.

Bani Luhi, S. A. 1378/1999. *Imam Khomeini dar Defa Moghaddas*. Tehran: Eeta Publishers.

Baniyaghoob, J. 2011/1390. *Zanan dar Bande 209 Evin*. Spanga: Baran.

Baradaran, M. 1386/2007. *Enak Shokaran (1)*. 6th ed. Tehran: Ravayat-e Fath.

2009. *The Massacre of Political Prisoners in Iran, 1988: An Addendum. Witness Testimonies and Official Statements*. Abdorrahman Boroumand Foundation, pp. 62–73.

Barkawi, T. and Brighton, S. 2011. Powers of War: Fighting, Knowledge, and Critique. *International Political Sociology*, 5, pp. 126–143.

Bartky, S. L. 2002. *Sympathy and Solidarity*. New York: Rowman & Littlefield.

Barz, G. F. 1997. Confronting the Field(Note) In and Out of the Field. In: G. F. Barz and T. J. Cooley, eds. *Shadows in the Field: New Perspectives for Fieldwork in Ethnomusicology*. New York: Oxford University Press, pp. 45–62.

Basij Jamaah Zanan-e Keshvar. 1391. *Taravat-e Jahad*. Tehran: Moaseseye farhangi ye honari ye Jannate Fakkeh.

Basmenji, K. 2005. *Tehran Blues: How Iranian Youth Rebelled against Iran's Founding Fathers*. London: Saqi.

Bauböck, R. 2010. Studying Citizenship Constellations. *Journal of Ethnic and Migration Studies*, 36(5), pp. 847–859.

Bauer, J. 1994. Conversations among Iranian Political Exiles on Women's Rights: Implications for the Community-Self Debate in Feminism. *Middle East Critique*, 3(4), pp. 1–12.

Baumel, J. T. 1999. Women's Agency and Survival Strategies during the Holocaust. *Women's Studies International Forum*, 22(3), pp. 329–347.

Bayat, A. 2010a. *Life as Politics: How Ordinary People Change the Middle East*. Stanford, CA: Stanford University Press.

2010b. Tehran: Paradox City. *New Left Review*, 66, pp. 99–122.

Bayatrizi, Z. 2010. Knowledge Is Not Power: State-Funded Research in Iran. *Current Sociology*, 58(6), pp. 811–832.

Beasley, C. and Bacchi, C. 2000. Citizen Bodies: Embodying Citizens – A Feminist Analysis. *International Feminist Journal of Politics*, 2, pp. 337–358.

Behrooz, M. 1999. *Rebels with a Cause: The Failure of the Left in Iran*. London: I. B. Tauris.

Benzecry, C. E. and Baiocchi, G. 2017. What Is Political about Political Ethnography? On the Context of Discovery and the Normalization of an Emergent Subfield. *Theory and Society*, 46(3), pp. 229–247.

Berger, M. T. 2004. After the Third World? History, Destiny, and the Fate of Third Worldism. *Third World Quarterly*, 25(1), pp. 9–39.

Berlant, L. and Warner, M. 1998. Sex in Public. *Critical Inquiry*, 24(2), pp. 547–566.

Berry, M. E. 2018. *War, Women, and Power*. Cambridge: Cambridge University Press.

Biersteker, T. J. and Weber, C. eds. 1995. *State Sovereignty as Social Construct*. Cambridge: Cambridge University Press.

Blumer, H. 1954. What Is Wrong with Social Theory? *American Sociological Review* 19(1), pp. 3–10.

Bolourchi, N. 2018. The Sacred Defense: Sacrifice and Nationalism across Minority Communities in Post-Revolutionary Iran. *Journal of the American Academy of Religion*, 86(3,) pp. 724–758.

Boltanski, L. 2011. *On Critique: A Sociology of Emancipation*. Cambridge: Polity Press. Translated by Gregory Elliott.

Bop, C. 2001. Women in Conflict: Their Gains and Their Losses. In: S. Meintjes, M. Turshen, and A. Pillay, eds. *The Aftermath: Women in Post-Conflict Transformation*. London: Zed Books, pp. 19–34.

Bowman, G. 2006. Death Revisited: Solidarity and Dissonance in a Muslim-Christian Palestinian Community. In: U. Makdisi and P. A. Silverstein, eds. *Memory and Violence in the Middle East and North Africa*. Bloomington and Indianapolis: Indiana University Press, pp. 27–49.

Boydston, J. 2008. Gender as a Question of Historical Analysis. *Gender & History*, 20, pp. 558–583.

Brinton, C. 1938. *The Anatomy of Revolution*. New York: W. W. Norton.

Brod, H. and Kaufman, M. eds. 1994. *Theorizing Masculinities*. London and New Delhi: Sage Publications.

Brookshaw, D. P. and Rahimieh, N. 2010. Introduction. In: D. P. Brookshaw and N. Rahimieh, eds. *Forugh Farrokhzad Poet of Modern Iran: Iconic Woman and Feminine Pioneer of New Persian Poetry*. London and New York: I. B. Tauris, pp. 1–6.

Brown, N. J. 2002. *Constitutions in a Nonconstitutional World*. Albany: State University of New York Press.

Brubaker, R. and Cooper, F. 2000. Beyond "Identity." *Theory and Society* 29(1), pp. 1–47.

Brumberg, D. and Farhi, F. 2016. Introduction: Politics of Contention and Conciliation in Iran's Semiautocracy. In: D. Brumberg and F. Farhi, eds. *Power and Change in Iran*. Indianapolis: Indiana University Press, pp. 1–33.

Burchell, G., Gordon, C., and Miller, P., eds. 1991. *The Foucault Effect: Studies in Governmentality*. Chicago: The University of Chicago Press.

Chatterjee, K. 2011. *Ali Shari'ati and the Shaping of Political Islam in Iran*. New York: Palgrave Macmillan.

Chatterjee, P. 2004. *The Politics of the Governed: Reflections on Popular Politics in Most of the World*. New York: Columbia University Press.

Chehabi, H. 1998. The Pahlavi Period. *Iranian Studies*, 31, pp. 495–502.

Closs Stephens, A. 2013. *The Persistence of Nationalism: From Imagined Communities to Urban Encounters*. London: Routledge.

Cohen, E. 2009a. *Semi-Citizenship in Democratic Politics*. Cambridge: Cambridge University Press.

——— 2014. Live Thinking, or the Psychagogy of Michel Foucault. *Differences: A Journal of Feminist Cultural Studies* 25(2), pp. 1–32.

Cohen, R. A. 2009. *The Rise and Fall of the Mojahedin Khalq 1987–1997*. Brighton and Portland: Sussex Academic Press.

Cohen, Y., Brown, B. R., and Organski, A. F. K. 1981. The Paradoxical Nature of State Making: The Violent Creation of Order. *The American Political Science Review*, 75(4), pp. 901–910.

Collier, D. 1993. The Comparative Method. In: Ada W. Finifter, ed. *Political Science: The State of the Discipline II*. Washington, DC: American Political Science Association, pp. 105–119.

Cooper, D. 2014. *Everyday Utopias: The Conceptual Life of Promising Space*. Durham and London: Duke University Press.

2015. Bringing the State Up Conceptually: Forging a Body Politics through Anti-gay Christian Refusal. *Feminist Theory*, 16(1), pp. 87–107.

2016. Enacting Counter-states through Play. *Contemporary Political Theory*, 15, pp. 453–461.

Cornell, D. and Seely, S. D. 2014. There's Nothing Revolutionary about a Blowjob. *Social Text 119*, 32(2), pp. 1–23.

Coronil, F. 1997. *The Magical State: Nature, Money, and Modernity in Venezuela*. Chicago: University of Chicago Press.

Cvetkovich, A. 2012. *Depression: A Public Feeling*. Durham: Duke University Press.

Dabashi, H. 1985. The Poetics of Politics: Commitment in Modern Persian Literature. *Iranian Studies*, 18(2/4), pp. 147–188.

1993. *Theology of Discontent: The Ideological Foundations of the Islamic Revolution in Iran*. New York: New York University Press.

Das, V. and Poole, D. eds. 2004. *Anthropology in the Margins of the State*. Oxford: James Currey.

Dashti, A. 1390/2011. *Parvaz-e Fereshteh-ha*. Ardabil: basij e jaameyeh Zanan.

Daulatzai, A. 2008. The Discursive Occupation of Afghanistan. *British Journal of Middle Eastern Studies*, 35(3), pp. 419–435.

Davis, K. 1997. Embody-ing Theory: Beyond Modernist and Postmodernist Readings of the Body. In: K. Davis, ed. *Embodied Practices: Feminist Perspectives on the Body*. London: Sage, pp. 1–23.

Deeb, L. 2006. *An Enchanted Modern: Gender and Public Piety in Shi'i Lebanon*. Princeton, NJ and Oxford: Princeton University Press.

2009. Emulating and/or Embodying the Ideal: The Gendering of Temporal Frameworks and Islamic Role Models in Shi''i Lebanon. *American Ethnologist*, 36(2), pp. 242–257.

Delaney, C. 1988. Mortal Flow: Menstruation in Turkish Village Society. In: T. Buckley and A. Gottlieb, eds. *Blood Magic: The Anthropology of Menstruation*. Berkeley: University of California Press, pp. 75–93.

Delaney, C. L. 1991. *The Seed and the Soil: Gender and Cosmology in Turkish Village Society*. Berkeley and Los Angeles: University of California Press.

Delanty, G. 1997. Models of Citizenship: Defining European Identity and Citizenship. *Citizenship Studies*, 1(3), pp. 285–303.

De Souza, M. L. and Lipietz, B. 2011. The "Arab Spring" and the City. *City*, 15(6), pp. 618–624, DOI: 10.1080/13604813.2011.632900.

Dissanayake, W. 1996. Introduction/Agency and Cultural Understanding: Some Preliminary Remarks. In: W. Dissanayake, ed. *Narratives of Agency: Self-Making in China, India, and Japan*. Minneapolis: University of Minnesota Press, pp. ix–xxi.

Doty, R. 2003. *Anti-immigrantism in Western Democracies: Statecraft, Desire and the Politics of Exclusion*. London: Routledge.

Dowlatabadi, M. 2011. *The Colonel.* London: Haus Publishing. Translated by Tom Patterdale.

2014. *Thirst.* London: Melville House Publishing. Translated by Martin E. Weir.

Dunn, Kevin C. 2010. There Is No Such Thing as the State: Discourse, Effect and Performativity. *Forum for Development Studies*, 37(1), pp. 79–92.

Ebtekar, M. 2000. *Takeover in Tehran: The Inside Story of the 1979 U.S. Embassy Capture.* Canada: Talonbooks.

Ehsani, K. 2009. The Urban Provincial Periphery in Iran: Revolution and War in Ramhormoz. In: Ali Gheissari, ed. *Contemporary Iran: Economy, Society, Politics.* Oxford: Oxford University Press, pp. 38–76.

2017. War and Resentment: Critical Reflections on the Legacies of the Iran-Iraq War. *Middle East Critique*, 26(1), pp. 5–24.

Ellis, N. 2015. *Territories of the Soul: Queered Belonging in the Black Diaspora.* Durham: Duke University Press.

Elshtain, J. B. 1987. *Women and War.* Brighton: Harvester Press.

2009. Women, the State, and War. *International Relations*, 23, pp. 289–303.

Englund, H. 2000. The Dead Hand of Human Rights: Contrasting Christianities in Post-Transition Malawi. *The Journal of Modern African Studies*, 38(4), pp. 579–603.

2004. Toward a Critique of Rights Talk in New Democracies: The Case of Legal Aid in Malawi. *Discourse & Society*, 15(5), pp. 527–551.

Enloe, C. 1989. *Bananas, Beaches & Bases: Making Feminist Sense of International Politics.* London and Sydney: Pandora Press.

1998. All the Men Are the Militias, All the Women Are Victims: The Politics of Masculinity and Femininity in Nationalist Wars. In: L. A. Lorentzen and J. Turpin, eds. *The Women and War Reader.* New York: New York University Press, pp. 50–62.

2000. *Manoeuvres: The International Politics of Militarizing Women's Lives.* Berkeley: University of California Press.

Esfandiari, H. 1994. The Majles and Women's Issues in the Islamic Republic of Iran. In: M. Afkhami and E. Friedl, eds. *In the Eye of the Storm: Women in Post-Revolutionary Iran.* New York: I. B. Tauris, pp. 61–79.

1997. *Reconstructed Lives: Women & Iran's Islamic Revolution.* Washington, DC: Woodrow Wilson Center Press.

Faist, T. 2000. Transnationalization in International Migration: Implications for the Study of Citizenship and Culture. *Ethnic and Racial Studies*, 23(2), pp. 189–222.

Fanon, F. 1970. The Fact of Blackness. In: F. Fanon, ed. *Black Skin, White Masks.* London: Paladin, pp. 77–99.

Farhadpour, L. 2012. Women, Gender Roles, Media and Journalism. In: T. Povey and E. Rostami-Povey, eds. *Women, Power and Politics in 21st Century Iran.* London: Ashgate, pp. 91–106.

Farhang, M. 1985. The Iran–Iraq War: The Feud, the Tragedy, the Spoils. *World Policy Journal*, 2(4), pp. 659–680.

Farhi, F. 1994. Sexuality and the Politics of Revolution in Iran. In: M. A. Tetreault, ed. *Women and Revolution in Africa, Asia, and the New World.* Columbia: University of South Carolina Press, pp. 252–271.

2004. The Antinomies of Iran's War Generation. In: L. B. Potter and G. G. Sick, eds. *Iran, Iraq, and the Legacies of War*. New York: Palgrave Macmillan, pp. 101–120.

Farjamfar, S. 1381/2002. *Kafsh-ha-ye Sargardan: Khaterat-e Soheila Farjamfar*. Tehran: Sourah Mehr.

Farzaneh, M. M. 2005. *Sorud-e Paydari*. Cologne: Forough.

Faulks, K. 2000. *Citizenship*. New York: Routledge.

Fazel, S. 1384/2005. *Az Zaban-e Sabr* (Words of Patience). Tehran: Sharaf.

Fineman, M. A. 2004. *The Autonomy Myth: A Theory of Dependency*. New York: The New Press.

Firouzkouhi, M. et al. 2012. Nurses experiences in chemical emergency departments: Iran–Iraq war, 1980–1988. *International Emergency Nursing*, http://dx.doi.org/10.1016/j.ienj.2012.03.002 [Accessed May 2016], pp. 1–6.

Flaskerud, I. 2004. Women as Ritual Performers: Commemorating Martyrdom in Female Gender-Specific Rituals in Shia-Islamic Iran. In: I. B. Maehle and I. M. Okkenhaug, eds. *Women and Religion in the Middle East and the Mediterranean*. Oslo: Unipub, pp. 115–134.

Foody, K. 2015a. Considering Public Criticism: Secularity, Citizenship, and Religious Argument in Contemporary Iran. *The Muslim World*, 105, pp. 299–311.

2015b. Interiorizing Islam: Religious Experience and State Oversight in the Islamic Republic of Iran. *Journal of the American Academy of Religion*, 83(3), pp. 599–623.

Friedl, E. 2009. New Friends: Gender Relations within the Family. *Iranian Studies*, 42(1), pp. 27–43.

Gallagher, S. 1995. Body Schema and Intentionality. In: J. L. Bermúdez, A. Marcel, and N. Eilan, eds. *The Body and Self*. London: MIT Press, pp. 225–44.

Gerami, S. 2003. Mullahs, Martyrs, and Men: Conceptualizing Masculinity in the Islamic Republic of Iran. *Men and Masculinities*, 5(3), pp. 257–274.

Ghamari-Tabrizi, B. 2009. Memory, Mourning, Memorializing: On the Victims of Iran-Iraq War, 1980–Present. *Radical History Review*, 105, pp. 106–121.

2016a. *Foucault in Iran: Islamic Revolution after the Enlightenment*. Minneapolis: University of Minnesota Press.

2016b. *Remembering Akbar: Inside the Iranian Revolution*. London: OR Books.

Ghasami, M. H. n.d. *Ketabak-e Moghavamat*. Qom: Hefz-e Asar va Nashr-e Arzeshhaye Defa-e Moghadas.

Gheissari, A. and Nasr, V. 2006. *Democracy in Iran: History and the Quest for Liberty*. Oxford: Oxford University Press.

Ghodsizad, P. 1383/2004. *Tarekh-e Shafahe-e Masjid Jalili*. Tehran: Entesharat-e Markaz-e Asnad-e Enghelab-e Islami.

Gianotti, T. J. 2011. Beyond Both Law and Theology: An Introduction to al-Ghazali's "Science in the Way of the Afterlife." *Reviving Religious Knowledge, The Muslim World*, 101(4), pp. 597–613.

Gongora, T. 1997. War Making and State Power in the Contemporary Middle East. *International Journal of Middle East Studies*, 29(3), pp. 323–340.

Gorky, M. 2018. *Mother*. Middletown, DE: iRead.

Gupta, A. 1995. Blurred Boundaries: The Discourse of Corruption, the Culture of Politics, and the Imagined State. *American Ethnologist*, 22(2), pp. 375–402.

Hadjebi-Tabrizi, V. 1383/2004. *Daade be Daad*. Cologne, Germany: Forough Books.

Hansen, T. 1999. *The Saffron Wave: Democracy and Hindu Nationalism in Modern India*. Princeton, NJ: Princeton University Press.

Hansen, T. and Stepputat, F. eds. 2001. *States of Imagination: Ethnographic Explorations of the Postcolonial State*. Durham and London: Duke University Press.

Harirchian, M. and Hashemi, S. 2015/1394. Be Marhemat-e Jang Hamsayeh Shodim [We Became Neighbors Courtesy of the War], in *Shahrat* 5. http://darbareyeshahr.ir/پرونده/به-مرحمت-جنگ-همسایه-شدیم-سرگذشتی-شهرکی/ [Accessed April 27, 2018].

Hartman, S. 2008. Venus in Two Acts. *Small Axe*, 12(2), pp. 1–14.

Hashemi, M. 2018. Tarnished Work: Dignity and Labour in Iran. *British Journal of Middle Eastern Studies*, 47(5), pp. 1–16.

Hasso, F. 2005. *Resistance, Repression, and Gender Politics in Occupied Palestine and Jordan*. Syracuse, NY: Syracuse University Press.

Hatem, M. 2000. The Pitfalls of the Nationalist Discourses on Citizenship in Egypt. In: S. Joseph, ed. *Gender and Citizenship in the Middle East*. Syracuse, NY: Syracuse University Press, pp. 33–57.

Hemmings, C. 2005. Invoking Affect. *Cultural Studies*, 19(5), pp. 548–567.

Hillmann, M. C. 1982. The Modernist Trend in Persian Literature and Its Social Impact. *Iranian Studies*, 15(1/4), pp. 7–29.

1987. *A Lonely Woman: Forugh Forrokhzad and Her Poetry*. Washington, DC: Mage Publishers and Three Continents Press.

Hiltermann, J. 2010. Deep Traumas, Fresh Ambitions: Legacies of the Iran-Iraq War. *Middle East Report* 257, pp. 6–15.

Hirst, W., and Manier, D. 2008. Towards a Psychology of Collective Memory. *Memory* 16(3), pp. 183–200.

Hoagland, S. L. 1988. *Lesbian Ethics*. Palo Alto, CA: Institute of Lesbian Studies.

Holliday, S. J. 2011. *Defining Iran: Politics of Resistance*. Farnham: Ashgate.

Homazadeh, M. 1382/2003. Az nahadsaze ta sazmanbazi. *Sureh*, 3, pp. 16–23.

Honig, B. 2008. Review: What Foucault Saw at the Revolution: On the Use and Abuse of Theology for Politics. *Political Theory*, 36(2), pp. 301–312.

Hoodfar, H. 1998. Volunteer Health Workers in Iran as Social Activists: Can "Governmental Non-governmental Organizations" Be Agents of Democratisation? Occasional Paper No. 10: Women Living under Muslim Law.

2008. Family Law and Family Planning Policy in Pre-and Post-Revolutionary Iran. In: K. M. Yount and H. Rashad, eds. *Family in the Middle East: Ideational Change in Egypt, Iran, and Tunisia*. London: Routledge, pp. 80–110.

Hoodfar, H. and Sadr, S. 2009. *Can Women Act as Agents of a Democratization of Theocracy in Iran?* [online] United Nations Research Institute for Social Development. Available at: www.unrisd.org/unrisd/website/document.nsf/

8b18431d756b708580256b6400399775/2e975aca2a81aa54c125765800287 35c/$FILE/ WebIran.pdf [Accessed December 18, 2010].

2010. Islamic Politics and Women's Quest for Gender Equality in Iran. *Third World Quarterly*, 31(6), pp. 885–903.

Hooper, C. 2001. *Manly States: Masculinities, International Relations, and Gender Politics*. New York: Columbia University Press.

Hosseini, S. A. 1388/2008. *Daa*. Tehran: Sourah Mehr.

Htun, M. and Weldon, S. L. 2012. The Civic Origins of Progressive Policy Change: Combating Violence against Women in Global Perspective 1975–2005. *American Political Science Review*, 106(3), pp. 548–569.

Ignatieff, M. 1994. *Blood & Belonging: Journeys into the New Nationalism*. London: Vintage.

Iqtidar, H. 2011a. Secularism beyond the State: The "State" and the "Market" in Islamist Imagination. *Modern Asian Studies*, 45(3), pp. 535–564.

——— 2011b. *Secularizing Islamists? Jama'at-e-Islami and Jama'at-ud-Da'wa in Urban Pakistan*. Chicago: University of Chicago Press.

Iran Human Rights Documentation Center. 2009. *Deadly Fatwa: Iran's 1988 Prison Massacre*. [online] Available at: www.iranhrdc.org/english/publi cations/reports/3158-deadly-fatwa-iran-s-1988-prison-massacre.html [Accessed March 12, 2012].

Isin, E. 2002. *Being Political: Genealogies of Citizenship*. Minneapolis: University of Minnesota Press.

——— 2004. The Neurotic Citizen. *Citizenship Studies*, 8(3), pp. 217–235.

——— 2005. Citizenship after Orientalism: Ottoman Citizenship. In: F. Keyman and A. Icduygu, eds. *Challenges to Citizenship in a Globalizing World: European Questions and Turkish Experiences*. London: Routledge, pp. 31–51.

——— 2008. Theorizing Acts of Citizenship. In: E. Isin and G. Nielsen, eds. *Acts of Citizenship*. London and New York: Zed Books, pp. 15–43.

——— 2009. Citizenship in Flux: The Figure of the Activist Citizen. *Subjectivity*, 29, pp. 367–388.

——— 2011. Ottoman Waqfs as Acts of Citizenship. In: P. Ghazaleh, ed. *Held in Trust: Waqf in the Muslim World*. Cairo: American University in Cairo Press, pp. 209–229.

——— 2012a. Citizens without Nations. *Environment and Planning D: Society and Space*, 30, pp. 450–467.

——— 2012b. Citizenship after Orientalism: An Unfinished Project. *Citizenship Studies*, 16(5–6), pp. 563–572.

Isin, E. and Turner, B. 2002. Citizenship Studies: An Introduction. In: E. Isin and B. Turner, eds. *Handbook of Citizenship Studies*. London: Sage, pp. 1–10.

Isin, E. and Ustundag, E. 2008. Wills, Deeds, Acts: Women's Civic Gift-Giving in Ottoman Istanbul. *Gender, Place and Culture*, 15(5), pp. 519–532.

Isin, E. and Wood, P. 1999. *Citizenship and Identity*. London: Sage.

Isurin, L. 2017. *Collective Remembering: Memory in the World and in the Mind*. Cambridge: Cambridge University Press.

Jabri, V. 2006. War, Security, and the Liberal State. *Security Dialogue*, 37(1), pp. 47–64.

2013. *The Postcolonial Subject: Claiming Politics/Governing Others in Late Modernity*. London: Routledge.

Jackson, S. 2006. Gender, Sexuality and Heterosexuality: The Complexity (and Limits) of Heteronormativity. *Feminist Theory*, 7, pp. 105–121.

Jacoby, T. A. 1999. Feminism, Nationalism and Difference: Reflections on the Palestinian Woman's Movement. *Women's Studies International Forum*, 22 (5), pp. 511–523.

Jafarian, G. 1381/2002. *Az Chande-La ta Jang: Khaterat-e Shamsy Sobhani* (From Chande-La to War: Memories of Shamsy Sobhani). Tehran: Sourah Mehr. 1396. *Roozhaaye be Ayneh*. Tehran: Sooremehr.

Jafarian, H. 1386/2007. *Niemey-e Penhan-e Mah (1)*. Tehran: Ravayat-e Fath.

Jaggar, A. M. 1989. Love and Knowledge: Emotions in Feminist Epistemology. In: A. M. Jagar and S. R. Bordo, eds. *Gender/Body/Knowledge: Feminist Reconstruction of Being and Knowing*. New Brunswick, NJ: Rutgers University Press, pp. 145–171.

Jahangiri, G. 2003. Memories. *Human Rights and Democracy for Iran.* www .iranrights.org/library/collection/120/prison-memoirs [Accessed 16 February, 2018].

Jalili, V. 1396/2017. *Shohada baraye che ofoghe jangedan?* Qom: daftar-e nashre moaref.

Jayawardena, K. 1986. *Feminism and Nationalism in the Third World*. London and Totowa, NJ: Zed Books.

Jones, K. B. 1990. Citizenship in a Woman-Friendly Polity. *Signs*, 15(4), pp. 781–812.

Joseph, G. M. and Nugent, D. 1994. Popular Culture and State Formation in Revolutionary Mexico. In: G. M. Joseph and D. Nugent, eds. *Everyday Forms of State Formation: Revolution and the Negotiation of Rule in Modern Mexico*. Durham and London: Duke University Press, pp. 3–23.

Joseph, S. 1994. Brother/Sister Relationships: Connectivity, Love, and Power in the Reproduction of Patriarchy in Lebanon. *American Ethnologist*, 21(1), pp. 50–73.

Joseph, S. ed. 2000. *Gender and Citizenship in the Middle East*. Syracuse, NY: Syracuse University Press.

Judaki, M. A. 1395/2016. *Naghshe Zanan dar Defa Moghaddas*. Tehran: Markaze Asnade Enghelabe Islami.

Kage, R. 2010. The Effects of War on Civil Society: Cross-national Evidence from World War II. In: E. Kier and R. Krebs, eds. *In War's Wake: International Conflict and the Fate of Liberal Democracy*. Cambridge: Cambridge University Press, pp. 97–120.

Kamari, A. 1385/2006. *Nameh-ha-ye Fahimeh*. Tehran: Daftar-e Adabiyat va Hon-ar-e Moqavemat.

Kamrava, M. 2000. Military Professionalization and Civil-Military Relations in the Middle East. *Political Science Quarterly*, 115(1), pp. 67–92.

Kanaaneh, R. 2005. Boys or Men? Duped or "Made"? Palestinian Soldiers in the Israeli Army. *American Ethnologist*, 32(2), pp. 260–275.

Kanafani, S. 2008. Leaving Mother-Land: The Anti-Feminine in Fida'i Narratives. *Identities*, 15(3), pp. 297–316.

Kandiyoti, D., ed. 1991. *Women, Islam, and the State*. Basingstoke: Macmillan.

Kantola, J. 2006. *Feminists Theorize the State*. New York: Palgrave.

Kar, M. 1379/2000. *Nakhl haye Sukhte*. Tehran: Roshangaran va motalate zanan.

Karimi-Hakkak, A. 1985. Of Hail and Hounds: The Image of the Iranian Revolution in Recent Persian Literature. *State, Culture, and Society*, 1(3), pp. 148–180.

Kashfi, S. A. 1385/2006. Ensan-e Razmandeh, Ensan-e Isargar. *Habil*, pp. 8–11. 1387/2008. Dar Jostojuye Cheshm Andaze Degar. *Habil*, 9, pp. 10–11.

Katouzian, H. 2010. Of the Sins of Forugh Farrokhzad. In: D. P. Brookshaw and N. Rahimieh, eds. *Forugh Farrokhzad Poet of Modern Iran: Iconic Woman and Feminine Pioneer of New Persian Poetry*. London and New York: I. B. Tauris, pp. 7–18.

Kaufman, J. and Williams, K. 2004. Who Belongs? Women, Marriage and Citizenship. *International Feminist Journal of Politics*, 6(3), pp. 416–435.

Kazruneyan, B. 1382/2003. *Ruzgaran (13): Ketab-e Zanan-e Khorramshahr*. Tehran: Ravayat-e Fath.

Keddie, N. 2000. Women in Iran since 1979. *Social Research*, 67(2), pp. 405–438.

Keyani, T. 1388/2009. *Haam Dush*. Isfahan: Gofteman-e Andesheh-ye Moaser.

Khatam, A. 2010. Struggles over Defining the Moral City: The Problem Called "Youth" in Urban Iran. In: L. Herrera and A. Bayat, eds. *Being Young and Muslim: New Cultural Politics in the Global South and North*. Oxford: Oxford University Press, pp. 207–221.

Khomeini, R. 1980. We Shall Confront the World with Our Ideology. *MERIP Reports*, 88, pp. 22–25. 1385/2006. *Sahife-ye Imam*. 4th ed. (The Imam's Book). Tehran: moassese Tanzim va Nashr-e Asar-e Imam Khomeini.

Khosravi, S. 2008. *Young and Defiant in Tehran*. Philadelphia: University of Pennsylvania Press. 2017. *Precarious Lives: Waiting and Hope in Iran*. Philadelphia: University of Pennsylvania Press.

Kohan-rooz, M. 1391/2012. An Roozha Poshtebane az Jang Bakhshe az Kare Roozaneh Zanane Irani bood. *Vijehnameh-ye Yadvareh Zanane Shahid-e Maazandaran*, pp. 55–57.

Koolaee, E. 2014. The Impact of Iraq-Iran War on Social Roles of Iranian Women. *Middle East Critique*, 23(3), pp. 277–291.

Korolczuk, E. and Graff, A. 2018. Gender as "Ebola from Brussels": The Anticolonial Frame and the Rise of Illiberal Populism. *Signs: Journal of Women in Culture and Society*, 43(4), pp. 797–821.

Kurzman, C. 2008. A Feminist Generation in Iran? *Iranian Studies*, 41(3), pp. 297–321.

Lamont, M. 2000. *The Dignity of Working Men: Morality and the Boundaries of Race, Class, and Immigration*. Cambridge, MA: Harvard University Press.

Landman, T. 2000. *Issue and Methods in Comparative Politics: An Introduction*. London: Routledge.

Leander, A. 2004. Wars and the Un-Making of States: Taking Tilly Seriously in the Contemporary World. In: S. Guzzini and D. Jung, eds. *Contemporary*

Security Analysis and Copenhagen Peace Research. London and New York: Routledge, pp. 69–80.

Ledeneva, A. 2001. Unwritten Rules: How Russia Really Works. http://cerlive .thomaspaterson.co.uk/sites/default/files/publications/attachments/pdf/2011/ e246_unwritten_rules-2203.pdf [Accessed February 20, 2018].

2006. *How Russia Really Works: The Informal Practices that Shaped Post-Soviet Politics and Business.* London: Cornell University Press.

Leezenberg, M. 2018. Foucault and Iran Reconsidered: Revolt, Religion, and Neoliberalism. *Iran Namag: A Bilingual Quarterly of Iranian Studies*, 3(2), pp. IV–XXVIII.

Lichterman, P. 1998. What Do Movements Mean? *Qualitative Sociology*, 2, pp. 401–418.

Lorde, A. 2007. Eye to Eye: Black Women, Hatred, and Anger. In: A. Lord, ed. *Sister Outsider: Essays and Speeches.* Berkeley, CA: The Crossing Press, pp. 145–175.

Lust, E. and Ndegwa, S. N. 2010. Governance Challenges in the Face of Transformation. *Middle East Law and Governance*, 2(2), pp. 113–123.

MacKinnon, C. 1989. *Toward a Feminist Theory of the State.* Cambridge, MA: Harvard University Press.

Mahbaz, E. 2008. *Faramusham Makon.* Sweden: Baran.

Mahdavi, P. 2007. Passionate Uprisings: Young People, Sexuality and Politics in Post-Revolutionary Iran. *Culture, Health & Sexuality*, 9, pp. 445–457.

2009. Who Will Catch Me If I Fall? Health and the Infrastructure of Risk for Urban Young Iranians. In: A. Gheissari, ed. *Contemporary Iran: Economy, Society and Politics.* Oxford: Oxford University Press, pp. 150–193.

Makaremi, C. 2013. *Aziz's Notebook: At the Heart of the Iranian Revolution.* Gallimard, Paris: Yoda Press.

Malarney, S. K. 2002. *Culture, Ritual and Revolution in Vietnam.* London: Routledge Curzon.

Mann, M. 1987. The Roots and Contradictions of Modern Militarism. *New Left Review*, 1(162), pp. 35–50.

Mantena, K. 2016. Popular Sovereignty and Anti-Colonialism. In: R. Bourke and Q. Skinner, eds. *Popular Sovereignty in Historical Perspective.* Cambridge: Cambridge University Press, pp. 297–319.

Marj, A. 1381/2002. *Nimey-e Penhan-e Mah (4)* (The Moon's Hidden Half). Tehran: Ravayat-e Fath.

Marjani, F. 1981. *Man and Islam: Dr. Ali Shariati.* Houston, TX: FILINC.

Markoff, J. 1996. *Waves of Democracy. Social Movements and Political Change.* Thousand Oaks, CA: Pine Forge.

Martin, D. and Miller, B. 2003. Space as Contentious Politics. *Mobilization: An International Journal*, 8(2), pp. 135–156.

Martin, V. 2007. *Creating an Islamic State: Khomeini and the Making of a New Iran.* London: I. B. Tauris.

Marwick, A., ed. 1988. *Total War and Social Changes.* New York: St. Martin's Press.

Masoumi, A. S. 1376/1997. *Zanan-e Jang* (The Women of War). Tehran: Hadaf.

Massumi, B. 2002. *Parables for the Virtual: Movement, Affect, Sensation.* Durham: Duke University Press.

Masters, C. 2008. Bodies of Technology and the Politics of the Flesh. In: J. L. Parpart and M. Zalewski, eds. *Rethinking the Man Question: Sex, Gender and Violence in International Relations*. London: Zed Books, pp. 87–107.

Maynes, M. J., Pierce, J. L., and Laslett, B. 2008. *Telling Stories: The Use of Personal Narratives in the Social Sciences and History*. London and Ithaca, NY: Cornell University Press.

Mazaheri, M. H. 1385/2006. Defa Moghaddas-e Dolati, Defa Moghaddas-e Mardomi. *Habil*, 12, pp. 4–7.

1392/2012. Khatar-e Soghut-e Bahman. *Habil*, 11(6), pp. 2–10.

McClintock, A. 1993. Family Feuds: Gender, Nationalism and the Family. *Feminist Review*, 44, pp. 61–80.

McDougall, J. 2006. Martyrdom and Destiny: The Inscription and Imagination of Algerian History. In: U. Makdisi and P. A. Silverstein, eds. *Memory and violence in the Middle East and North Africa*. Indianapolis: Indiana University Press, pp. 50–72.

McDowall, D. 1996. *A Modern History of the Kurds*. London: I. B. Tauris.

McRobbie, A. 2009. *The Aftermath of Feminism: Gender, Culture and Social Change*. London: Sage.

Mesdaghi, Iraj. 1383/2004. *Descent of Sunrise: Memories of Prison* (Volume 1/in Farsi). Kista: Alfabet Maxima Publishing.

Meyer, B. 2004. Christianity in Africa: From African Independent to Pentecostal Charismatic Churches. *Annual Review of Anthropology*, 33, pp. 447–474.

Miettinen, R. 1999. The Riddle of Things: Activity Theory and Actor Network Theory as Approaches of Studying Innovations. *Mind, Culture, and Activity*, 6(3), pp. 170–195.

Migdal, J. S. 2001. *State in Society: Studying How States and Societies Transform and Constitute One Another*. Cambridge: Cambridge University Press.

Milani, F. 1982. Love and Sexuality in the Poetry of Forugh Farrokhzad: A Reconsideration. *Iranian Studies*, 15(1/4), pp. 117–128.

1992. *Veils and Words: The Emerging Voice of Iranian Women Writers*. Syracuse, NY: Syracuse University Press.

Mir-Hosseini, Z. 2000. *Islam and Gender: The Religious Debate in Contemporary Iran*. London: I. B. Tauris.

2017. Islam, Gender, and Democracy in Iran. In: J. Cesari and J. Casanova, eds. *Islam, Gender, and Democracy in Comparative Perspective*. Oxford: Oxford University Press, pp. 211–236.

Mirsepassi, A. 1396/2018. Taghi Arani. *Azadeye Andesheh*, 5, pp. 18–41.

Mirzaeian, S. n.d. Dar Kenar-e oo: Goft to go ba Akram Farahzadi (Next to Him: A Conversation with Akram Farahzadi). *Kaman*, 94.

Mitchell, T. 1991. The Limits of the State: Beyond Statist Approaches and Their Critics. *The American Political Science Review*, 85, pp. 75–96.

2002. *Rule of Experts: Egypt, Techno-politics, Modernity*. Berkeley: University of California Press.

Moallem, M. 2005. *Between Warrior Brother and Veiled Sister: Islamic Fundamentalism and the Politics of Patriarchy in Iran*. Los Angeles: University of California Press.

Moghadam, V. M. 1988. Women, Work, and Ideology in the Islamic Republic. *International Journal of Middle East Studies*, 20(2), pp. 221–243.

1992. Revolution, Islam and Women: Sexual Politics in Iran and Afghanistan. In: A. Parker et al., eds. *Nationalisms and Sexualities*. New York: Routledge, pp. 424–446.

Mohammadi, L. 1381/2002a. *Dokhtaran-e OPD: Khaterat-e Mina Kamaii* (The OPD Girls: Memories of Mina Kamaii). Tehran: Sourah Mehr.

1381/2002b. *Didar -e- Zakhmaha: Khaterat-e Masoomeh Mirzai* (Visiting Wounds: The Memories of Masoomeh Mirzai). Tehran: Sourah Mehr.

Mohseni, P. 2013. The Islamic Awakening: Iran's Grand Narrative of the Arab Uprisings. *Middle East Brief*, 71, pp. 1–9. Brandeis University: Crown Center for Middle East Studies.

Mojab, S. 1999. Vengeance and Violence: Kurdish Women Recount the War. *Canadian Woman Studies*, 19(4), pp. 89–94.

2007. Years of Solitude, Years of Defiance: Women Political Prisoners in Iran. In: A. Agah, S. Parsi, and S. Mehr, eds. *We Lived to Tell: Political Prisoner Memoirs of Iranian Women*. Canada: McGillian Books.

Momen, M. 1985. *An Introduction to Shi'i Islam: The History and Doctrines of Twelver Shi'ism*. New Haven, CT: Yale University Press.

Mookherjee, M. 2005. Affective Citizenship: Feminism, Postcolonialism and the Politics of Recognition. *Critical Review of International Social and Political Philosophy*, 8, pp. 31–50.

Morgana, M. S. 2018. The Islamic Republican Party of Iran in the Factory: Control over Workers' Discourse in Posters (1979–1987). *Iran: Journal of the British Institute of Persian Studies*, 56(2), pp. 1–13.

Mortazavi, Z. and Safeiyeh, H. 1382/2003. *Ghessi-e Baray-e Sajjad (A Story for Sajjad)*. Tehran: Boustan-e Fadak.

Moshtagh, Z. 1385/2006. *Talebi: Ba Revayat-e Hamsar Shahid (Talebi: The Martyr's Wife's Narration)*. Tehran: Ravayat-e Fath.

Motahhari, M. 1386/2007. *Ayandeye Enghelabe Islami ye Iran*. 26th ed. Tehran: Sadra Publishers.

Mottahedeh, R. 2000. *The Mantle of the Prophet: Religion and Politics in Iran*. Oxford: One World.

Mouri, L. and Batmanghelichi, K. S. 2015. Can the Secular Iranian Women's Activist Speak? Caught between Political Power and "Islamic Feminism." In: G. Ozyegin, ed. *Sexuality in Muslim Cultures*. Aldershot: Ashghate Publishing, pp. 331–354.

Najmabadi, A. 2005. *Women with Moustaches and Men without Beards: Gender and Sexual Anxieties of Iranian Modernity*. Berkeley: University of California Press.

2006. Beyond the Americas: Are Gender and Sexuality Useful Categories of Historical Analysis? *Journal of Women's History*, 18, pp. 11–21.

Nicolini, D. 2013. *Practice, Theory, Work: An Introduction*. Oxford: Oxford University Press.

Nielsen, G. M. 2008. Answerability with Cosmopolitan Intent: An Ethics-Based Politics for Acts of Urban Citizenship. In: E. F. Isin and G. M. Nielsen, eds. *Acts of Citizenship*. London: Zed Books, pp. 266–286.

Noori, N. 2012. Rethinking the Legacies of the Iran–Iraq War: Veterans, the Basij, and Social Resistance in Iran. *Political and Military Sociology*, 40, pp. 119–140.

Noruzi, P. and Nouri, M. 1386/2007. Ravande ru be roshte shakhes haaye hozehye din dar sal e 1385. *Barnameh*, 252.

Nouraie-Simone, F. 2005. Wings of Freedom: Iranian Women, Identity, and Cyberspace. In: F. Nouraie-Simone, ed. *On Shifting Ground: Muslim Women in the Global Era*. New York: Feminist Press at the City University of New York, pp. 61–79.

Nyers, P. 2011. Forms of Irregular Citizenship. In: V. Squire, ed. *The Contested Politics of Mobility: Borderzones and Irregularity*. London: Routledge, pp. 184–198.

O'Neill, K. L. 2010. *City of God: Christian Citizenship in Postwar Guatemala*. London and Berkeley: University of California Press.

Ong, A. 1996. Cultural Citizenship as Subject-Making: Immigrants Negotiate Racial and Cultural Boundaries in the United States [and Comments and Reply]. *Current Anthropology*, 37(5), pp. 737–762.

2011. Translating Gender Justice in Southeast Asia: Situated Ethics, NGOs, and Bio-Welfare. *Journal of Women of the Middle East and the Islamic World*, 9, pp. 26–48.

Osanloo, A. 2009. *The Politics of Women's Rights in Iran*. Princeton, NJ: Princeton University Press.

2014. Khomeini's Legacy on Women's Rights and Roles in the Islamic Republic of Iran. In: A. Adib-Moghaddam, ed. *A Critical Introduction to Khomeini*. Cambridge: Cambridge University Press, pp. 239–255.

Paidar, P. 1995. *Women and the Political Process in Twentieth-Century Iran*. Cambridge: Cambridge University Press.

1997. *Women and the Political Process in Twentieth-Century Iran*. Cambridge: Cambridge University Press.

Parker, A., Russo, M., Sommer, D., and Yaeger, P. eds. 1992. *Nationalisms and Sexualities*. New York: Routledge.

Parsipur, S. 2013. *Kissing the Sword: A Prison Memoir*. New York: The Feminist Press at CUNY. Translated by Sara Khalili.

Parvaz, N. 2002. *Beneath the Narcissus*. Stockholm: Nasim.

Parvaz, N. and Namazie, M. 2003. Beneath the Narcissus: A Woman's Experience of Iranian Prisons and Beyond. *Feminist Review*, 73, pp. 71–85.

Pourreza, N. 1397/2018. Shekl Gereye Shahrvande Gaame dar Jahate Hokmrani ye Shahree. *Hamshahri*.

Povey, T. 2012. The Iranian Women's Movement in Its Regional and International Context. In: T. Povey and E. Rostami-Povey, eds. *Women, Power and Politics in 21st Century Iran*. London: Ashgate, pp. 168–182.

Povey, T. and Rostami-Povey, E. eds. 2012. *Women, Power and Politics in 21st Century Iran*. London: Ashgate.

Prunhuber, C. 2010. *The Passion and Death of Rahman the Kurd: Dreaming Kurdistan*. Bloomington: iUniverse.

Rahnema, A. 1998. *An Islamic Utopian: A Political Biography of Ali Shariati*. London: I. B. Tauris.

Raissi, R. 1383/2003. *Khabarnegar-e Jangi: Khaterat-e Maryam Kazamzadeh*. Tehran: Yad Banu.

Reeves, M. 1989. *Female Warriors of Allah: Women and the Islamic Revolution*. New York: E. P. Dutton.

Rejali, D. M. 1994. *Torture & Modernity: Self, Society, and State in Modern Iran*. Boulder, CO, San Francisco, and Oxford: Westview Press.

Rivetti, P. Forthcoming. *Political Participation and Iranian Post-Revolutionary Reformism*. New York: Palgrave McMillan.

Robertson, G. 2011. The Massacre of Political Prisoners in Iran, 1988. Abdorrahman Boroumand Foundation. www.iranrights.org/english/docu ment-1380.php. [Accessed March 1, 2020].

Saalmee nejad, abdalreza. 1391. *Dokhtari Kenare Shaat*. Tehran: faathaan.

Sabet, F. 1383. *Yaadhaa-ye Zendan*. Paris: Khavaran.

Sadeghi, F. 2008. Negotiating with Modernity: Young Women and Sexuality in Iran. *Comparative Studies of South Asia, Africa, and the Middle East*, 28(2), pp. 250–259.

2009. Foot Soldiers of the Islamic Republic's "Culture of Modesty." *Middle East Report*, 250, pp. 50–55.

Sadiqi, F. and Ennaji, M. 2006. The Feminization of Public Space: Women's Activism, the Family Law, and Social Change in Morocco. *Journal of Middle East Women's Studies*, 2(2), pp. 86–114.

Sadr, S. 2011. Shekanje va Khoshunat-e Jensi Alayhe Zendaneyan-e Siaysi-ye Zan dar Jomhuri-ye Islami. *Edalat baray-e Iran*.

Sadri, M. 2001. Sacral Defense of Secularism: The Political Theologies of Soroush, Shabestari, and Kadivar. *International Journal of Politics, Culture, and Society*, 15(2), pp. 257–270.

Saeidi, F. 1382/2003. *Ghermez, Rang-e Khun-e Baba-m* (Red, The Colour of My Dad's Blood). Tehran: Boustan Fadak.

Saeidi, S. 2008. Only Five Female Martyrs on Streets of Tehran. Translated from Farsi, *Iranian.com*. www.iranian.com/main/blog/shirin-saeidi/only-5-female-martyrs-streets-tehran [Accessed December 2014].

2017. Becoming Hezbollahi: Religion and the Unintended Consequences of Propaganda in Post-2009 Iran. POMEPS Studies 28, pp. 20–25.

Safavi, R. 1389/2010. *Zanan va Defa-e Moghadas*. www.sajed.ir/new/index.php? option=com_content&view=article&id=17418:1389-02-15-14-58-58& catid=780:women-and-sacred-defense&Itemid=555 [Accessed 2014].

Saghafi, M. 1378/1999. Enghelab, Jang, va Gardesh-e Nokhbegan dar Jamaeh. *Goft-e Gu*, pp. 35–55.

2001. Crossing the Desert: Iranian Intellectuals after the Islamic Revolution. *Critique: Critical Middle Eastern Studies*, 10(18), pp. 15–45.

Sameti, M., Ataei, Z., and Esmaeili, Z. 1382/2003. *Harfahash be del Mineshast* (His Words Were Appealing). Tehran: Bourstan-e Fadak.

Sanadjian, M. 1996. A Public Flogging in South-Western Iran: Juridical Rule, Abolition of Legality and Local Resistance. In: O. Harris, ed. *Inside and Outside the Law: Anthropological Studies of Authority and Ambiguity*. New York: Routledge, pp. 157–183.

Sarhangi, M. 1381/2002. *Banu-ye Mah (2)* (Lady of the Moon). Tehran: Kaman. 1384/2005. *Banu-ye Mah (5)* (Lady of the Moon). Tehran: Kaman.

1385/2006. *Banu-ye Mah (6): Goft-o Gu ba Parvin Daepour Hamsar Sardar Shahid Hossein Baghari.* Tehran: Kaman.

Sartori, G. 1970. Concept Misformation in Comparative Politics. *American Political Science Review,* LXIV(4), pp. 1033–1053.

Sayer, A. 2005. Class, Moral Worth and Recognition. *Sociology,* 39(5), pp. 947–963.

Sayigh, R. 1998a. Gender, Sexuality, and Class in National Narrations: Palestinian Camp Women Tell Their Lives. *Frontiers: A Journal of Women Studies,* 19(2), pp. 166–185.

1998b. Palestinian Camp Women as Tellers of History. *Journal of Palestine Studies,* 27(2), pp. 42–58.

2002. Remembering Mothers, Forming Daughters: Palestinian Women's Narratives in Refugee Camps in Lebanon. In: N. Abdo and R. Lentin, eds. *Women and the Politics of Military Confrontation: Palestinian and Israeli Gendered Narratives of Dislocation.* New York and Oxford: Berghahn Books, pp. 56–71.

Schayegh, C. 2010. Seeing Like a State. *International Journal of Middle East Studies,* 42, pp. 37–61.

Sciolino, E. 2000. *Persian Mirrors: The Elusive Face of Iran.* London and New York: The Free Press.

Scott, J. W. 1988. *Gender and the Politics of History.* New York: Columbia University Press.

Sedghi, H. 2007. *Women and Politics in Iran: Veiling, Unveiling, and Reveiling.* Cambridge: Cambridge University Press.

Shaditalab, J. 2005. Iranian Women: Rising Expectations. *Critique: Critical Middle East Studies,* 14(1), pp. 35–55.

Shaditalab, J., ed. 1397/2018. Special Issue on Gender and Quality of Life. *Haft Shahr: Journal of Urban Development and Organization,* 4(61), pp. 1–348.

Shaery-Eisenlohr, R. 2008. *Shiite Lebanon: Transnational Religion and the Making of National Identity.* New York: Columbia University Press.

Shahbani, G. 1386/2007. *Hoghughe Asasi va Sakhtare Hokumate Jomhuri ye Islami ye Iran.* 28th ed. Tehran: Etelaat Publishers.

Shaheed, A. 2012. Report of the Special Rapporteur on the Situation of Human Rights in the Islamic Republic of Iran. United Nation's Human Rights Council HRC/19/66, p. 13.

Shahidian, H. 1994. The Iranian Left and the "Woman Question" in the Revolution of 1978–79. *International Journal of Middle East Studies,* 26(2), pp. 223–247.

1996. Iranian Exiles and Sexual Politics: Issues of Gender Relations and Identity. *Journal of Refugee Studies,* 9(1), pp. 43–72.

1997. Women and Clandestine Politics in Iran, 1970–1985. *Feminist Studies,* 23(1), pp. 7–42.

Shahrokni, N. and Dokouhaki, P. 2012. A Separation at Iranian Universities, *MERIP,* 18 October. www.merip.org/mero/mero101812 [Accessed 2016].

Shams, F. 2018. The Village in Contemporary Persian Poetry. *Iranian Studies,* 51 (3), pp. 1–23. DOI: 10.1080/00210862.2018.1431045

Shapiro, M. J. 2000. National Times and Other Times: Re-Thinking Citizenship. *Cultural Studies,* 14(1), pp. 79–98.

Shariati, A. 1348/1969 (1391/2012). *Ommat-o-Imammat*. Tehran: Teribon Mostazafin.

1356/1977. *Fatima Fatima ast* (Fatima Is Fatima). Tehran: Ḥusayniyya-i Irshad.

Sharoni, S. 1988. Rethinking Women's Struggles in Israel-Palestine and in the North of Ireland. In C. O. N. Moser and F. C. Clark, eds. *Victims, Perpetrators or Actors? Gender, Armed Conflict and Political Violence*. London: Zed Books, pp. 85–98.

Sheridan, A., trans. 1988. *Michel Foucault: Politics, Philosophy, Culture*. London: Routledge.

Shirazi, A. 1387/2008. *Nameh-haye Deltangi*. Tehran: Sureh Mehr.

Shirkhani, A. and Zare, A. 1384/2005. *Tahavolat-e Houzeh-ye Elmieh-ye Qom* (Developments of Qom's Seminaries). Tehran: Markaz-e Asnad-e Enqelab-e Islami.

Sika, N. and Khodary, Y. 2012. One Step Forward, Two Steps Back? Egyptian Women within the Confines of Authoritarianism. *Journal of International Women's Studies*, 13(5), pp. 91–100.

Silone, I. 2005. *Bread and Wine*. New York: Signet Classics. Translated by Eric Mosbacher.

Singh, J. 2018. *Unthinking Mastery: Dehumanism and Decolonial Engagements*. Durham, NC: Duke University Press.

Sjoberg, L. and Gentry, C. E. 2007. *Mothers, Monsters, Whores: Women's Violence in Global Politics*. London: Zed Books.

Skocpol, T. 1988. Social Revolutions and Mass Military Mobilization. *World Politics*, 40(2), pp. 147–168.

Slaby, J., Mühlhoff, R., and Wüschner, P. 2019. Concepts as Methodology: A Plea for Arrangement Thinking in the Study of Affect. In: A. Kahl, ed. *Analyzing Affective Societies: Methods and Methodologies*. New York: Routledge, pp. 27–42.

Sohrabi, N. 2011. The Power Struggle in Iran: A Centrist Comeback. *Middle East Brief*, 53, pp. 2–3.

2016. Books as Revolutionary Objects in Iran. *Age of Revolutions*. https://ageofrevolutions.com/2016/04/04/books-as-revolutionary-objects-in-iran/ [Accessed May 24, 2018].

2019. Remembering the Palestine Group: Global Activism, Friendship, and the Iranian Revolution. *International Journal of Middle East Studies*, 51, pp. 281–300.

Soleimani, N. 1381/2001. *Gol-e Simin*. Tehran: Sourah Mehr.

Sreberny-Mohammadi, A. 1995. Global News Media Cover the World. In: J. Downing, A. Mohammadi, and A. Sreberny-Mohammadi, eds. *Questioning the Media: A Critical Introduction*. London: Sage Publications, pp. 428–443.

Stanley, L. and Wise, S. 1993. *Breaking Out Again: Feminist Ontology and Epistemology*. London and New York: Routledge.

Starr, A., Fernandez, L., and Scholl, C. 2011. *Shutting Down the Streets: Political Violence and Social Control in the Global Era*. New York: New York University Press.

Stempel, J. D. 1981. *Inside the Iranian Revolution*. Bloomington: Indiana University Press.

Strauss, J. and Cruise O'Brien, D., eds. 2007. *Staging Politics: Power and Performance in Asia and Africa*. London: I. B. Tauris.

Swidler, A. 2001. *Talk of Love: How Culture Matters*. Chicago: The University of Chicago Press.

Tabari, A. and Yeganeh, N. 1982. *In the Shadow of Islam: The Women's Movement in Iran*. London: Zed Press.

Tagavi, J. 1985. The Iran-Iraq War: The First Three Years. In: B. M. Rosen, ed. *Iran Since the Revolution: Internal Dynamics, Regional Conflict, and the Superpowers*. New York: Columbia University Press, pp. 63–82.

Taghvaei, N. 2000. *Chai Talkh*. Tehran: Tofigh Afarin.

Talebi, S. 2011. Who Is Behind the Name? A Story of Violence, Loss, and Melancholic Survival in Post-revolutionary Iran. *Journal of Middle East Women's Studies*, 7(1), pp. 39–69.

2014. Children as Protectors: The Conditions of Parenthood in a Political Prison in Iran. *Champ pénal/Penal field* XI. https://doi.org/10.4000/champpenal.8770 [Accessed February 15, 2018].

Tawasil, A. 2015. Toward the Ideal Revolutionary Shi'i Woman: The Howzevi (Seminarian), the Requisites of Marriage and Islamic Education in Iran. *Journal of Women of the Middle East and the Islamic World*, 13, pp. 99–126.

Tazmini, G. 2009. *Khatami's Iran: The Islamic Republic and the Turbulent Path to Reform*. London: I. B. Tauris.

Tetreault, M. A. 1994. *Women and Revolution in Africa, Asia, and the New World*. Columbia: University of South Carolina Press.

Thaler, D. E. et al. 2010. *Mullahs, Guards, and Bonyads: An Exploration of Iranian Leadership Dynamics*. Arlington, VA: National Defense Research Institute (RAND).

Thomas, J. L. and Bond, K. D. 2015. Women's Participation in Violent Political Organizations. *American Political Science Review*, 109(3), pp. 488–506.

Tilly, C. ed. 1975. *The Formation of National States in Western Europe*. Princeton, NJ: Princeton University Press.

Tilly, C. 1985. War Making and State Making as Organized Crime. In: P. Evans, D. Rueschemeyer, and T. Skocpol, eds. *Bringing the State Back In*. Cambridge: Cambridge University Press, pp. 169–191.

1990a. *Coercion, Capital and European States, A.D. 990–1992*. Cambridge: Blackwell.

1990b. Where Do Rights Come From? Working Paper 98. Center for Studies of Social Change: New School for Social Research.

2006. Afterward: Political Ethnography as Art and Science. *Qualitative Sociology*, 29, pp. 409–412.

Torab, A. 1996. Piety as Gendered Agency: A Study of Jalaseh Ritual Discourse in an Urban Neighbourhood in Iran. *Journal of the Royal Anthropological Institute*, 2(2), pp. 235–252.

Touba, J. R. 1987. The Widowed in Iran. In: H. Z. Lopata, ed. *Widows Volume I: The Middle East, Asia, and the Pacific*. Durham: Duke University Press.

True, J. 1996. Feminism. In: S. Burchill and A. Linklater, eds. *Theories of International Relations*. New York: St. Martin's Press, pp. 210–251.

Turner, B. 2008. Acts of Piety: The Political and the Religious, or a Tale of Two Cities. In: E. F. Isin and G. M. Nielsen, eds. *Acts of Citizenship*. London: Zed Books, pp. 121–136.

Vahdat, F. 2003. Post-Revolutionary Islamic Discourses on Modernity in Iran: Expansion and Contraction of Human Subjectivity. *International Journal of Middle East Studies*, 35(4), pp. 599–631.

Valadi, M. H. 1386/2007. *Aflakian-e Zamin*. Tehran: Nashr Shahid.

Varzi, R. 2006. *Warring Souls: Youth, Media, and Martyrdom in Post-Revolutionary Iran*. Durham and London: Duke University Press.

Velleman, D. 2013. *Foundations for Moral Relativism*. Cambridge: Open Book Publishers.

Vickers, J. 2006. Bringing Nations In: Some Methodological and Conceptual Issues in Connecting Feminisms with Nationhood and Nationalisms. *International Feminist Journal of Politics*, 8(1), pp. 84–109.

—— 2008. Gendering the Hyphen: Gender Dimensions of Modern Nation-State Formation in Euro-American and Anti- and Post-Colonial Contexts. In: Y. Abu-Laban, ed. *Gendering the Nation-State: Canadian and Comparative Perspectives*. Vancouver: UBC Press, pp. 21–45.

Voynich, E. L. 2018. *The Gadfly*. Middletown, DE.

Waetjen, T. 2001. The Limits of Gender Rhetoric for Nationalism: A Case Study from Southern Africa. *Theory and Society*, 30(1), pp. 121–152.

Walters, W. 2008. Acts of Demonstration: Mapping the Territory of (non-) Citizenship. In: E. F. Isin and G. M. Nielsen, eds. *Acts of Citizenship*. London: Zed Books, pp. 182–206.

Weiss, M. 2011. The Epistemology of Ethnography: Method in Queer Anthropology. *GLQ: A Journal of Lesbian and Gay Studies*, 17(4), pp. 649–664.

Wickramasinghe, M. 2010. *Feminist Research Methodology*. New York: Routledge.

Yahosseini, S. G. 1387/2008. *Zeiton-e Sorkh: Khaterat-e Nahid Yousefian* (The Red Olive: Memories of Nahid Yousefian). Tehran: Soureh Mehr.

Yeganeh, N. 1982. Women's Struggles in the Islamic Republic of Iran. In A. Tabari and N. Yeganeh, eds. *In the Shadow of Islam: The Women's Movement in Iran*. London: Zed Books, pp. 26–74.

Zaghyan, M. 1386/2007. *An Su-ye Devar-e Del*. Tehran: bonyad-e hafz-e Asar va Arzesh-ha-ye Defa-e Moghaddas.

Zahidi, S. and Shariflu, S. 1391/2012. *Negah-e Por Baran*. Tehran: Fatehan Publishers.

Zarabizadeh, B. 1396. *Dokhtare Shina*. Tehran: Sooremehr.

Zerilli, L. 2005. *Feminism and the Abyss of Freedom*. Chicago: University of Chicago Press.

Zibakalam, S. 1385/2006. Avalin Jazbehye Aam dar Ketabhaaye Defa Moghaddas. *Habil*, 12, p. 21.

Zubaida, S. 2001a. *Islam, the People and the State*. London: I. B. Tauris.

—— 2001b. Islam and the Politics of Citizenship and Community. *Middle East Report*, 221, pp. 20–27.

Index

Books in the Series

CPSIA information can be obtained
at www.ICGtesting.com
Printed in the USA
LVHW080821310822
727263LV00004B/187